TRADE
in Services
TRADE
Agreements

Bulk Sales

Get to know more about SAGE

TRADE
in Services
TRADE
Agreements
Perspectives from INDIA
and the European Union

Edited By

ARPITA MUKHERJEE
RUPA CHANDA
TANU M. GOYAL

$SAGE   www.sagepublications.com
Los Angeles • London • New Delhi • Singapore • Washington DC

First published in 2016 by

SAGE Publications India Pvt Ltd
B1/I-1 Mohan Cooperative Industrial Area
Mathura Road, New Delhi 110 044, India
www.sagepub.in

SAGE Publications Inc
2455 Teller Road
Thousand Oaks, California 91320, USA

SAGE Publications Ltd
1 Oliver's Yard, 55 City Road
London EC1Y 1SP, United Kingdom

SAGE Publications Asia-Pacific Pte Ltd
3 Church Street
#10-04 Samsung Hub
Singapore 049483

Published by Vivek Mehra for SAGE Publications India Pvt Ltd, typeset at 10/13 pts Times by Diligent Typesetter, Delhi and printed at Chaman Enterprises, New Delhi.

Library of Congress Cataloging-in-Publication Data

Trade in services and trade agreements : perspectives from India and the European Union / edited by Arpita Mukherjee, Rupa Chanda, Tanu M. Goyal.
    pages cm
Includes bibliographical references and index.
    1. Service industries—India. 2. Service industries—European Union countries. 3. India—Commercial policy. 4. European Union countries—Commercial policy. 5. India—Commerce—European Union countries. 6. European Union countries—Commerce—India. I. Mukherjee, Arpita, editor. II. Chanda, Rupa, editor. III. Goyal, Tanu M. editor.
    HD9987.I42T734   382'.45—dc23   2016   2015026389

ISBN: 978-93-515-0324-8 (HB)

The SAGE Team: N. Unni Nair, Neha Sharma, Anju Saxena and Ritu Chopra

Contents

CHAPTER 1
Introduction   1
Arpita Mukherjee, Rupa Chanda and Tanu M. Goyal

PART I

CHAPTER 2
The Services Sector in India and the EU   19
Ramneet Goswami

CHAPTER 3
Trade and Investment in Services: Reflections from India and
    the EU   53
Ramneet Goswami

PART II

CHAPTER 4
Expanding Collaboration in Logistics: The BTIA and Beyond   85
Smita Miglani

List of Tables

List of Figures

List of Boxes

Foreword

The services sector has emerged as the largest and fastest-growing sector in the world economy, contributing significantly to global output and employment. Several countries and regions, both emerging and advanced, are important players in the global services market. Notable among these are India and the European Union (EU). In both these economies, the services sector is the largest contributor to the gross domestic product (GDP) and plays a significant role in trade and FDI flows.

The importance of services is palpable in the relationship between India and the EU. Bilateral trade in services has grown more than fourfold since 2003 in spite of the global slowdown. Today, the EU is India's largest trading partner in services and accounts for around 13 per cent of India's services trade. The EU is one of the major sources of foreign investments and technology transfer into India.

Underpinning the bilateral economic engagement are the complementarities between the two economies. While India possesses a large, young and well-educated English-speaking workforce that can offer services at globally competitive rates, the EU faces skill shortages and adverse demographic conditions. The large and growing Indian market is in sharp contrast to the saturated market of many EU member states. There are also complementarities with regard to areas of interest and strength across services and modes of delivery. India's competitiveness in skilled labour-intensive sectors such as IT, health and business services complements EUs strength in capital and technology-intensive infrastructure services such as telecommunications, energy and transport services. Several EU companies are keen on accessing the Indian market in a range of service sectors such as infrastructure, business and social services.

Numerous agreements between India and EU have already been signed, although the one that could be transformational is the Bilateral Trade and Investment Agreement (BTIA) that covers a wide range of issues and sectors, including goods, services, investment, government procurement, sustainable development and labour standards, among others. The BTIA negotiations began in June 2007 and have been conducted in the backdrop of languid economic reforms in India and lacklustre performance of many Eurozone countries due to the economic crisis. If signed, the BTIA will be India's first agreement with a major advanced regional bloc and a major trading partner. For the EU, it will be its first agreement with a large emerging market. The agreement has enormous potential to deepen bilateral trade and investment relations and to lock in reform. It could also have spillover impacts on other trading nations given the size of the two economies.

In 2014, India's new government committed to reform and has taken several initiatives such as liberalising the FDI limits in railways and insurance to push ahead the reform agenda. The government is also encouraging foreign companies to come and set up manufacturing bases in India through its 'Make in India' initiative. This is likely to create demand for allied services such as logistics services. Once India initiates some key reforms and the EU is able to emerge from the crisis, the setting and context of the trade negotiations will change for the better.

India and EU are independently active participants in bilateral and regional trade agreements, reflecting in part slow progress in the World Trade Organization (WTO). In part it reflects a desire to advantage from increased trade and investment flows. Against this backdrop, this book is a timely contribution to the existing body of knowledge on domestic reforms and trade agreements in services. Based on extensive primary and secondary information, the analysis breaks new ground in attempting to understand the trade complementarities in the service sector between a developing country and a developed region. The political economy challenges in the context of such a broad based agreement are also addressed. Besides a rich overview of the service sectors in both economies, the book focuses on carefully selected sectors that represent not only the plenty of potential for increased bilateral engagement, but also the possibility of joint operations in third country markets. The selected services cover broad clusters, namely infrastructure (logistics and energy), business

(IT-ITeS and retail), professional (accountancy) and social (health and environment) services, with some services cutting across clusters. Sector-specific discussion captures the existing regulatory structure, barriers faced and opportunities at hand in each other's markets along with an analysis of the domestic reforms that will allow India and the EU to realise those opportunities. The analysis in the book also looks beyond sector-specific issues in that it examines the commitments made by India and the EU in their existing bilateral agreements and implications for the ongoing negotiations for the BTIA.

The Indian Council for Research on International Economic Relations (ICRIER) has been at the vanguard of research on 'Trade and Investment in Services'. It forms one of the key focus areas of the ICRIERs research and this book is the result of hard work and scholarship spread over the better part of two years. I am sure the book will offer students, researchers, academics, businesses and industry bodies interesting and analytical insights on the subject of globalisation of services. I have no doubt that the book will also enhance knowledge and understanding among policy-makers in India and the EU. With many regional trade negotiations such as the Regional Comprehensive Economic Partnership (RCEP), Trans-Pacific Partnership (TPP) and Transatlantic Trade and Investment Partnership (TTIP) underway, the book will also serve to inform future negotiations that involve India and the EU.

Economic integration in services, as opposed to merchandise trade, is a more difficult and sensitive issue, and it will be counterproductive to not recognise this dimension. I hope that the book will generate debate on issues around India–EU BTIA negotiations as well as on broader issues relating to enhancing the global competitiveness and efficiency of services, including development of services value chains between developed and developing countries. ICRIER gratefully acknowledges the support of Konrad-Adenauer-Stiftung (KAS), Germany, for sponsoring the research on which the book is based. The editors of the book and chapter authors have been involved in the India–EU BTIA negotiations and, thus, have a ring side view of the policy process. A lot of that experience is reflected in the writing, making it a worthy addition to the existing literature on the subject.

Rajat Kathuria
Director and Chief Executive, ICRIER, New Delhi

Acknowledgements

We express our gratitude to Rajat Kathuria, Director and Chief Executive, Indian Council for Research on International Economic Relations (ICRIER) for giving us the opportunity to work in this area and for his encouragement and support. We would like to thank KAS for funding this study. Without the support of Beatrice Gorawantschy, former Resident Representative, KAS (India) and her team of Malte Gaier and Pankaj Madan, this project would not have been completed in such a short time.

The book has received input from several Indian and European policymakers and industry experts. Sumanta Chaudhuri, Sudhanshu Pandey, Sonia Pant, Amit Yadav, Sangeeta Godbole, Peter Young, Ignacio Garcia Bercero and Sanchita Chatterjee improved our understanding of the India–EU trade relationships. Afaq Hussain of the Bureau of Research on Industry and Economic Fundamentals (BRIEF) and his team efficiently conducted the primary survey. We would also like to thank Manab Majumdar of the Federation of Indian Chambers of Commerce and Industry (FICCI), who helped us organise the stakeholder's consultations for the study.

Our administrative team at ICRIER, particularly Rajeev Kapil, Manmeet Ahuja and their teams, deserves special mention for the strong administrative support throughout the study and publication work. Anu Mohandas and Hilda Kathuria who coordinated meetings and appointments, Chhaya Singh who helped with documentation and Raj Kumar Shahi who provided IT support deserve our unconditional gratitude.

We are extremely grateful to the contributing authors who met the tight deadlines despite their busy schedules. Renu Gupta deserves notable praise for her expert copyediting and for bringing uniformity to the writing styles of several authors. Last but not the least, we would like to thank our families for their constant support while we worked late nights and for handling our project-related stress.

1

Introduction*

*Arpita Mukherjee, Rupa Chanda
and Tanu M. Goyal*

In the past two decades, the services sector has emerged as the largest and fastest growing sector of the global economy, accounting for more than 60 per cent of global output and one-third of global employment. There has been increased trade in services as a result of globalisation, technological developments, new business outsourcing models, establishment of services value chains and liberalisation of markets through domestic reforms. Consequent to the rise in services trade, there has also been an increased thrust on enabling a more liberal trading environment for services trade.

Services became a part of multilateral negotiations under the auspices of the World Trade Organization (WTO) during the Uruguay Round of negotiations through the General Agreement on Trade in Services (GATS).[1] Due to the slow progress of the second Round of WTO negotiations—the Doha Round—there has been a proliferation of free trade agreements (FTAs) and increasingly, a trend towards comprehensive agreements which cover services, investment and a range of other issues such as cooperation, government procurement, sustainable development

---

*Following symbols have been used for currencies: Indian Rupees (INR) = ₹; Euro = €; US Dollar = $ or US$.

[1] The GATS, which came into force in January 1995, established rules and disciplines governing trade in services.

and trade facilitation that have a bearing on trade. Today, most trading nations, especially large services trading nations such as the United States (US) and the European Union (EU), are negotiating such comprehensive trade agreements. This has not only widened the scope for services liberalisation, but has also complicated bilateral negotiations because services are now covered not only under the services chapters of the agreements but also under the chapters on investment cooperation, government procurement and Intellectual Property Rights (IPR), among others.

There is a significant body of literature on the proliferation of trade agreements. For instance, the slow progress of the WTO's Doha Round of negotiations, snowballing and domino effects where countries did not want to be left behind and political and strategic reasons, among others, have encouraged WTO members to enter into FTAs and PTAs (preferential trade agreements) (Brown and Stern, 2011; Horn et al., 2010). Baldwin (1993) explains the emergence of bilateral and regional trade agreements as a domino phenomenon that reflects trade diversion concerns among countries. Baier and Bergstrand (2003) cite *pure economic* factors such as a gain in welfare as one of the main drivers of these *new age* agreements. Ornelas (2003) highlights *rent dissipation* as a major contributing factor for such FTAs and Woolcock (2007) has shown that there are mixed motives behind FTAs that include both political and commercial concerns.

Studies have also focused on the treatment of services in multilateral and bilateral trade agreements. These studies analyse the type of scheduling, depth of commitments and linkages of services sector commitments with other areas of trade negotiations and also compare commitments across trade agreements and with the applied domestic regime. For instance, Marchetti and Roy (2008) and Horn et al. (2010) analyse the scope and commitments in services under multilateral and bilateral agreements and note that the latter contain *WTO-plus* provisions in the case of services; the agreements of developed countries such as the EU attempt to secure regulatory certainty along with market access liberalisation. When they compared the commitments under trade agreements with the applied domestic regime, the studies found that some trade agreements, especially those by the US and the EU, seek forward-looking commitments and promote future domestic reforms. Fink and Molinuevo (2008) analyse the architecture of trade agreements and find that the design of bilateral agreements covering services can be different from the GATS architecture. They conclude that what is relevant is not the design but the extent of actual liberalisation. Countries like Singapore have used FTAs (US–Singapore FTA) to push for domestic reforms, while others like India prefer to undertake domestic reform first and then bind them in trade agreements (Mukherjee, 2008).

Several studies have shown that there are high welfare gains resulting from trade liberalisation. Ghemawat (2011) argues that the gains from liberalising barriers in global merchandise trade would amount to 0.5 per cent of the world gross domestic product (GDP), which is estimated at US$300 billion. Additionally, by removing barriers to the movement of people, the gains would be almost 100 per cent of the GDP. As per another study, in case of the EU alone, global welfare gains from liberalisation at the level of EU's offer in the Doha Round are estimated at 0.5–0.8 per cent of the GDP.[2] A large part of these gains will be directed to developing countries in Asia and Africa. The study further shows that gains from liberalising global trade in services would be 0.8 per cent of the GDP and those from liberalising services in India would be 1.8 per cent of the GDP.

However, while the overall welfare gains and losses arising from liberalisation of services have been studied, it is difficult to quantify sector-specific gains and losses arising from services trade liberalisation in the context of bilateral trade agreements between the developed and developing countries. One such important case in the present-day scenario is the India–EU Broad-based Trade and Investment Agreement (India–EU BTIA). Both the EU, a regional bloc consisting of 28 countries that includes many developed countries, and India, an important developing and emerging economy, are actively engaged in negotiating bilateral and regional agreements with third countries around the world. The two are also currently negotiating a BTIA to broaden bilateral commercial and economic relations with each other. The BTIA is a comprehensive WTO plus agreement that will cover trade in goods, services, investment, trade facilitation measures, government procurement, labour standards and sustainable development, among others. If successfully negotiated, this

---

[2] The study defines welfare gains as increase in global consumption. For details see http://erhvervsstyrelsen.dk/file/3852/Economic_effects.pdf (accessed on 24 November 2014).

will be the EU's first trade agreement with a large and growing emerging market. This will also be India's first trade agreement with a large bloc of developed nations, which also feature among its largest trading and investment partners. This legally binding agreement would cover almost one-fifth of the world's population and, therefore, its impact and implications (both positive and negative) would be significant (Singh, 2009). However, this agreement, which has been under negotiation since June 2007, has progressed very slowly in the aftermath of the global financial crisis and the subsequent Eurozone crisis. The slow pace of reforms in India over the past few years has also contributed to the stalling of these negotiations.

With the coming into power of a majority government at the centre in May 2014, the prospects for reforms in India have improved. The new Indian Government has declared its commitment to reforms, such as liberalisation of foreign direct investment in the insurance sector and introduction of a single Goods and Services Tax (GST), among other proposed reforms. In the interim, while these proposed reforms remain pending and await consensus and clearance through the Parliamentary process, in order to signal its binding commitment to the reform process, the government has issued several ordinances to keep the momentum going. The government has also announced that it will reduce the cost of doing business by removing/replacing the outdated regulation and by streamlining clearance procedures.

The EU on its part is slowly recovering from the economic crisis, though some countries like Greece remain in a difficult economic position. This could provide some impetus to the bilateral trade negotiations, though recovery on a more firm footing in the Eurozone countries would help facilitate these discussions. Another positive development is the recent consensus reached on the issue of trade facilitation between India and the EU. Hence, given a more dedicated outlook for reforms in India and some signs of recovery in the EU, the prospects for the India–EU BTIA have improved and a new look into the likely contours of this agreement and an understanding of the core areas of interest on both sides can help provide useful policy directions for the ongoing negotiations.

A successful conclusion would increase the competitiveness of both partners in the global arena. The agreement would strengthen the EU's trade ties in Asia as well as the EU's role as a global actor and revive market confidence in the Eurozone. India would gain greater market access to 28 EU Member States (Khandekar and Sengupta, 2012). Since India is a high tariff country, the BTIA is expected to lead to tariff reductions in India. As a result, companies from EU Member States would be able to secure a comparative export advantage in the Indian market vis-à-vis companies from other countries such as China and the US. Apart from increasing trade volumes between India and the EU, the BTIA would enable technology and knowledge transfer between a developed and developing nation, help to develop infrastructure in India through investment from EU Member States, improve supply chains, link production networks between Indian and the EU companies, create job opportunities, increase competitiveness of companies in both economies and enhance skill development. The EU companies would be able to access the low-cost skilled workforce of India. This would not only help to mitigate their labour shortages but also enable them to improve their global competitiveness. All these could help deepen their bilateral ties (Upadhyay, 2012). This would also enable India and the EU to become part of the global value chain in services. As per the Eurostat data, the EU outsources knowledge-intensive services including research and development (R&D) services to India, as a part of its global value chain. The BTIA is likely to enhance India–EU collaborations in the global value chain.[3] Additionally, with the 'Make in India' campaign (www.makeinindia.gov.in), the Indian government has initiated steps to encourage foreign investments in the Indian manufacturing sector and services that support manufacturing. This is likely to benefit companies from the EU Member States. India is in the process of developing infrastructure including economic corridors, and countries like the United Kingdom (UK) have already expressed interest in investing in developing economic corridors such as the Delhi–Mumbai Industrial Corridor. The Indian government is encouraging foreign companies to develop industrial clusters in these corridors. India is also planning to launch a 'Serve from India' campaign which will encourage foreign companies to enter the market and provide services from India.

Further, the BTIA is expected to facilitate trade flows by address-ing some non-tariff barriers, such as differences in product standards. In

---

[3] http://epp.eurostat.ec.europa.eu/statistics_explained/index.php/Global_value_chains_-_international_sourcing_to_China_and_India (accessed on 24 November 2014).

addition, the BTIA is expected to significantly increase bilateral invest-ment flows. EU companies, which are facing a slowdown and a saturated domestic market, are exploring investment opportunities in growing emerging markets like India, and Indian companies are exploring invest-ment opportunities in the EU to acquire technology and get the benefits of being treated as a EU company.[4] A trade agreement will provide security to investors.

Policy-makers in the EU and India recognise the trade and investment complementarities between the two economies and the likely benefits of a bilateral trade agreement. The EU has moved from an aid-oriented strategy to a trade-oriented strategy for emerging markets like India (European Commission, 2006c). More recently, with the new government in India, a series of policy reforms have been enacted in sensitive sectors like railways and defence to facilitate bilateral trade and investment. Given these developments, this book examines the cross-cutting issues that affect bilateral prospects in core areas of interest in services for the two trading partners and analyses the implications of liberalising trade in services between the two. As it is often difficult to quantify services trade and its associated gains, the book makes use of anecdotal evidence, discussions with experts and practitioners in different sectors and secondary evidence to illustrate the likely gains and losses from bilateral liberalisation of services trade and investment. Considering the present focus on international integration, liberalisation and reforms in both markets, this book suggests a negotiation strategy and looks beyond the India–EU BTIA to deepen bilateral relations between the two economies.

The Importance of Services Liberalisation in the India–EU BTIA

Both the EU and India are proponents of liberalising services trade in the WTO and under bilateral trade agreements. The EU is considered a suc-cessful regional bloc in terms of market integration. Among developed countries, the EU and among large developing countries, India have been active players in the recent *global race* for the *new age* FTAs.

---

[4] Foreign companies that invest in the EU are treated at par with EU companies.

The EU market for goods is integrated and the EU is in the process of integrating the internal services market. If it is integrated, the EU will offer one of the largest services markets. In India, the services sector is growing faster than the country's GDP, and India offers a large and unsaturated market to global service providers. India seeks greater market access for its service providers through bilateral trade agreements, but the services sector in India faces several restrictions including restrictions on foreign direct investment. If the services sector is liberalised, the two economies will jointly offer a large market of more than 1.7 billion consumers for their service providers.[5] At the same time, both India and the EU are negotiating a number of trade agreements that will have implications for the market integration of global services; for example, the EU is negotiating a Trans-Pacific Partnership (TPP) Agreement with the US and India is negotiating the Regional Comprehensive Economic Partnership Agreement (RCEP) with the Association of Southeast Asian Nations (ASEAN) Member States and Australia, China, Japan, Korea and New Zealand.

The importance of services in their respective trade agreements stems from the fact that this constitutes the largest sector in both economies. In 2012, services contributed about 56.5 per cent to India's GDP and 73.4 per cent to the EU's GDP. It employs about 28 per cent of the workforce in India and 71.8 per cent of the workforce[6] in the EU in 2011.[7] Since the 1990s, EU Member Countries and India have autonomously liberalised the services sector. Both are global players in the services market, with growing trade in services. In 2011, services trade contributed 25.9 per cent and 22.4 per cent of total trade for India and the EU, respectively. In 2011, the EU was the largest exporter of services among WTO member countries, accounting for around 24.7 per cent of the world's total exports of services, while India was ranked 8th with a share of 3.3 per cent (WTO, 2012).

---

[5] Based on the population estimate given in the CIA World Economic Factbook.

[6] The figure is for organised employment. The sector is highly unorganised and it is difficult to get information on it.

[7] The World Factbook (July 2014), Central Intelligence Agency (CIA), available at https://www.cia.gov/library/publications/the-world-factbook/geos/ee.html (accessed on 29 July 2013).

In terms of the market and governance, India and the EU have similar structures. Both are multicultural democracies with a quasi-federal governance structure. India consists of 28 states with several state-specific policies and the EU has 28 Member States with different national policies. In India, some services like retail are under state jurisdiction, while the EU Member States have different policies for services sectors like accountancy services. Thus, both India and the EU do not have a single market for services in terms of their governance structure and regulations.

India and the EU started liberalising their services sectors in the 1990s. As a result, several services in the two markets have evolved from the government-controlled monopolies to competitive services with strong and growing private sector participation. The two economies face similar challenges in allowing private participation in sectors like education and health services that require strong government involvement due to their public goods nature, and they can learn from each other's regulatory experiences. Recently, India has further liberalised its services sector with the view to attract foreign investments. Foreign direct investment (FDI) limit in defence has been increased to 49 per cent under the government route, and the investor with more than 49 per cent share will be given approval by Cabinet Committee on Security on a case-by-case basis, based on technology transfer. Additionally, FDI in railways has also been permitted for construction, operation and maintenance of high speed trains and sub-urban corridors. In December 2014, the Department of Industrial Policy and Promotion (DIPP) released a list of initiatives being undertaken for easing the environment for doing business in India. Some of the steps included simplifying the design and process of application, creating a dynamic portal (eBiz) with online payment facility and initiating the process for simplifying and rationalising operating environment.[8]

There are important differences between the two markets. These include differences in demographics, growth prospects and the standard of living. Compared to the EU, India has a much younger population. In 2010, the median age of India's population was 25.1 years, while the median age in the EU ranged between 34.2 years (Cyprus) and 44.3 years

---

[8] DIPP, Government of India; also see http://dipp.nic.in/English/Investor/Doing_BusinessInitiative.pdf (accessed on 17 December, 2014) for details.

(Germany).[9] Compared to the EU, the Indian market has been growing at a faster pace. In 2012, while India's GDP grew at 4 per cent, the EU's GDP declined by 0.2 per cent. In 2016, the Indian market is expected to grow by 7.5 per cent, while the EU is expected to grow by 1.9 per cent (IMF, 2015). Further, the EU market is reaching its saturation point, while the Indian market continues to grow.

These differences result in strong trade and investment complementarities between the two economies in the services sector. India, on the one hand, can offer its human capital and access to a large and growing domestic market to EU companies that are increasingly looking at extra-regional markets given their rapidly ageing population and saturation in their regional market. The EU, on the other hand, can provide the capital and technology required for India's economic development and for sustaining a high growth rate. The trade and investment complementarities between the two are reflected in the actual trade and investment flows. The EU is India's largest trading partner in services, and bilateral services trade has shown an upward trend. Between 2004 and 2012, bilateral trade in services increased from US$9.82 billion to US$29.3 billion.[10] In 2010, the EU contributed 11 per cent to India's services trade, followed by the US (10 per cent).[11] In comparison, India's share in the EU's bilateral trade in services is low. Among Asian countries, in 2011, India was ranked 4th among the services exporters and importers of the EU (after China, Japan and Singapore), accounting for 1.9 per cent of the EU's exports and for 2.2 per cent of the EU's imports, respectively.[12]

The EU is a large investor in the Indian market and is one of the largest sources of technology transfer for India. Between April 2000 and April 2013, total cumulative FDI inflows (including goods and services)

[9] Compiled from International Human Development Indicators available at http://hdrstats.undp.org/en/tables/ (accessed on 31 July 2013). The median age in Cyprus is the lowest and Germany is the highest. The source does not give a median age for the EU as a whole.

[10] Compiled from Eurostat, 'Table: International Trade in Services (since 2004), available at http://appsso.eurostat.ec.europa.eu/nui/show.do?dataset=bop_its_det&lang=en (accessed on 23 September 2013).

[11] The share was calculated from UNCTAD 'Statistics on International Trade: Services' and OECD 'Statistics on International Trade in Services by Partner Country (EBPOS, 2002)', available athttp://stats.oecd.org/Index.aspx?DatasetCode=TIS (accessed on 25 July 2013).

[12] Extracted from WTO (2013), Table 1.2, p. 22.

from the EU were US\$49 billion, which accounted for 25 per cent of cumulative FDI inflows during this period.[13] Investment data by sector from the Reserve Bank of India (RBI) shows that between April 2008 and June 2011, the services sector accounted for the largest share of cumulative FDI inflows from the EU (43.6 per cent). Between July 2007 and June 2013, Indian investment in the EU was US\$39.1 billion and services accounted for 64 per cent of this investment.[14] In India, preference is given to foreign investments that are accompanied by technology transfer. The EU is the largest source of technology transfer in India. Three EU Member States—Germany, the UK and Italy—accounted for 30.6 per cent of the total technology transfer approvals in India in 2010.[15] A trade agreement with a large trading partner in services and between two economies with strong investment and technology linkages is going to be mutually beneficial. The governments of the two economies recognise the existence of trade and investment complementarities and have taken several initiatives to facilitate trade and investment flows.

Inter-government Efforts to Facilitate Trade and Investment

The inter-governmental relationship between India and EU dates back to 1962 when India was among the first set of countries to set up diplomatic relations with the European Economic Community (EEC) to foster economic cooperation, trade and development. In 1983, the European Commission (EC) delegation was set up in New Delhi, India, thus providing a basis for continuous engagement by the EU in the Indian market. This relationship deepened in the 1990s when both India and the EU started liberalising and globalising. The relationship took a new turn in the Lisbon Summit of June 2000 where the focus was on building a Strategic Partnership.

---

[13] Compiled from DIPP (2013a), Annex-A, p. 5.

[14] Calculated from the RBI database on 'Overseas Indian Direct Investment', available at http://www.rbi.org.in/scripts/Data_Overseas_Investment.aspx (accessed on 18 July 2013).

[15] Extracted from DIPP (2010), Table III.B: Country-wise Foreign Technology Transfer Approvals, p. 5.

In the 5th Summit at The Hague in November 2004, the relationship was upgraded from an economic to a strategic partnership. India was the sixth country (after the US, Russia, China, Japan and Canada) to have a strategic partnership with the EU. The EU's Galileo project—a global navigation satellite system—is an important example of strategic partnership between the two sides. Over the past decade, the two economies have signed several cooperation agreements. These include the India and EU Science and Technology Agreement of 2001, which was renewed in 2009. In 2010, India, the European Commission and EU Member States launched a pilot initiative through the strategic forum for International Science and Technology Cooperation (SFIC) towards greater convergence of their priorities and strategies in the field of water and bio-resources. On 29 September 2008, the EU and India signed a Horizontal Aviation Agreement and the two economies are also negotiating a maritime agreement.

In the 6th EU–India Summit in September 2005, a High-Level Trade Group (HLTG) was established to explore ways to deepen and widen the bilateral trade and investment relationship. This HLTG recommended a BTIA in the 7th Summit in Helsinki, Finland. Based on this recommendation, in June 2007, the EU and India began negotiations on the BTIA in Brussels, Belgium. As of October 2013, 16 rounds of negotiations of this comprehensive trade agreement have been completed. In the last quarter of 2014, the Indian government met with the EU ambassador to take a stock of the negotiations from where they had left.[16]

Studies on the India–EU BTIA

Studies that examine the likely impact of the India–EU BTIA using both secondary evidence and survey approaches show that the India–EU BTIA will be mutually beneficial (see Centre for the Analysis of Regional Integration at Sussex [CARIS] and Consumer Unity and Trust Society [CUTS], 2007; ECORYS, CUTS and Centre for Trade and Development [Centad], 2009; Mukherjee and Goswami, 2011). These studies also highlight several barriers to bilateral trade in services that

[16] http://articles.economictimes.indiatimes.com/2014-09-10/news/53770416_1_india-and-eu-eu-ambassador-eu-side (accessed on 16 December 2014).

can be addressed under the bilateral trade agreement. While India tends to impose market access barriers, rigid regulations in the EU restrict the entry and operation of foreign service providers and companies. India, the EU and its Member States including Germany, France, Italy, Sweden and the UK[17] are already engaged in several collaborations at different levels—between governments, between industry associations and between businesses. The India–EU BTIA will help consolidate the inter-government collaborations and provide liberal access to each other's companies in two large markets. The HLTG recognised this and has laid down the blueprints for the bilateral trade negotiations. It proposed that a comprehensive trade agreement with substantial liberalisation would benefit both India and the EU. The EU's strategy towards India shows a marked change in its 2006 report, 'Global Europe: Competing in the World'[18] in which it emphasised that the EU should enter into trade agreements with emerging markets that have high levels of protectionism, such as India. The 2006 document focused on promoting bilateral trade through competition rather than on aid for emerging markets like India, which was identified as a country in which EU companies have a strong interest in entering and operating.

About the Book

Most studies on the India–EU relationship focus on their strategic relationship (Baroowa, 2007; Sachdeva, 2009) and a few like Mukherjee and Goswami (2011) focus on the liberalisation of the services sector. Other studies like Stichele and Singh (2009) examine the liberalisation of specific services sectors like financial services. However, there are no studies that look beyond the India–EU BTIA to provide a comparative analysis of the trade agreements of India and the EU.

This book addresses some gaps in the research by examining the India–EU trade and investment relationship in services before and after the global slowdown. The objective is to develop an understanding of

---

[17] For details, see http://www.oir.iitm.ac.in/wp-content/uploads/2013/05/Overview.pdf (accessed on 1 October 2013).
[18] Available at http://trade.ec.europa.eu/doclib/docs/2006/october/tradoc_130376.pdf (accessed on 1 June 2015).

the existing trade and investment complementarities between India and the EU, and assess how a trade agreement between the two economies can help realise the opportunities created by such complementarities. It examines the scope for increasing market access and removing barriers for service providers and companies in each other's market. This book gives a holistic perspective covering key service sectors of interest to both India and the EU in light of the changing policy space in both markets.

Precisely, the book makes three potential contributions to the literature.

1. It looks at the pattern of services trade between a developed and a developing economy, both of which are actively engaged in negotiating comprehensive trade agreements. It covers an important trade agreement, the India–EU BTIA, which would be the EU's first agreement with a large emerging market and India's first agreement with a major developed country trade bloc. Since such an agreement is likely to have an impact on other large trading nations like the US and China through trade agreements such as the TPP Agreement and the RCEP, a close examination of the BTIA would be an important contribution to the literature on trade agreements and trade policy.

2. It provides a comprehensive coverage of the services sector in India and the EU, including a discussion of trends and patterns in services trade and regulatory developments across a wide range of service sectors. It also highlights the concerns and potential in individual services and examines cross-sectoral issues and challenges that affect bilateral relations in services. Hence, this book is a useful reference for scholars interested in the services sector in general, those interested in learning more about specific services and scholars interested in the Indian and EU economies.

3. This book provides an up-to-date account of developments in the global economy, the euro zone and the Indian economy and their impact on the services sector in the EU and India. It also brings to the fore emerging debates and challenges in services integration in the wake of the current recessionary environment. This book would provide valuable information to policy-makers and industry about the prevailing regulatory regimes for services in India

and the EU and the sensitivities and debates surrounding regulatory reforms in services. Such inputs would help policy-makers to formulate their negotiating strategies and also help industry design its *go-to-market* strategy.

The book is divided into three parts with 11 chapters. Part I provides an overview in two chapters; Chapter 2 provides an overview of the services sector in the two economies, while Chapter 3 examines trends and recent developments in trade and investment in services.

Part II consists of seven chapters on different sectors of interest to either the EU or India or both. The sectors have been selected based on their importance in the India–EU BTIA as well as the need to cover different types of services, namely infrastructure services, business services, social services and other services. The sector studies follow a common format. They focus on trends and recent developments in the specific sector in the Indian and EU markets and examine their global and bilateral trade patterns. Since bilateral trade data are not available, the sector studies rely on findings from in-depth interviews and discussions with stakeholders in each sector and substantiate the findings with an analysis of secondary data. These studies also identify trade complementarities within each sector, potential areas for bilateral trade, investment and collaboration and sector-specific regulatory and other barriers to developing bilateral relations. They also suggest reform measures to strengthen relations in the sector and present sector-specific negotiation strategies.

Infrastructure services play a crucial role in boosting economic growth, enhancing the productivity and competitiveness of domestic industries, facilitating trade and linking the economy to the rest of the world. This book covers two key infrastructure services, logistics in Chapter 4 and energy services in Chapter 5, where Indian and EU companies have significant trade complementarities. EU companies are large investors in both these sectors in India. Recently, the policy focus of the Indian government has been to attract foreign investments in developing infrastructure particularly in the logistics sectors. To this effect, several developments have occurred in the Indian markets that are noteworthy.

Both India and the EU have focused on exports of business services, which are based on skilled human resources. These include services like software and professional services. Chapter 6 covers IT/ITeS services, which is one of the most important export sectors for both India and the EU, while Chapter 7 covers accountancy services, which is a key professional service for which EU companies are seeking market access in India. The chapters address several issues related to the movement of professionals such as harmonisation of qualifications that can be addressed through bilateral agreements.

Social services such as healthcare help in human capital development and inclusive growth. In India and the EU, the government plays a key role in providing these services to ensure equitable distribution. However, with globalisation, the role of private players in the provision of healthcare has increased, thereby creating opportunities for bilateral trade and investment flows as highlighted in Chapter 8. Chapter 9 focuses on a key social service—environment services—a sector of interest to the EU in trade agreements. All trade agreements signed by the EU contain a chapter on sustainable development in addition to addressing the liberalisation of environment services separately under the services chapter; the chapter on sustainable development focuses on the environmental and social impact of trade agreements. In a trade agreement between the EU and a developing country such as India, the European Commission, the EU Parliament and other organisations closely monitor the social and environmental impact.

Other services cannot be classified under the three categories above, but they have strong links with other sectors of the economy and can enhance growth and employment. One such service is retail, which is a key component of the supply chain and production network. Until retail is liberalised, production networks and end-to-end supply chains between the two economies cannot be established. Although India's large consumer market is of significant interest to EU companies, retail is one of the few sectors in India where there are restrictions on FDI along with regulatory hurdles. The EU is seeking market access commitments from India in retail services and India has so far taken a defensive position. Chapter 10 examines the potential for liberalising this sector under the India–EU BTIA.

Part III consolidates the key findings of the book and moves beyond the India–EU BTIA. As a benchmark for the India–EU BTIA, Chapter 11 analyses the offers made by India and the EU in the Uruguay Round and the progress made in the Doha Round of the WTO and in their commitments in the existing trade agreements to highlight their respective expectations and likely demands from each other in the ongoing BTIA negotiations. It examines the framework used by India and the EU in drafting their agreements and, hence, the likely architecture of a bilateral agreement between the two economies. It also examines the prospects for India–EU inter-governmental cooperation at three levels: multilateral, bilateral and between India and individual EU Member States. Based on the sector studies, it summarises the scope for liberalising and enhancing bilateral trade, investment and collaboration in services between India and the EU and the key challenges. It then presents a roadmap to look beyond the India–EU BTIA so that the two economies continue to engage in trade, investment and collaboration in services beyond the formal legal architecture provided by this prospective trade agreement.

Ultimately, this book attempts to present a roadmap for enhancing bilateral trade, investment and economic cooperation between India and the EU in the light of recent developments in both the trading partners. As a way forward, it goes beyond the BTIA to examine other ways of improving bilateral relations that go further than what is legally envisioned under the BTIA.

PART I

PART I

2
The Services Sector in India and the EU

Ramneet Goswami

Introduction

India and the EU, although very differently placed in terms of their levels of per capita income and in terms of their institutional, social and human development indicators, share similarities in the services sector. Europe is often described as a 'service economy', while in India services is often regarded as the 'mainstay of the economy'.[1] In both India and the EU, the services sector started to grow in the mid-1980s with growth accelerating in the 1990s. Today, services is the main contributor to the GDP and to overall growth in both India and EU Member States. It also contributes a significant share to employment in both economies; in the EU, the services sector is the largest employer, and in India services is the second largest employer after agriculture (Bhattacharya and Mitra, 1990, Kochhar et al., 2006). The main factors that have contributed to the growth of this sector in both economies are liberalisation of the services sector, economic development and technological advances (Ansari, 1995;

[1] European Commission (2009) and Planning Commission (2008). However, the path by which the two economies reached here is different. In the EU, the shift towards services has followed the normal paradigm of economic growth and structural change with a gradual transition from agriculture to industry to services, whereas India has leapfrogged from agriculture to services.

Banga, 2005; Banga and Goldar, 2004; Bhattacharya and Mitra, 1990; Chanda, 2002; Gordon and Gupta, 2003; Hansda, 2001; Jain and Ninan, 2010; Kemekliene and Watt, 2010). The sector has been the focus of significant reforms and liberalisation in both economies over the past two decades. India and the EU are also similar in terms of their governance structures. Both have a quasi-federal institutional structure (both India and EU have 28 states/Member States) and the services sector is jointly governed by the centre (the central government in India and the European Commission in the EU) and by the state (state governments in India and individual Member States in the EU).

The institutional, macro-economic and regulatory framework in India and the EU is explored in this chapter. These aspects have an important bearing on the bilateral relation between India and the EU.

Governance Structure in India and the EU

Multiple governing bodies often lead to slow reforms (Mandel and Carew, 2013) and regulatory complexities. Both India and the EU have multiple jurisdictions governing the services sector, creating complexities in their bilateral relations in services. India has a quasi-federal governance structure and according to the Constitution of India, some services are under the jurisdiction of the central government (Union List), some are under state governments (State List) and the remainder are under the joint administration of the central and state governments (Concurrent List) (Figure 2.1). At the central level, multiple ministries and government departments regulate different services. For instance, in India, energy is regulated by the Ministry of Power, the Ministry of Coal, the Ministry of Oil and Natural Gas, and the Ministry of New and Renewable Energy at the centre. Yet, there is no nodal ministry for sectors such as construction and retail. Professional bodies regulate professions such as medical, architecture and accountancy services.

The EU also has a quasi-federal institutional structure (Kelemen, 2006) and the governance of services comes under both the Union and individual Member States. At the EU level, there are five types of governing institutions: (1) European Commission, (2) Council of the European Union, (3) European Council, (4) European Parliament and (5) European Court

Figure 2.1
Jurisdiction of Services Sectors in the Constitution of India

UNION LIST

- Telecommunications, postal, broadcasting, financial services (including insurance and banking), national highways and mining services

STATE LIST

- Health and related services, real-estate services, retail, services incidental to agriculture, hunting and forestry

CONCURRENT LIST

- Professional services (legal, accounting, auditing and bookkeeping, taxation, architectural, engineering, integrated engineering, urban planning and landscape architectural, medical and dental services and service provided by midwives, nurses, etc., education, printing and publishing, and electricity

Source: Extracted from Mukherjee (2012).

of Justice (Figure 2.2). The European Commission is the main executive authority of the EU, which has legislative as well as administrative powers. The European Commission comprises 28 Commissioners—one from each Member State—who are responsible for specific policy areas

Figure 2.2
Regulatory Structure of the EU

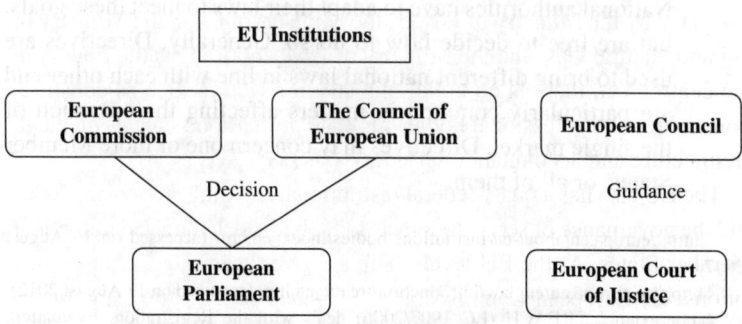

Source: Extracted from Demuro (2008), Figure: EU Institutions.

such as foreign affairs, education and transport. The main role of the European Commission is to propose (to Parliament and the Council), implement and enforce EU laws (jointly with the Court of Justice) and represent the EU at international negotiations. The Council of the European Union represents the individual Member States and its role includes the adoption of European laws and concluding/finalising international agreements between the EU and other foreign countries or international organisations. The European Council became an official EU institution under the Treaty of Lisbon in 2009. Its main function is to set up the EU's policy and to resolve issues between Member States. The European Parliament was established in 1979 with three main roles: (1) passing European laws (jointly with the Council), (2) exercising democratic supervision over other EU institutions and (3) adopting or rejecting the EU budget (jointly with the Council). The European Court of Justice ensures that the EU legislations are interpreted and applied uniformly in all the EU Member States. It also settles legal disputes among the EU Member States, EU institutions, businesses and individuals.[2]

In the EU, legislations or regulations are adopted in the form of EU laws. Every Member State is obliged to implement these laws or legislation in their national law.[3] The EU laws can be in the form of:

1. **Regulations:** These are the most direct form of EU law that become immediately enforceable as law in all Member States simultaneously. Regulations[4] override all national laws of Member States that deal with the same subject matter.

2. **Directives:** These lay down guidelines or results that must be achieved by every Member State within a given timeframe. National authorities have to adapt their laws to meet these goals, but are free to decide how to do so. Generally, Directives are used to bring different national laws in line with each other and are particularly common in matters affecting the operation of the single market. Directives may concern one or more Member States, or all of them.

---

[2] http://europa.eu/about-eu/institutions-bodies/index_en.htm (accessed on 16 August 2012).

[3] http://ec.europa.eu/eu_law/introduction/treaty_en.htm (accessed on 17 August 2012).

[4] For example, REACH (EC 1907/2006) deals with the Registration, Evaluation, Authorisation and Restriction of Chemical Substances.

3. **Decisions:** This is a legal instrument that is addressed to an individual Member State. They are generally passed either by the Council of the European Union (sometimes jointly with the European Parliament) or by the European Commission.[5]

Every individual Member State has the freedom to enact acts and regulations related to the services sector; for example, work permits and visas are under the purview of individual Member States. Due to the implementation of policies at the state level, regulations can vary significantly across Member States. The speed of implementation of Directives varies markedly across Member States and the extent of market integration varies across different services. For instance, while telecommunications and energy have been opened up fully to market competition, postal services remain relatively regulated (Keune et al., 2008). Although the Directive on electricity came into force in February 1999, five years later the Directorate General Energy and Transport (2004) found that full competition was present only in the UK, Sweden, Finland, Norway and Denmark (Keune et al., 2008).

In the same way, there are differences in how regulations in services are implemented across Indian states. Thus, service markets and regulations in both India and the EU are not integrated and this needs to be kept in mind when examining the services sector of the two economies. It is also important to note that the services sector is not homogenous and that it covers a wide range of activities from sophisticated information technology (IT) to simple services provided by workers in the informal sector.

Classification of Services in India and the EU

The services sector can be classified in accordance with the United Nations Central Product Classification (UNCPC), which is used for international negotiations such as the World Trade Organization's (WTO) General Agreement on Trade in Services (GATS) negotiations. India uses the classification provided by the National Industrial Classification (NIC)

---

[5] http://ec.europa.eu/eu_law/introduction/what_decision_en.htm (accessed on 17 August 2012).

and at present the NIC 2008 classification is in use. In the EU, the classification of the services sector is based on the European Classification of Economic Activities (NACE) and at present the NACE Revision 2 is being used in the EU.

There are broad similarities in the classification and coverage of services in India and the EU (see Appendix A, Table 2A.1 for details). The main difference is that the EU coverage is broader for services in wholesale and retail trade and education. Neither classification includes *Construction* as a services sector.

In India, disaggregated data for several services subsectors is not available. Even where data is available, it suffers from deficiencies related to definition, method of collection, suitability for pricing, construction of indices, and much more. In the past few years, different government departments such as the Central Statistical Office (CSO), the National Sample Survey Organisation (NSSO) under the Ministry of Statistics and Programme Implementation (MOSPI) and the Reserve Bank of India (RBI) have been trying to collect and collate data at the disaggregated level. However, since several services such as retail and construction are largely in the non-corporate sector (the informal or unorganised sector), the data is misreported and/or underreported.

In the EU, Eurostat provides sector-specific data on different services sectors. The data is available under Structural Business Statistics (SBS)[6] according to the NACE classification. The SBS does not cover the education and health sectors. Thus, the coverage is not comprehensive. Nevertheless, since most services in the EU are in the corporate sector unlike in India and as the compilation of data is uniform across all EU Member States, there is a lower likelihood of data mismatches and misreporting of data.

Overview of the Services Sector in India and the EU

India and the EU are among the largest economies in the world. In 2013, the EU was the world's largest economy with a GDP of US$17.35 trillion,

---

[6] The data is available at http://epp.eurostat.ec.europa.eu/portal/page/portal/european_business/data/database (accessed on 29 August 2012).

while India was ranked 10th with a GDP of US$1.8 trillion.[7] Among EU Member States, Germany was the fourth largest economy with a share of 5.1 per cent of world GDP, followed by France (5th at 4 per cent), the UK (7th at 3.5 per cent) and Italy (8th at 3.2 per cent).[8] Although the EU's GDP is almost nine times larger than India's, it has been growing much more slowly than India (Table 2.1).

Contribution of Services to GDP

The services sector contributes to more than 50 per cent share of GDP in India and over 70 per cent in the EU. Liberalisation of services, changes in demand patterns, the high income elasticity of demand for services, technological advances, the availability of high-skilled manpower and rising government expenditures on services are the main factors that have contributed to the growth of services in India and its rising contribution to India's GDP (Ansari, 1995; Banga, 2005; Banga and Goldar, 2004; Bhattacharya and Mitra, 1990; Chanda, 2002; Gordon and Gupta, 2003; Hansda, 2001; Jain and Ninan, 2010). Until the early 1980s, India was an agrarian economy. Agriculture was the main contributor to India's GDP (46 per cent share compared to 33 per cent share of services). The services sector started to grow rapidly in the mid-1980s and its growth accelerated during the 1990s, eventually making it the largest sector of the economy. In 2011, services contributed to 56.4 per cent of India's GDP (Table 2.1).

In the EU, the contribution of the services sector increased from 63.3 per cent in the 1990s to 70 per cent in 2000 and accounted for 73.5 per cent of GDP in 2010 (Table 2.1). The increased services intensity of the EU economy has been driven by several factors including the high income elasticity of demand for services, the rise in demand for intermediate services that helps to set up the production networks and global value chains and structural changes, among others (Havlik, 2006; Kemekliene and Watt, 2010).

There is, however, considerable variation in the pattern of services growth and the contribution of services at the sub-national level across states in India and at the sub-regional level across member countries in

---

[7] Calculated from IMF (2013).
[8] Compiled and calculated from IMF (2012).

Table 2.1
Select Macroeconomic Indicators for India and the EU

Indicators	India								EU							
	1990	2000	2005	2008	2010	2011	2012	2013	1990	2000	2005	2008	2010	2011	2012	2013
GDP (at current prices) (US$ billion)	327	477	834	1,224	1,708	1,880	1,859	1,877	7,334	8,524	13,851	18,377	16,341	17,671	16,444	17,353
GDP (annual % growth)	5.5	3.8	9.3	3.9	10.3	6.6	4.7	5.0	2.7	3.9	2.2	0.4	2.0	1.6	-0.4	0.1
Agriculture (% of GDP)	29.0	23.0	18.8	17.8	18.2	17.9	17.5	18.2	3.5	2.3	1.8	1.6	1.6	1.5	1.5	1.5
Agriculture (annual % growth)	4.0	0.0	5.1	0.1	8.6	5.0	1.4	4.7	4.2	-0.5	-5.1	3.9	-3.9	0.7	-5.3	-0.6
Manufacturing (% of GDP)	16.2	15.3	15.4	15.4	14.8	14.7	14.1	12.9	NA	18.6	16.5	15.7	15.1	15.1	14.8	14.5
Manufacturing (annual % growth)	4.8	7.3	10.1	4.3	8.9	7.4	1.1	-0.7	N.A.	5.3	2.1	-2.3	10.3	4.4	-1.6	-0.7
Industry (% of GDP)	26.5	26.0	28.1	28.3	27.2	27.2	26.2	24.8	32.8	28.0	26.4	26.2	25.0	24.8	24.4	24.1
Industry (annual % growth)	7.3	6.0	9.7	4.4	7.6	7.8	1.0	0.4	2.5	4.1	1.5	-1.7	5.8	1.6	-2.1	-1.1
Services (% of GDP)	44.5	51.0	53.1	53.9	54.6	54.9	56.3	57.0	63.3	69.7	71.8	72.2	73.4	73.7	74.1	74.4

Indicator																
Services (annual % growth)	4.9	5.1	10.9	10.0	9.7	6.6	7.0	6.8	3.3	4.1	2.6	1.3	1.1	1.8	0.4	0.5
Trade (% of GDP)	15.2	26.4	41.3	52.3	48.3	54.1	54.7	53.2	54.5	72.1	73.3	81.0	79.5	84.8	84.6	82.1
Trade in services (% of GDP)	3.3	7.6	11.9	15.8	13.6	14.0	14.8	N.A.	11.0	15.6	16.5	18.3	18.9	19.4	20.1	N.A.
Merchandise trade (% of GDP)	12.7	19.7	29.1	42.1	33.8	40.5	42.1	N.A.	43.6	58.4	59.5	66.4	64.3	69.7	70.0	N.A.
Total exports (% of GDP)	6.9	12.8	19.3	23.6	22.0	23.9	24.0	24.8	27.0	36.1	37.0	40.7	40.2	42.9	43.2	42.2
Total exports (annual % growth)	11.1	18.2	26.1	14.6	19.6	15.6	5.0	8.4	4.8	12.6	6.0	1.5	11.0	6.3	2.3	1.3
Total imports (% of GDP)	8.3	13.7	22.0	28.7	26.3	30.2	30.7	28.4	27.5	36.0	36.3	40.3	39.3	41.9	41.4	39.9
Total imports (annual % growth)	3.4	4.6	32.6	22.7	15.6	21.1	6.6	-2.5	4.2	11.7	6.1	1.1	9.9	4.2	-0.2	0.4
Population (in billion)	0.87	1.04	1.13	1.17	1.21	1.22	1.24	1.25	0.48	0.49	0.50	0.50	0.50	0.51	0.51	0.51
Population growth (annual %)	2.04	1.67	1.48	1.33	1.29	1.28	1.26	1.24	0.33	0.16	0.40	0.38	0.24	0.28	-0.08	0.22
Total labour force (in billion)	0.33	0.41	0.47	0.47	0.47	0.48	0.48	N.A.	0.22	0.23	0.24	0.24	0.24	0.25	0.25	N.A.

(Table 2.1 Continued)

(Table 2.1 Continued)

Indicators	India								EU							
	1990	2000	2005	2008	2010	2011	2012	2013	1990	2000	2005	2008	2010	2011	2012	2013
Employment in agriculture (% of total employment)	N.A.	59.9	55.8	N.A.	51.1	N.A.	47.2	N.A.	N.A.	7.8	6.2	5.2	5.2	5.0	5.1	N.A.
Employment in industry (% of total employment)	N.A.	16.0	19.0	N.A.	22.4	N.A.	24.7	N.A.	N.A.	29.3	27.5	27.3	25.2	25.0	25.0	N.A.
Employment in services (% of total employment)	N.A.	24.1	25.2	N.A.	26.6	N.A.	28.1	N.A.	N.A.	62.6	66.0	67.2	69.1	69.4	69.6	N.A.
Unemployment (% of total labour force)	N.A.	4.3	4.4	N.A.	3.5	N.A.	3.6	N.A.	N.A.	9.2	8.9	6.9	9.6	9.6	10.5	N.A.

Source: Compiled from ADB (2012), MOSPI (2011), World Bank (2012). Table extracted from Eurostat, http://appsso.eurostat.ec.europa.eu/nui/show.do?dataset=une_rt_a&lang=en (accessed on 30 August 2012).

Notes: N.A. = data is not available; World Bank (2014), *World Development Indicators 2014*, http://data.worldbank.org/products/wdi

the EU. Some Indian states and some EU Member Countries lie much above the country or regional average with regard to the contribution of services in their economies. Also, there are wide differences across the different subsectors of services in terms of their contributions as is reflected in Table 2.2. Trade, hotels and restaurants and transport, storage and communication services contribute to a substantial share of GDP in India, while business activities and financial services contribute the major share of GDP in the EU.

Table 2.2
Per cent Share of Services Sectors in the GDP of India and the EU

Services	2005	2008	2010	2011	2012
India					
Trade, hotels and restaurants	16.7	16.9	17.3	17.4	17.2
Transport, storage and communications	8.2	7.8	7.3	7.3	7.5
Financial services (banking and insurance)	5.4	5.6	5.7	5.7	5.9
Real estate and business services	9.1	10.3	10.4	10.7	11.4
Public administration and defence services	5.6	5.8	6.1	5.9	6.0
Other services	7.9	7.5	7.9	7.8	8.2
EU					
Wholesale and retail trade, transport, accommodation services	19.5	19.3	18.9	19.0	19.1
Financial and insurance services	5.6	5.4	5.8	5.7	5.7
Information and communication services	4.9	4.8	4.8	4.8	4.8
Arts, entertainment and recreation and other services	3.4	3.5	3.6	3.7	3.7
Professional, scientific and technical activities; administrative and support services	9.7	10.4	10.2	10.3	10.3
Public administration, defence, education, health, etc.	18.4	18.3	19.4	19.3	19.4
Real estate services	10.2	10.5	10.6	10.9	11.1

Source: MOSPI (2014) and Table: National Accounts by 10 branches—aggregates at current prices (NACE Rev. 2), Eurostat, available at http://epp.eurostat.ec.europa.eu/portal/page/portal/national_accounts/data/database (accessed on 7 December 2014).

Employment in the Services Sector

In India, the services sector is the second largest employer after agriculture. In 2010, 26.5 per cent of workers were employed in the services sector (Table 2.1). In 2009–2010, employment in services accounted for around 62 per cent of employment in the organised sector;[9] however, within services, the majority of employment is in the unorganised, informal or non-corporate sector. Sectors such as financial, real estate and business services and community, social and personal services largely provide organised sector employment, while retail and wholesale trade largely provide non-corporate sector employment.[10] In the EU, as in India, the services sector is the largest employer. In 2010, about 69 per cent was employed in services (Table 2.1), but unlike India, in the EU, employment in services is mostly in the formal or organised sector (Kemekleine et al., 2007).

The expansion of service sector employment in both India and the EU is driven by factors such as structural change (from goods to services), technological advances, services liberalisation and cross-border mobility of workers and services providers (Kemekliene and Watt, 2010). However, employment trends differ in India and the EU. Unlike the EU, in India, employment in services has not risen commensurately with its growing share in India's GDP (Bhattacharya and Mitra, 1990; Kochhar et al., 2006), nor has there been a marked shift from informal to formal employment within the services sector. This leads to under-reporting of service sector employment in India since there is no official system to collect data for the informal sector.

Over time, there has also been a change in the pattern of employment within the services sector in both India and the EU. Wholesale trade and retail trade account for a substantial part of services sector employment in both economies. In India, the change in the production structure from agriculture to services is one of the main reasons for the increase in employment in the services sector, but in the EU, the rise

---

[9] The organised sector is also called the corporate or formal sector. It consists of registered companies or units. These are professionally managed with a transparent accounting system and follow government regulations and legislations such as labour laws.

[10] Calculated from MOSPI (2011).

in services employment is mainly driven by increases in real estate, renting and business activities. In the EU, the growth in employment in business services is mainly due to restructuring in the manufacturing sector, since several service-related occupations in manufacturing have been fragmented and outsourced, thus moving over to the services sector.[11]

Recent Developments and Growth Prospects

Since 2008, the weakening of global growth and the sovereign debt crisis in several EU Member States has pushed the region into a recession. The EU registered a decline of 0.2 per cent in the GDP in 2012 and the unemployment rate rose to 9.7 per cent in 2011. Despite measures such as the European Stability Mechanism, an expansionary monetary policy and the adoption of a second programme for Greece to address the euro crisis and to revive growth (European Commission, 2013) forecasts for 2014 by the European Commission and the IMF remain tepid at 1.6 per cent and 1.2 per cent, respectively, with the unemployment rate predicted to rise to 11 per cent in 2014. However, the services sector is expected to play a growing role in the EU region. The share of services in the EU's GDP is projected to rise to 74 per cent in 2020 and to 74.7 per cent in 2030 (Kemekleine et al., 2007).

Compared to the EU, India has been less affected by the 2008 crisis, mainly due to its lower dependence on trade and relatively closed capital market. However, since 2011, the economic growth has slowed down and the country is facing high inflation and fiscal deficit, reduction in FDI inflows, among others. The IMF's World Economic Outlook[12] for the year 2014 has projected the growth rate for India to be 5.6 per cent in 2014 with an improved growth rate of 6.4 per cent in 2015. As in the case of the EU, services will continue to play an important role in India's GDP and exports due to the increase in per capita income, a growing middle class, rising literacy rates and further opening up of the Indian economy.

---

[11] For details, see Kemekliene and Watt (2010).

[12] http://www.imf.org/external/pubs/ft/weo/2014/02/pdf/text.pdf (accessed on 24 January 2015).

Services Sector Liberalisation and Future Regulations

Both India and the EU initiated reforms in services in the 1980s, a process that gained momentum in the 1990s. In both economies, the reform process is still ongoing. However, although both economies see services reforms as an integral part of their economic policies, an examination of their regulatory frameworks and policy initiatives indicates important differences in their long-term and strategic orientation towards the services sector.

India

The main elements of services reforms in India have been the dismantling of public monopoly in sectors such as air transport, telecommunications and financial services and the opening up of various sectors to foreign investment and streamlining approval procedures. In recent months, there has been a renewed thrust on liberalising the service sector, including (a) liberalising FDI restrictions in sectors such as insurance, railways, defence and air transport; (b) setting up regulatory frameworks and independent regulators in sectors such as coal, railways and postal services that are currently public monopolies but which may be privatised in the future; (c) introducing regulations in new services such as direct selling, express delivery and cloud computing that are not covered under the existing regulations; and (d) amending outdated regulations in sectors such as postal services. As a result of these initiatives, with the exception of a few sectors such as legal and postal that remain closed to FDI, almost all the other services sectors have been opened up to foreign investment, either on an automatic basis or subject to approval. Public–private partnerships have also been encouraged in several sectors, especially infrastructure services, to improve their efficiency, productivity and quality and to enhance the overall competitiveness of the Indian economy given the significance of such services in the production process. The Indian government is also in the process of introducing several new Bills such as the Direct Taxes Code Bill, 2012 which are likely to impact the services sector.

Despite the significant policy changes in services, there is still no comprehensive policy or strategy for the services sector in India. There are sector-specific laws, regulations and regulatory bodies for different services. Some services are covered under several different legislations, reflecting their complex nature and inter-linkages with goods. For instance, energy is regulated by the Coal Mines (Nationalisation) Act, 1973, the Petroleum and Natural Gas Regulatory Board (PNGRB) Act, 2006 and the Electricity Act, 2003, among others. Apart from these sector-specific regulations, the services sector is also impacted by cross-cutting regulations such as the Companies Act (1956), which lays down conditions for establishing a company.

The EU

Like India, the EU initiated its liberalisation and privatisation policies in the 1980s. In Central and Eastern Europe, the state-controlled socialist countries turned to capitalism at the end of the 1980s, resulting in the rapid liberalisation and privatisation of state-owned enterprises. In Western Europe, the UK, under Prime Minister Margaret Thatcher, introduced economic liberalisation and privatisation during the 1980s and the early 1990s. Other Western European countries pursued liberalisation and deregulation to varying degrees (Keune et al., 2008).

However, unlike India, the EU has a comprehensive services sector policy to integrate the regional services market. The main aim of the Directive on Services (2006/123/EC) is to harmonise or create a single market for the services sector across EU Member States. In addition, there are sector-specific Directives for services such as telecommunications, broadcasting, transport, electricity, gas and postal services. Directives relating to the movement of people such as the Blue Card Directive (2009/50/EC) and the Single Permit Directive (2011/98/EU) impact the ability of third-country nationals to provide services in EU Member States (see Appendix B for details on EU Directives on the services sector).

This integrated strategy towards services is also reflected in a variety of sector-specific and cross-cutting initiatives and proposals introduced by the EU in recent years with a bearing on the EU's service sector and its competitiveness and the creation of a single market for services. In 2010, the EU came up with a 10-year growth strategy—Europe 2020 Strategy—that focused on employment, research and innovation, education, poverty reduction and climate/energy that have implications for the services sector. The strategy also introduced seven flagship initiatives that include initiatives such as broadband access to all by 2013 and enhancing the international attractiveness of Europe's universities. It recommended full implementation of the Services Directive (2006/123/EC) and stated that, if implemented, the Directive could increase trade in commercial services by 45 per cent and in FDI by 25 per cent, bringing an increase of between 0.5 per cent and 1.5 per cent in GDP (European Commission, 2010a). The EU is in the process of implementing new regulations as well as amending various Directives such as the Services Directive (2006/123/EC). In May 2012, the European Commission proposed measures to improve the implementation of the Services Directive (2006/123/EC) (European Commission, 2012a).

For easier movement of people, in May 2010, the European Commission put forward a proposal on the 'conditions of entry and residence of third-country nationals in the framework of intra-corporate transferees (ICT) such as manager, specialist and graduate trainee' (European Commission, 2010b). In this proposal, the European Commission defined the concept of *intra-corporate transferee* based on the EU's commitment under GATS and bilateral trade agreements. The proposal also emphasised the introduction of a transparent and fast-track entry procedure for short durations (about 30 days) to process applications and a single application for work and residence permits. The European Commission recommended that economic need tests or labour market tests[13] should be removed. The proposed Directive is aimed at enabling the EU companies to get better and faster access to global talent in order to meet the shortage of managers, specialists and graduate trainees in the EU market and to create new employment opportunities.[14] The proposed Directive is expected to complement the EU Blue Card Directive (2009/50/EC) and Single Permit Directive (2011/98/EU). In December 2011, the European Commission proposed to amend Directive 2005/36/EC on the Recognition of Professional Qualifications and the Regulation on Administrative

[13] Economic needs test or labour market test is a test that tries to establish whether there is an economic need or labour market need for a particular supply of a service in a specific mode of supply. A service supplier is allowed to supply the service if the competent authority or regulatory body decides that there is an economic need for such a supply.

[14] http://europa.eu/rapid/pressReleasesAction.do?reference=MEMO/10/324&type=HTML (accessed on 24 August 2012).

Cooperation through the Internal Market Information System (European Commission, 2011a) to facilitate easier labour mobility of architects, nurses and midwives. It also proposed to introduce the European professional card, systematic screening and a mutual evaluation exercise for all regulated professions in the Member States.

The EU has sector-specific action plans for certain services, namely the Financial Services Action Plan,[15] the European Retail Action Plan,[16] the Transport Action Plan[17] and Flightpath 2050: Europe's Vision for Aviation.[18]

Hence, both India and the EU have taken various measures to reform their services sectors to foster its growth and competitiveness. However, the EU has formulated a long-term vision or strategy for the service sector, particularly for the region, whereas India still lacks a comprehensive long-term service sector strategy at the national level both for services growth and for services exports.

Conclusion

Services are a major driving force behind the growth of the Indian and EU economies. Services contribute a significant share to the GDP and employment of both economies. Projections indicate that the services sector will continue to drive growth in both India and the EU, despite the macroeconomic and financial challenges that both economies are facing. There are also similarities between India and the EU in other respects, such as their quasi-federal governance structures and their adoption of liberalisation policies and reforms over the past two decades.

However, there are important differences between the two economies in terms of the nature of their services growth and their broader strategy

---

[15] For details, see http://europa.eu/legislation_summaries/internal_market/single_market_services/financial_services_general_framework/l24210_en.htm (accessed on 24 August 2012).

[16] For details, see http://ec.europa.eu/internal_market/retail/index_en.htm#maincontentSec1 (accessed on 24 August 2012).

[17] For details, see http://ec.europa.eu/transport/its/road/action_plan/action_plan_en.htm (accessed on 24 August 2012).

[18] For details, see http://ec.europa.eu/transport/air/doc/flightpath2050.pdf (accessed on 24 August 2012).

and orientation towards services growth and exports. While in the EU the bulk of the services sector is in the organised corporate segment and generates employment in the organised sector, in India a large part of the services sector lies in the unorganised or non-corporate segment. India's approach to services reforms has been sector specific, focusing primarily on liberalising FDI in specific services and on introducing sector-specific regulations and legislation. The EU's approach has been more broad-based and cross-cutting, focusing on efficient service delivery and harmonising regulatory regimes at the regional level through EU-level service sector Directives so as to facilitate the creation of a single services market.

The differences and similarities between India and the EU in the patterns and trends in their services sectors have several implications for developing India–EU relations in services. First, given the significance of services to both economies, this is clearly a sector where there is likely to be mutual interest and scope to deepen relations. Second, given the EU's efforts to create a single regional market for services by easing the barriers to intra-regional trade and movement of labour and capital through different Directives, there could be benefits to extra-regional service providers, including from India, in accessing the wider EU market in services. At the same time, it could also create discriminatory conditions for extra-regional service providers and increase competition from lower cost suppliers within the EU. Third, since the services sector remains governed by the national and EU-level Directives with some sectors outside the services Directive such as the mobility of service providers, which is still governed by EU Member Country laws, there will be complexities and tensions between the regional and the sub-regional frameworks in negotiating services with the EU. Finally, the lack of a long-term coherent strategy for promoting services growth and exports in India would affect the country's ability to capitalise on the opportunities and challenges in the EU's services market. Ultimately, the prospects for India–EU relations in services will depend on the EU's growth prospects, its macroeconomic and financial stability and its ability to recover from the present economic slowdown as well as on India's ability to overcome its current macroeconomic and structural challenges, to attract FDI in its liberalised services and to create a more transparent and predictable policy environment.

Appendix A

Table 2A.1

Classification and Coverage of Services in India and the EU

Services Category	India (NIC 2008)	EU (NACE Version 2)
Wholesale and retail trade; repair of motor vehicles and motorcycles (G)	√	√
• Sale of motor vehicles		
• Maintenance and repair of motor vehicles		
• Sale of motor vehicle parts and accessories		
• Wholesale on a fee or contract basis		
• Wholesale of agricultural raw materials and live animals; food, beverages and tobacco; household goods; machinery, equipment and supplies		
• Other specialised wholesale		
• Non-specialised wholesale trade		
• Retail sale in non-specialised stores		
• Retail sale of food, beverages and tobacco; automotive fuel; information and communications equipment; other household equipment; cultural and recreation goods; and other goods in specialised stores		
• Retail sale via stalls and markets		
• Retail trade not in stores, stalls or markets		
• Sale, maintenance and repair of motorcycles and related parts and accessories	×	√
• Wholesale of information and communication equipment	×	√
Transportation and storage (H)	√	√
• Transport via railways; via pipeline		
• Sea and coastal water transport		
• Inland water transport		
• Other land transport		
• Passenger and freight air transport		

(Table 2A.1 Continued)

(Table 2A.1 Continued)

Services Category	India (NIC 2008)	EU (NACE Version 2)
• Warehousing and storage		
• Support activities for transportation		
• Postal and courier activities		
• Freight transport by road and removal services	×	√
• Inland passenger and freight water transport	×	√
Accommodation and food service activities (I)	√	√
• Hotels and similar accommodation		
• Camping grounds, recreational vehicle parks and trailer parks		
• Other accommodation		
• Restaurants and mobile food service activities		
• Event catering and other food service activities		
• Beverage serving activities		
• Short-term accommodation activities	×	√
Information and communication (J)	√	√
• Publishing of books, periodicals and other publishing activities		
• Software publishing		
• Motion picture, video and television programme activities		
• Sound recording and music publishing activities		
• Radio broadcasting		
• Television programming and broadcasting activities		
• Wired and wireless telecommunications activities		
• Satellite telecommunications and other telecommunications activities		
• Computer programming, consultancy and related activities		
• Data processing, hosting and related activities		
• Other information service activities		

(Table 2A.1 Continued)

(Table 2A.1 Continued)

Services Category	India (NIC 2008)	EU (NACE Version 2)
Financial and insurance activities (K)	√	√
• Monetary intermediation		
• Activities of holding companies		
• Trusts, funds and other financial vehicles		
• Other financial service activities		
• Insurance		
• Reinsurance		
• Pension funding		
• Activities auxiliary to financial service activities; insurance and pension funding		
• Fund management activities		
Real estate activities (L)	√	√
• Real estate activities with own or leased property		
• Real estate activities on a fee or contract basis		
Professional, scientific and technical activities (M)	√	√
• Legal activities		
• Accounting, bookkeeping and auditing activities		
• Management consultancy activities		
• Architectural and engineering activities and related technical consultancy		
• Technical testing and analysis		
• Research and experimental development on natural sciences and engineering		
• Research and experimental development on social sciences and humanities		
• Advertising		
• Market research and public opinion polling		
• Specialised design activities		
• Photographic activities		
• Other professional, scientific and technical activities		
• Veterinary activities		

(Table 2A.1 Continued)

(Table 2A.1 Continued)

Services Category	India (NIC 2008)	EU (NACE Version 2)
Administrative and support service activities (N)	√	√
• Renting and leasing of motor vehicles; personal and household goods; machinery, equipment and tangible goods		
• Leasing of non-financial intangible assets		
• Activities of employment placement agencies		
• Temporary employment agency activities		
• Human resources provision and management of human resources functions		
• Travel agency and tour operator activities		
• Other reservation service activities		
• Private security activities		
• Security systems service activities		
• Investigation activities		
• Combined facilities support activities		
• Cleaning activities		
• Landscape care and maintenance service activities		
• Office administrative and support activities		
• Activities of call centres		
• Organisation of conventions and trade shows		
• Business support service activities N.E.C.		
Public administration and defence; compulsory social security (O)	√	√
• Administration of the State, and the economic and social policy of the community		
• Provision of services to the community as a whole		
• Compulsory social security activities		
Education (P)	√	√
• Primary education		
• Secondary education		

(Table 2A.1 Continued)

(Table 2A.1 Continued)

Services Category	India (NIC 2008)	EU (NACE Version 2)
• Higher education		
• Other education		
• Educational support services		
• Pre-primary education	×	√
Human health and social work activities (Q)	√	√
• Hospital activities		
• Medical and dental practice activities		
• Other human health activities		
• Nursing care facilities		
• Residential care activities for mental retardation, mental health and substance abuse; and elderly and disabled		
• Other residential care activities N.E.C.		
• Social work activities		
Arts, entertainment and recreation (R)	√	√
• Creative, arts and entertainment activities		
• Libraries, archives, museums and other cultural activities		
• Gambling and betting activities		
• Sports activities		
• Other amusement and recreation activities		
Other service activities (S)	√	√
• Activities of business, employers and professional membership organisations; and other membership organisations		
• Activities of trade unions		
• Repair of computers and communication equipment; and personal and household goods		
• Other personal service activities		
Activities of extraterritorial organisations and bodies (U)	√	√

Source: Extracted from MOSPI (2008) and European Commission (2008).

Notes: √ indicates sectors that are covered by India and the EU in their classification.

x indicates that the sector is not covered by either India or the EU.

Appendix B: Important Directives in the EU and Their Impact

- *Directive on Services (2006/123/EC)*[19]

Box 2B.1: List of Services Sectors Covered and Excluded in the Services Directive (2006/123/EC)

Services That Are Covered

- Business services (such as management consultancy services, event organisation, advertising and recruitment services, printing, publishing, etc.)
- Professional services (such as legal and tax advisers, architects, engineers, accountants and surveyors, services provided by midwives, etc.)
- Construction services
- Distribution trade (including retail and wholesale)
- Real estate services
- Rental and leasing services
- Travel and tourism services
- Leisure services (including sport centres and amusement parks)
- Education services

Services That Are Excluded

- Financial services
- Telecommunications services
- Energy services
- Transport services
- Healthcare services
- Audiovisual services
- Social services
- Private security services
- Gambling

Source: Compiled from *Services Directive*, and *http://ec.europa.eu/internal_market/services/services-dir/guides_en.htm* (accessed on 17 August 2012).

---

[19] The full text of the Directive is available at http://eur-lex.europa.eu/LexUriServ/LexUriServ.do?uri=OJ:L:2006:376:0036:0068:en:PDF (accessed on 17 August 2012).

This Directive is part of the economic reform launched by the Lisbon European Council with a view to making the EU the most competitive and dynamic knowledge-based economy in the world by 2010.[20] It was adopted in 2006. The Directive aims to remove obstacles and ensure the freedom of establishment of nationals/companies of a Member State in another Member State and the free movement of services providers across all Member States. It aimed to extend the scope of liberalisation to a broader range of services, and it covers a large number of services sectors including business services, real estate, retail and wholesale distribution, construction and tourism (Box 2B.1). These services contribute to around 45 per cent of the EU's GDP and employment.

The Directive requires each EU Member State to put in various measures and reform national laws in accordance with the different provisions of the Directive. It focuses on simplifying administrative procedures and prohibits several discriminatory and burdensome requirements. To enhance the rights of consumers and strengthen their confidence in the internal market, the Directive obliges Member States to remove regulatory obstacles for service recipients wanting to buy services supplied by providers established in other Member States. It also ensures that consumers can make informed choices when buying services in other Member States by means of information obligations that apply to both providers and Member States' authorities. Article 20 of the Directive prohibits discrimination against service recipients on the basis of their nationality or country of residence. Some important articles of the Directive that will facilitate market integration are given in Box 2B.2.

---

[20] For details, see page L 376/36-37 of the Services Directive available at http://eur-lex.europa.eu/LexUriServ/LexUriServ.do?uri=OJ:L:2006:376:0036:0068:en:PDF   (accessed on 17 August 2012).

Box 2B.2: Important Articles of the Services Directives (2006/123/EC)

Article 14: Prohibited Requirements

- Prohibition on
  - having discriminatory requirements (i.e. national requirements, residency requirements, and so on),
  - having an establishment in more than one Member State or on being entered in the registered/enrolled with professional bodies/associations of more than one Member State or
  - having requirements on the form of establishment—an agency, branch or subsidiary on an economic needs test.

- Ban on
  - obligation to obtain a financial guarantee or insurance from an operator established in the same Member State,
  - involvement of competing operators in the decision of competent authorities or
  - having previously registered/previously exercised the activity for a given period in the same Member State.

Article 15: Requirements to Be Evaluated

- Quantitative or territorial restrictions.
- Obligation for the service provider to take a specific legal form of establishment.
- Requirements relating to the shareholding of companies.
- Ban on having more than one establishment.
- Obligation to apply fixed, minimum or maximum tariffs.

Article 16: Freedom to Provide Services

- Ensures free access to and free exercise of a service activity in the territory of a Member State for providers established in another Member State.

(Box 2B.2 Continued)

(Box 2B.2 Continued)

- Obligation to have an establishment in the territory of the Member State where the service is provided.
- Obligation to obtain an authorisation, including entry in a register or registration with a professional body or association.
- Ban on the provider setting up a certain form or type of infrastructure in their territory (including an office or association in their territory).
- Obligation to obtain a special identity document issued by competent authorities.

Article 20: Non-discrimination

- Member States shall ensure that the recipient is not made subject to the discriminatory requirements based on his nationality or residency.
- Member States shall ensure that the general conditions of access to a service, which are made available to the public at large by the provider, do not contain discriminatory provisions relating to the nationality or place of residence of the recipient, but without precluding the possibility of providing for differences in the conditions of access where those differences are directly justified by objective criteria.

Article 24: Commercial Communications by the Regulated Professions

- Member States shall remove all total prohibitions on commercial communications by the regulated professions.
- Member States shall ensure that commercial communications by the regulated professions comply with professional rules, in conformity with Community Law, which relate, in particular, to the independence, dignity and integrity of the profession, as well as to professional secrecy, in a manner consistent with the specific nature of each profession. Professional rules on commercial communications shall be non-discriminatory, justified by an overriding reason relating to the public interest and proportionate.

Source: Extracted from *EU Directive on Services in the Internal Market,* available at *http://eur-lex.europa.eu/LexUriServ/LexUriServ.do?uri=OJ:L:2006:376:0036:0068: en:PDF* (accessed on 17 August 2012).

Although the Directive is a step towards the integration of the services market, it does not affect/interfere with the national laws of individual Member States such as criminal and labour laws. It also excludes national regulations related to services sectors that are not covered by the Directive such as financial services, audio-visual services, transportation and telecommunications services.

As of August 2012, the Services Directive has been fully transposed by all Member States (European Commission, 2012b). Several Member States have removed a number of restrictions to adhere to this Directive. For example, Spain has removed nationality and residence requirements for casual trading and Romania has removed the nationality requirement for tourist guides. Several Member States including Belgium, France and Luxembourg have removed the requirement for an economic needs test, while Austria, France and Greece have removed quantitative and territorial restrictions. The obligation to obtain financial guarantees in the Member State of establishment has been removed by Greece (in the tourism sector) and Portugal (in professional services, construction, real estate and tourism). Certain EU Member States such as Belgium, Germany and Greece have abolished the minimum capital requirements in the tourism sector (European Commission, 2012b).

Some EU Member States have made the legal form requirements less rigid. For instance, in Poland, lawyers and tax advisers can now exercise their activities as a joint stock limited partnership. One major barrier for service providers is the requirement to be established in the country before they can provide services; Portugal and Sweden have abolished this requirement. Specific establishment requirements have also been abolished in the construction sector in Austria and Germany, in professional services in Greece and in travel agencies in Belgium and Spain (European Commission, 2012b).

- *Directive on Conditions of Entry and Residence for Third-country Nationals for purposes of High Qualified Employment or Blue Card Directive (2009/50/EC)*

The EU has a shortage of high-skilled workers due to the low fertility rate, ageing population, and much more.[21] In order to meet the shortage

---

[21] http://ec.europa.eu/home-affairs/doc_centre/immigration/docs/studies/emn_highly_skilled_workers_study_synthesis_report_may07.pdf (accessed on 19 August 2012).

of high-skilled workers and to attract high-skilled labour from foreign countries, the European Commission adopted the Blue Card Directive (2009/50/EC)[22] in May 2009. It lays down the framework for easier entry, residency and transposition of third-country nationals across all EU Member States. All EU Member States, with the exception of Denmark, the UK and Ireland, are bound by the Directive. The Directive provides a common and simplified procedure applicable in all EU Member States (Box 2B.3).

Box 2B.3: Key Features of the Blue Card Directive (2009/50/EC)

- The Directive is designed to
  - facilitate the admission of highly qualified workers/labourers by harmonising entry and residence conditions throughout the EU,
  - simplify admission procedures and
  - improve the legal status of highly qualified workers/labourers already residing in the EU.
- The Directive applies to highly qualified third-country nationals seeking to be admitted to the territory of a Member State for more than three months for the purpose of employment as well as to their family members.
- The Directive does not prevent Member States from having their own system of national residence permits for highly skilled migrants, but such national permits cannot grant the right of residence in other EU Member States that is included under the Blue Card Directive [Article 4 (2)].
- The validity of the Blue Card will be between one and four years [Article 7 (2)].
- Entry Conditions for Third-country Highly Skilled Workers
  - A valid work contract or binding job offer of at least one year in the Member State concerned.
  - A gross annual salary should be at least 1.5 times the average gross annual salary paid in the Member State concerned (Member States may lower the salary threshold to 1.2 times for certain professions where there is a particular need of third-country workers) [Article 5(3) and (5)].

(Box 2B.3 Continued)

[22] The full text is available at http://eur-lex.europa.eu/LexUriServ/LexUriServ.do?uri= OJ:L:2009:155:0017:0029:en:PDF (accessed on 19 August 2012).

(Box 2B.3 Continued)

- A valid travel document and a valid residence permit or a national long-term visa [Article 5(1-d)].
  - Proof of sickness insurance [Article 5(1-e)].
  - For regulated professions, a document attesting fulfilment of the conditions set out under national laws of the EU Member State in the work contract or binding job offer; for unregulated professions, a document attesting the relevant higher professional qualifications in the occupation or sector specified in the work contract or binding offer [Article 5(1-b,c)].
  - Required to provide residential address in the Member State concerned [Article 2].
  - Once a Member State grants a Blue Card to a third-country national, and after two years that person may benefit from free access to highly qualified employment positions in that Member State; and may also move to another EU Member State where their skills may be needed [Article 12(1-2)].
- EU Blue Card holders shall receive equal treatment like nationals, i.e. working conditions; social security; pensions; recognition of diplomas, education and vocational training (minimum employment experience must be two years) [Article 14 (1)];
- After 18 months of legal residence in the first Member State, a EU Blue Card holder (including family members) may move to other Member State for highly qualified employment [Article 18 (1)];

Source: Compiled from *Blue Card Directive,* available at *http://eur-lex.europa.eu/ LexUriServ/LexUriServ.do?uri=OJ:L:2009:155:0017:0029:en:PDF* (accessed on 17 August 2012).

The deadline for full transposition of the Directive was June 2011. As of August 2012, all EU Member States (except Slovenia) had fully transposed the Directive in their national laws.[23]

- *Directive on a Single Application Procedure for a Single Permit for Third-country Nationals to Reside and Work in the Territory*

---

[23] http://europa.eu/rapid/pressReleasesAction.do?reference=IP/12/529& (accessed on 19 August 2012).

of a Member State and on a Common Set of Rights for Third-country Workers Legally Residing in a Member State or Single Permit Directive (2011/98/EU).

In order to free the entry of third-country nationals, the EU adopted the Single Permit Directive (2011/98/EU) in December 2011. This Directive seeks to establish a simplified and harmonised procedure for a non-EU migrant or third-country national to obtain a work and residence permit in an EU Member State. It also defines a common set of rights such as working conditions, recognition of educational and professional qualifications, taxation, vocational training, access to social security, including unemployment benefits, and the transfer of acquired pensions awarded to third-country workers/migrants. One key feature of the Directive is to have a single permit that covers both residence and work permits. The Directive excludes posted third-country workers[24] and intra-corporate transferees. This is an important step in facilitating free intra-EU mobility along with equal treatment as given to EU nationals.

As of August 2012, the EU Member States were in the process of implementing this Directive.[25]

- *Sector-specific Regulations and Directives*

The EU also has sector-specific regulations and Directives for sectors not covered under the Services Directive (2006/123/EC). Some examples are given in Box 2B.4.

[24] This Directive does not prevent a third-country nationals who are legally residing and working in a Member State and posted to another Member State from continuing to enjoy equal treatment with respect to nationals of the Member State of origin for the duration of their posting.

[25] http://www.epc.eu/documents/uploads/pub_1398_eu_single_permit_directive.pdf (accessed on 29 August 2012).

**Box 2B.4: Select EU Legislation Applicable to Different
Services Sectors (as of August 2012)**

Financial

- Directive 2006/48/EC relating to the taking up and pursuit of the business of credit institutions.

Energy

- Directive 2003/55/EC on common rules for the internal market in natural gas.
- Directive 2009/72/EC on common rules for the internal market in electricity.

Transport and Logistics

- Council Regulation (EEC) No 4055/86 applying the principle of freedom to provide services to maritime transport between Member States and between Member States and third countries.
- Council Regulation (EEC) No 3921/91 laying down the conditions under which non-resident carriers may transport goods or passengers by inland waterway within a Member State.
- Directive 2003/55/EC on common rules for the internal market in natural gas.
- Council Regulation (EEC) No 3577/92 on applying the principle of freedom to provide services to maritime transport within Member States (maritime cabotage).
- Council Regulation (EC) No 1356/96 on common rules applicable to the transport of goods/passengers by inland waterway between Member States with a view to establishing freedom to provide such transport services.
- Regulation (EC) No 1370/2007 on public passenger transport services by rail and by road.
- Regulation (EC) No 1008/2008 on establishing common rules for the operation of air services in the Community.
- Regulation (EC) No 1072/2009 on common rules for access to the international road haulage market.

(Box 2B.4 Continued)

(Box 2B.4 Continued)

- Regulation (EC) No 1073/2009 on common rules for access to the international market for coach and bus services.
- Regulation (EU) No 913/2010 on European rail network for competitive freight.
- Council Directive 91/440/EEC on the development of the Community's railway.
- Council Directive 96/67/EC on access to the ground handling market at Community airports.
- Directive 2002/39/CE on opening to competition of Community postal services.

Information Technology (IT) and Information Technology Enabled Services (ITeS)

- Directive 2000/31/EC on certain legal aspects of information society services, in particular electronic commerce, in the Internal Market or 'Directive on electronic commerce'.
- Directive 2002/20/EC on the authorisation of electronic communications networks and services or 'Authorisation Directive'.
- Directive 2002/58/EC concerning the processing of personal data and the protection of privacy in the electronic communications sector or 'Directive on privacy and electronic communications'.

Telecommunications

- Directive 2002/19/EC on access and interconnection of electronic communications networks and associated facilities.
- Directive 2002/20/EC on the authorisation of electronic communications networks and services (Authorisation Directive).
- Directive 2002/21/EC on a common regulatory framework for electronic communications networks and services.
- Directive 2002/22/EC on universal service and users' rights relating to the electronic communications networks and services.
- Directive 2002/58/EC on the processing of personal data and the protection of privacy in electronic communications sector (Directive on privacy and electronic communications).

(Box 2B.4 Continued)

(Box 2B.4 Continued)

Professional and Business Services

- Directive 98/5/EC on facilitating the practice of the profession of lawyer on a permanent basis in a Member State other than that in which the qualification was obtained.
- Directive 2005/36/EC on the recognition of professional qualifications.
- Directive 2005/71/EC on specific procedure for admitting third-country nationals for the purposes of scientific research.
- Directive 2009/50/EC on conditions of entry and residence of third-country nationals for the purposes of highly qualified employment or 'Blue Card Directive'.

Source: Compiled from Annex I a—EU Legislation Applying to Services Sector, pp. 85–87, European Commission (2012b) and different EU Directives.

3

Trade and Investment in Services: Reflections from India and the EU

Ramneet Goswami

Introduction

S ervices are a growing component of global trade and investment and India and the EU are key players in the international market thereof. Technological advancements, greater mobility of people and cheaper transmission and communication costs along with liberalisation of domestic policy regimes have led to an increase in global services trade. Between 2001 and 2011, global services trade increased almost three times—from US$1.5 trillion to US$4.2 trillion (WTO, 2012). Among WTO member countries, the EU has the topmost position in global services trade, while India ranks among the top 10 member countries. India and the EU, thus occupy a prominent position in services trade.

The report of the EU–India High-Level Trade Group (2006)[1] highlighted that the EU and India constitute strategically important markets

---

[1] For details, see http://trade.ec.europa.eu/doclib/docs/2006/september/tradoc_130306.pdf (accessed on 23 September 2013).

for each other's companies in terms of both immediate opportunities in services as well as future potential. Interestingly, both India and the EU started liberalising their services sector in the 1990s. Liberalisation, along with the economic integration of the EU increased global concatenation of the two economies in services. The EU is trying to integrate the services market within EU Member States, India is in the process of liberalising its foreign direct investment (FDI) regime in services to attract more investment into services sectors such as insurance.

This is further facilitated by the complementarity that India and the EU enjoy in services sectors (Chakraborty and Kumar, 2012; Khandekar and Sengupta, 2012; Mukherjee and Goswami, 2011; Wouters et al., 2013). The EU market, especially Western Europe, is becoming saturated, whereas the Indian market is growing. India is a large economy with a democratic set-up, while the EU represents the largest market in the world in terms of GDP. The need for infrastructure investment in India complements the core competence of EU companies in sectors such as energy and transportation. India needs technology and global best practices that EU companies can provide. The large low-cost skilled workforce of India can complement the EU's growing demand for a workforce due to its ageing population. These trade and investment complementarities and mutual gains justify the need for greater India–EU engagement in trade and investment.

In terms of treatment of services under their trade agreements, both India and the EU are proponents of liberalisation of trade in services in the ongoing Doha Round of WTO negotiations and in their respective bilateral trade agreements. Both India and the EU are keen to negotiate trade agreements that are comprehensive and include services and investment.

Given the strong interest of the two economies in liberalising trade in services and the huge potential for India–EU bilateral trade and investment in services, this chapter presents an overview of trade and investment between India and the EU looking at the trends and patterns of trade in services in global and bilateral context. It assesses the export competitiveness in services and highlights the issues faced and reforms required to tap the trade and investment potential between India and the EU.

India–EU Global Trade in Services

The global services trade of India and the EU has increased substantially in the past two decades. Services trade also contributes a significant share to GDP and total trade for both India and the EU. In the 1990s, the share of services trade to GDP for India and the EU stood at 3.3 per cent and 14 per cent, respectively. In 2011, this share for India and the EU increased to 14 per cent and 18.7 per cent, respectively (see Table 2.1 in Chapter 2). The share of services trade in total trade has increased—from 22.2 per cent in 1991 to 25.9 per cent in 2012 in India's total trade and 20.3 per cent to 22.4 per cent in the EU's total trade (see Table 3A.1 in Appendix). Thus, although the share of services trade in GDP is higher for the EU, the increase in contribution of services to total trade and GDP is much faster for India.

According to UNCTAD Trade Statistics, India's services trade has increased from US$11 billion in 1991 to US$40.5 billion in 2002 and US$274 billion in 2012.[2] Between 2002 and 2012, India's services trade grew at a compound annual growth rate (CAGR) of 21.1 per cent, which is much higher than the 10.3 per cent annual growth in global services trade. In 2012, India's services exports and imports reached US$148.1 billion and US$125.9 billion, respectively (see Table 3A.2 in Appendix). Between 2002 and 2012, India's services exports grew at a CAGR of 22.5 per cent, compared to 19.5 per cent growth in its merchandise trade and 10.5 per cent growth in global services exports. Thus, India's services exports have grown more rapidly than its merchandise exports and also relative to global services exports.

The EU is the largest player in services trade. The EU's services trade increased from US$888 billion in 1992 to US$1,364 billion in 2002 and to US$3,351 billion in 2012.[3] Between 2002 and 2012, the EU's services

---

[2] Compiled and calculated from UNCTAD Statistics on International Trade in services, available at http://unctadstat.unctad.org/ReportFolders/reportFolders.aspx (accessed on 5 September 2013).

[3] Compiled and calculated from UNCTAD Statistics on International Trade in services, available at http://unctadstat.unctad.org/ReportFolders/reportFolders.aspx (accessed on 5 September 2013). *Note*: Due to the expansion of the EU, the data is calculated differently. Between 1992 and 2004, there were 15 EU Member States; in 2005, there were 25 EU Member States and from 2008 to 2012, data is given for EU-27. Croatia became an EU Member on 1 July 2013; therefore, it is not included.

trade grew at a CAGR of 9.4 per cent. The EU's services exports grew at the rate of 10.1 per cent compared to the growth rate of 8.9 per cent for merchandise exports in 2002–2012. Overall, although the EU is a much larger player in services trade than India, its services trade is growing at a slower rate than India's. Both India and the EU have a positive trade balance in services.

Export Competitiveness of India and the EU in Services

The ranking and market share in export and import of different services for India and the EU are presented in Table 3.1. The EU occupies the top position in exports and imports of most services, while India is still

Table 3.1

Exports and Imports of India and the EU in Different Services in 2012 (ranks and % share)

	Exports		Imports	
Service Category	India	EU-27	India	EU-27
Commercial services	6th (3.3%)	1st (42.5%)	7th (3.1%)	1st (37.9%)
Travel services	11th (1.6%)	1st (33.2%)	N.L.	1st (34.1%)
Transportation services	10th (1.9%)	1st (41.8%)	4th (5.2%)	1st (29.5%)
Other commercial services				
Audiovisual and related services	6th (1.7%)	1st (77.7%)	N.L.	1st (64.0%)
Communications services	7th (1.9%)	1st (66.2%)	N.L.	1st (68.9%)
Computer services	2nd (22.4%)	1st (62.2%)	6th (2.0%)	1st (61.2%)
Construction services	N.L.	1st (40.0%)	N.L.	1st (40.4%)
Financial services	6th (1.8%)	1st (51.5%)	3rd (4.3%)	1st (62.4%)
Insurance services	6th (2.4%)	1st (63.1%)	5th (4.5%)	2nd (25.0%)
Other business services	4th (4.9%)	1st (56.2%)	7th (3.7%)	1st (57.7%)
Personal, cultural and recreational services	6th (2.2%)	1st (74.4%)	N.L.	1st (58.4%)
Telecommunications services	5th (2.4%)	1st (61.9%)	7th (1.7%)	1st (67.7%)

Source: Compiled from WTO (2013 and 2014).
Notes: N.L. = not in list.
    2. Per cent share is given in parentheses.

a marginal player in transport and travel service exports, but has evolved as a major exporter of computer and information services. If we look at the ranks, among WTO member countries, India's rank has improved over time. In 2001, India was ranked 24th on services exports and 20th on services imports, but in 2012, its rank improved to 5th and 7th for exports and imports, respectively.[4]

India and the EU's export competitiveness in different services sub-sectors can be calculated from their Revealed Comparative Advantage (RCA)[5] using the Balassa Index. Table 3.2 shows that although India has a strong comparative advantage in export of computer and information services, the EU has a comparative advantage in transportation, communications, financial services, insurance, and personal, cultural and recreational services.

Table 3.2
RCAs for India and the EU in Exports of Services

	India					EU				
Service Sector	*2001*	*2006*	*2010*	*2011*	*2012*	*2001*	*2006*	*2010*	*2011*	*2012*
Transportation	0.53	0.50	0.52	0.63	0.61	0.98	0.99	1.01	1.01	1.03
Travel	0.60	0.47	0.47	0.52	0.50	0.90	0.91	0.82	0.82	0.80
Other Services										
Communications	2.79	1.27	0.51	0.50	0.51	1.07	1.09	1.18	1.19	1.23
Computer and Information	9.72	6.88	5.81	5.52	5.38	1.24	1.23	1.22	1.21	1.17
Construction	0.18	0.38	0.17	0.25	0.24	1.21	1.06	0.99	0.97	0.85
Financial	0.29	0.44	0.65	0.63	0.58	1.12	1.16	1.10	1.15	1.18
Government services	1.46	0.18	0.23	0.25	0.20	0.85	0.74	0.68	0.64	0.60
Insurance	0.85	0.76	0.58	0.84	0.78	1.27	1.13	1.35	1.25	1.33

(Table 3.2 Continued)

[4] Calculated from WTO (2012), Tables A8 and A9, pp. 220–227.

[5] The formula for calculating RCA is $RCA_{ij} = (x_{ij}/X_{it})/(x_{wj}/X_{wt})$, where x_{ij} and x_{wj} are the values of a country's exports of services sector j and world's exports of services sector j, and X_{it} and X_{wt} refer to the country's total exports and world total exports. If the RCA is greater than 1 for any sector, the country is said to have a comparative advantage vis-à-vis the rest of the world in that sector.

(Table 3.2 Continued)

	India					EU				
Service Sector	2001	2006	2010	2011	2012	2001	2006	2010	2011	2012
Other business services	0.61	1.51	1.10	1.11	1.25	1.17	1.09	1.10	1.11	1.11
Personal, cultural and recreational	0.00	0.53	0.33	0.30	0.47	1.30	1.28	1.49	1.52	1.51
Royalties and Licence fees	0.04	0.01	0.02	0.03	0.03	0.52	0.64	0.81	0.81	0.78

Source: Calculated from UNCTAD Statistics on International Trade in services, available at http://unctadstat.unctad.org/ReportFolders/reportFolders.aspx (accessed on 25 August 2013).

Notes: Due to the expansion of the EU, the data is calculated differently. For the year 2001, data is for EU-15; for 2006, the data is for EU-25; and from 2010 to 2012, the data is for EU-27.

This discussion shows that services trade in both India and the EU has increased manifold over the years. Both economies have an export interest in several services sectors and have trade complementarities. For instance, the EU has the potential to export transportation and *other business services (such as financial, insurance, etc.)* to India, whereas India has the potential to export computer and information services to the EU. However, there is considerable difference between the two economies in the absolute size of their services trade, which indicates an asymmetry in their relative positions in the world market and consequently their unequal bargaining power in trade agreements, even though both are proponents of services liberalisation. Moreover, the EU seems to have a more diversified export basket than India.

India–EU Bilateral Trade in Services

Given the trade complementarities between India and the EU, it is important to examine their bilateral trade patterns. In India, bilateral services trade data is not available by service categories. Therefore, mirrored data on bilateral services trade between India and the EU has been obtained

Figure 3.1
India–EU Trade in Services.

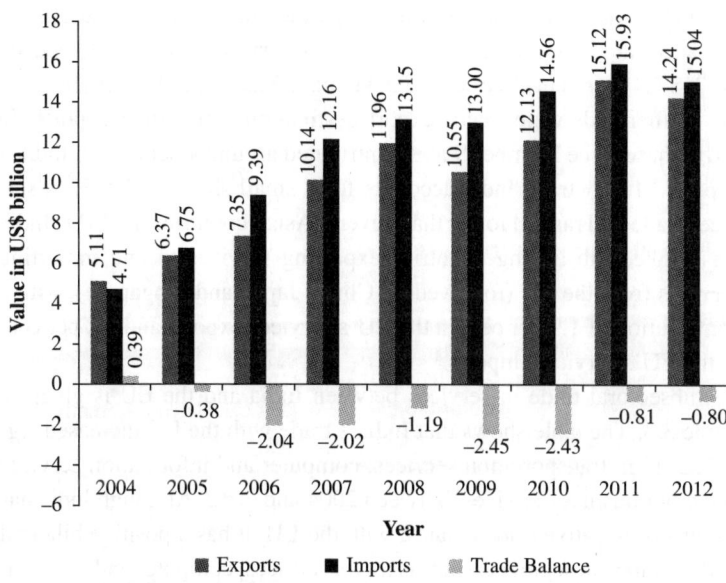

Source: Compiled from Eurostat Table: International Trade in Services (since 2004), available at http://appsso.eurostat.ec.europa.eu/nui/show.do?dataset=bop_its_det&lang=en (accessed on 23 September 2013).

Notes: Values are converted from euro to US dollar. Exchange rates: for 2003, €1 = US$1.13208 (average); 2004, €1 = US$1.24386 (average); 2005, €1 = US$1.24539 (average); 2006, €1 = US$1.25622 (average); 2007, €1 = US$1.40 (average); 2008, €1 = US$1.47134 (average); 2009, €1 = US$1.3937 (average); 2010, €1 = US$1.3267 (average); 2011, €1 = US$1.3943 (average). Extracted from historical exchange rates, Oanda currency converter, http://www.oanda.com/currency/historical-rates/

from the European database, Eurostat. Figure 3.1 shows that bilateral trade in services between India and the EU has increased almost three times—from US$9.8 billion in 2004 to US$29.3 billion in 2012. Between 2004 and 2012, bilateral trade in services grew at a CAGR of 14.6 per cent. India's services exports and imports increased from US$5.1 billion and US$4.7 billion, respectively, in 2004 to US$14.2 billion and US$15 billion, respectively, in 2012. Between 2004 and 2012, India's imports grew at a higher growth rate (15.6 per cent) than India's exports to the

EU (13.7 per cent). India has a positive trade balance in services with the rest of the world but it has a negative trade balance with the EU.

The EU is India's largest trading partner in services. In 2010, the EU accounted for 11 per cent of India's services trade, followed by the US (10 per cent).[6] Among EU Member States, the UK, France and the Netherlands were major export destinations for Indian exports. In 2010, these three Member States contributed around 4 per cent in India's exports.[7] In contrast, India accounts for a small share of the EU's services trade and ranked lower than several Asian countries. In 2011, India was ranked 4th among countries exporting services to and importing services from the EU (followed by China, Japan and Singapore), with a contribution of 1.9 per cent in the EU's services exports and 2.2 per cent in the EU's services imports.[8]

Subsectoral trade in services between India and the EU is given in Table 3.3. The table shows that India's trade with the EU increased significantly in transportation services, computer and information services and other business services[9] between 2004 and 2012. Although India has an overall negative trade balance with the EU, it has a positive bilateral trade balance in segments such as travel services, computer and information and other business services.

This discussion shows that bilateral trade between India and the EU has increased substantially after liberalisation and that the composition of this trade has shifted from traditional to modern services. The economic reforms in general and liberalisation of foreign policies in particular have

[6] The share was calculated from UNCTAD Statistics on International Trade: Services and 'OECD Statistics on International Trade in Services by Partner Country (EBPOS 2002)', available at http://stats.oecd.org/Index.aspx?DatasetCode=TIS (accessed on 25 July 2013).

[7] Compiled and calculated from 'OECD Statistics on International Trade in Services by Partner Country', available at http://stats.oecd.org/Index.aspx?DatasetCode=TIS (accessed on 14 September 2012).

[8] Extracted from, WTO (2013), Table 1.2, p. 22.

[9] 'Other business services' include services such as legal, accounting, architectural, engineering, management consulting, public relations services, advertising, market research and public opinion polling services research and development services, placement of personnel, security and investigation services, translation and interpretation, photographic services, building cleaning services, agricultural, mining and on-site processing services; and operational leasing services (rental) without operators services (i.e. resident/non-resident leasing and charters of ships, aircraft, and transportation equipment such as railway cars, containers, rigs, etc. without crew).

Table 3.3
Bilateral Trade between India and the EU by Services—2004 and 2012 (in US$ billion)

Services	2004				2012			
	Exports	Imports	Total Trade	Trade Balance	Exports	Imports	Total Trade	Trade Balance
Transportation	1.32	1.84	3.16	–0.52	2.78	4.89	7.67	–2.11
Travel	1.84	0.99	2.83	0.85	2.24	2.07	4.31	0.17
Other Services	1.95	1.89	3.84	0.06	9.20	8.04	17.24	1.16
Communications	0.16	0.09	0.24	0.07	0.32	0.45	0.77	–0.13
Computer and information	0.44	0.19	0.63	0.24	2.78	1.98	4.76	0.80
Construction	0.08	0.24	0.32	–0.16	0.21	0.42	0.62	–0.21
Financial	0.04	0.18	0.22	–0.15	0.17	0.42	0.58	–0.25
Government	0.05	0.22	0.27	–0.17	0.08	0.19	0.27	–0.12
Insurance	0.05	0.05	0.10	–0.01	0.16	0.23	0.39	–0.07
Other business services	1.10	0.82	1.92	0.27	5.33	3.78	9.11	1.55

(Table 3.3 Continued)

(Table 3.3 Continued)

Services	2004				2012			
	Exports	Imports	Total Trade	Trade Balance	Exports	Imports	Total Trade	Trade Balance
Personal, cultural and recreational	0.01	0.01	0.02	0.00	0.04	0.06	0.10	−0.02
Royalties and licence fees	0.03	0.08	0.12	−0.05	0.11	0.51	0.62	−0.39
Total services	5.11	4.71	9.82	0.39	14.24	15.04	29.28	−0.80

Source: Compiled from Eurostat, Table: International Trade in Services (since 2004), available at http://appsso.eurostat.ec.europa.eu/nui/show.do?dataset=bop_its_det&lang=en (accessed on 23 September 2013).

Notes: Values are converted from euro to US dollar. Exchange rates: for 2003, €1 = US$1.13208 (average); 2004, €1 = US$1.24386 (average); 2005, €1 = US$1.24539 (average); 2006, €1 = US$1.25622 (average); 2007, €1 = US$1.40 (average); 2008, €1 = US$1.47134 (average); 2009, €1 = US$1.3937 (average); 2010, €1 = US$1.3267 (average); 2011, €1 = US$1.3943 (average). Extracted from historical exchange rates, Oanda currency converter, http://www.oanda.com/currency/historical-rates/

positively affected FDI in both economies. With its high GDP growth and large market, India has emerged as a favoured destination for foreign investment and the EU is among the major investors in the world, thereby creating an important source of complementarity between the two economies.

India and EU's Global Investments

India and the EU are at different levels of development and their requirements for capital differ. There are several studies comparing different countries in terms of their attractiveness for foreign investment. AT Kearney (2012a) in its FDI Confidence Index ranked India as the second most attractive destination in 2012 for FDI after China from among 25 countries. Among EU Member States, Germany was ranked 5th, the UK was 8th, France was 17th, and Poland, Spain and the Netherlands were at 23rd, 24th and 25th ranks, respectively. Thus, according to this index, India seems to rank higher than several EU Member States as a destination for FDI. However, the Index considers only a small group of countries and does not include all EU Member States.

UNCTAD publishes various indices that are based on surveys of Transnational Corporations (TNCs) and Investment Promotion Agencies (IPAs). According to the UNCTAD FDI Attraction Index 2011, India was ranked 59th out of 182 FDI host countries in 2011. Among the Member States, there is wide variation in ranking. Member States such as Belgium, Luxembourg and Ireland were ranked among the top five FDI host countries (2nd, 4th and 5th, respectively), others such as the UK, Poland, Bulgaria, Malta and Spain had a higher rank than India (29th, 40th, 45th and 58th, respectively) and France, Germany, Italy, Sweden, Denmark, Finland and Greece had a lower rank than India.[10] UNCTAD's Inward FDI Potential Index (UNCTAD, 2012: Table 32a) ranks India third among 182 countries in 2011 in terms of its potential for hosting FDI. Among EU Member States, Germany, France and the UK were ranked 8th, 11th and 16th, respectively.

---

[10] Among FDI host countries in the Index, the ranks were: France (77), Germany (86), Italy (97), Sweden (99), Denmark (112), Finland (122) and Greece (142). Source: UNCTAD (2012), Table 31.

Due to the large and unsaturated market, India is a more attractive FDI destination than several EU Member States, but its relative performance in terms of actually attracting FDI is weaker than several EU Member States. Additionally, since the EU was worse affected by the global slowdown compared to India, there has been a loss of confidence among global investors as regards the EU Member States. It is, therefore, important to study long-term trends and patterns in the global FDI inflows and outflows in India and the EU.

Global FDI Inflows to India and the EU

Economic reforms in general and liberalisation of FDI in particular have affected the magnitude and pattern of FDI inflows received by India and the EU. The FDI inflows of India and the EU have increased manifold after they liberalised their economies. In the 1990s, India's FDI inflows were valued at US$0.20 billion, which increased to US$5.5 billion in 2001 and reached a peak of US$31.5 billion in 2011. Similarly, the EU's FDI inflows reached US$420.7 billion in 2011 from US$97.31 billion in the 1990s (see Table 3A.3 in Appendix for details). It is worth mentioning that while India's share in global FDI inflows has increased, the EU's share in global FDI inflows has declined in the past two decades. In 2011, India received 2.07 per cent in terms of FDI inflows compared to 0.66 per cent in the 1990s. Over the same period, the EU's share in FDI inflows declined from 47 per cent to 27.6 per cent.[11]

The services sector is a key area for attracting FDI inflows in India and the EU. Between 2000 and 2012, the services sector[12] accounted for around 64 per cent of the FDI inflows in India (Pal and Hsu 2013), and in the EU the services sector accounted for 66.6 per cent of FDI inflows in 2009.[13]

[11] Calculated from UNCTAD Statistics on 'Foreign Direct Investment', available at http://unctadstat.unctad.org/ReportFolders/reportFolders.aspx (accessed on 25 July 2013).

[12] Including financial, non-financial, construction, energy, telecommunications, computer software and hardware, hotels and tourism, trade, transport, information and broadcasting, consultancy, etc.

[13] Extracted from Eurostat, Table: EU direct investment flows, breakdown by partner country and economic activity (NACE Rev.2) (bop_fdi_flow_r2), available at http://epp.eurostat.ec.europa.eu/portal/page/portal/balance_of_payments/data/database (accessed on 22 September 2013).

Global FDI Outflows from India and the EU

In the past two decades, FDI outflows from India and the EU have increased. Over time, the EU has emerged as a major investor abroad and companies from EU Member States are now investing in developing countries to establish their production networks and services value chains. India's outward investment has also increased, especially in the past decade. In the 1990s, India had minimal FDI outflows, but by 2001 these amounted to US$1.4 billion and reached US$14.75 billion in 2011. While India's share in global FDI outflows increased from 0.01 per cent in the 1990s to 0.87 per cent in 2011, the EU's share declined from 54 per cent to 33.1 per cent over the same period.[14]

The services sector accounts for a large share of FDI outflows for both India and the EU. Between 2006–2007 and 2010–2011, India's outward FDI was valued at US$57 billion, of which US$29 billion or around 50 per cent was in the services sector, US$23 billion was in manufacturing and the balance in agriculture and allied activities (Pal and Hsu, 2013). In the EU, the services sector accounted for 71.4 per cent of its FDI outflows in 2009.[15]

There are a couple of interesting findings here. First, services account for a large share of FDI inflows and outflows for both India and the EU. Within services, the focus is on financial, business and transport services, because trade in services and FDI flows are closely linked to global manufacturing value chains that depend on technological developments, innovative business models and the removal of trade barriers (OECD and WTO, 2013).

India–EU Bilateral Investment Collaborations

There has been a considerable increase in investment flows between India and the EU over the past two decades. To promote and protect bilateral investments, India has signed Bilateral Investment Promotion and

[14] Calculated from UNCTAD Statistics on 'Foreign Direct Investment', available at http://unctadstat.unctad.org/ReportFolders/reportFolders.aspx (accessed on 25 July 2013).

[15] Extracted from Eurostat Table: EU direct investment flows, breakdown by partner country and economic activity (NACE Rev.2) (bop_fdi_flow_r2), available at http://epp.eurostat.ec.europa.eu/portal/page/portal/balance_of_payments/data/database (accessed on 22 September 2013).

Protection Agreement (BIPA) with 22 EU Member States.[16] The objective of this Agreement is to promote and protect the interests of investors and create conditions favourable for fostering greater investment by investors of one country in the territory of the other country. India also has a Double Taxation Avoidance Agreement (DTAA) with 24 EU Member States[17] to promote investment by eliminating dual taxes. These measures have resulted in increased bilateral investments between India and the EU. Against this background, this section first discusses FDI inflows from the EU to India and then Indian investments in EU Member States.

The EU's Investments in India

The EU investors in India have either invested directly or through third country such as Mauritius, Singapore and Cyprus. It is therefore difficult to capture the actual investments from the EU to India. According to statistics released by the Department of Industrial Policy & Promotion (DIPP), under the Ministry of Commerce and Industry, Government of India, the EU is the second largest investor in India. Between April 2000 and April 2013, total cumulative FDI inflows (including goods and services) from the EU were valued at US$49 billion, which accounted for 25 per cent of cumulative FDI inflows into India during this period. Among EU Member States, the UK, Netherlands, Germany and France are the major investors. Between April 2000 and April 2013, these four EU Member States accounted for 18.3 per cent of India's cumulative FDI inflows.[18] The services sector is the largest recipient of FDI inflows from the EU. According to the DIPP (2011), equity-based FDI inflows from the EU in India's services sector (including construction) were valued at US$10 billion and accounted for 24.27 per cent in India's total cumulative FDI inflows from the EU between January 2000 and December 2011.

[16] The BIPA encourages, promotes and protects bilateral investments by enforcing the legal rights of investors and by guaranteeing fair and equitable treatment to the investment of the bilateral partner. The EU Member States are Austria, Belgium, Bulgaria, Cyprus, the Czech Republic, Denmark, Finland, France, Germany, Hungary, Italy, Latvia, Lithuania, Netherlands, Poland, Portugal, Romania, Slovakia, Slovenia, Spain, Sweden and the UK. For details, see http://finmin.nic.in/bipa/bipa_index.asp (accessed on 30 July 2013).

[17] The DTAA covers taxes on income proposed on behalf of each contracting state. It protects taxpayers against double taxation. It also provides reduced tax rates on dividends, interest, royalties and technical service fees received by residents of one country from those in the other. For details of EU Member States, see Note 16.

[18] Compiled from DIPP (2013a), Annex-A, p. 5.

The EU is one of the major sources of technology transfer to India. Between August 1991 and December 2009, India approved 8,106 proposals for the transfer of foreign technology. The US was ranked first with 1,841 approvals, followed by Germany with 1,116 approvals, the UK with 876 approvals and Italy with 489 approvals. Together, the three EU Member States accounted for 30.6 per cent of the technology transfer approvals in India, which is higher than the US' share of 22.7 per cent share.[19]

Indian Investments in the EU

India's total investments (including goods and services) in the EU, although small, have increased significantly in the past decade. According to Eurostat, in 2011, Indian investments in the EU increased to US$1.3 billion from US$97 million in 2001.[20] Over time, India's share in the EU's extra-EU FDI inflows has also increased. While in 2001, India contributed to 0.1 per cent of the extra-EU's FDI inflows, in 2011 the share increased to 0.4 per cent. India's rank among extra-EU investing countries improved from 27th in 2001 to 15th in 2011.[21]

Table 3.4 shows that between July 2007 and June 2013, Indian investments in the EU were valued at US$39.1 billion. Among EU Member States, the Netherlands, the UK and Cyprus are the preferred investment destinations for Indian companies. Between July 2007 and June 2013, Indian investments in these three EU Member States were valued at US$35.3 billion, which accounted for 90 per cent of Indian investments in the EU and 25 per cent share in India's total overseas investments.

The services sector is a key sector for India's outward investments to the EU. Between July 2007 and June 2013, services contributed to around 64 per cent of India's total FDI outflows to the EU. Among EU Member States, there are wide variations with regard to investment in services.

[19] Extracted from DIPP (2010), Table III.B: Country-wise Foreign Technology Transfer Approvals, p. 5,

[20] Calculated from Eurostat, Table: EU direct investment inward flows by extra EU investing country, http://epp.eurostat.ec.europa.eu/tgm/table.do?tab=table&init=1&plugin=1&language=en&pcode=tec00048 (accessed on 24 July 2013). Values are converted from euro to US dollar. Exchange rates: for 2001, €1 = US$ 0.8962 (average) and 2011, €1 = US$1.3943 (average). Extracted from historical exchange rates, Oanda currency converter, http://www.oanda.com/currency/historical-rates/

[21] Calculated from Eurostat, Table: EU direct investment inward flows by extra EU investing country, http://epp.eurostat.ec.europa.eu/tgm/table.do?tab=table&init=1&plugin=1&language=en&pcode=tec00048 (accessed on 24 July 2013).

Table 3.4
Indian Investments in Different Sectors in EU Member States (July 2007 to June 2013) (values in US$ million)

EU Member States	Community, Social and Personal Services (A)	Construction (B)	Financial, Insurance, Real Estate and Business Services (C)	Transport, Storage and Communication Services (D)	Wholesale, Retail Trade, Restaurants and Hotels (E)	Total Services (A + E)	Agriculture, Hunting, Forestry, Fishing and Mining	Manufacturing	Miscellaneous	Electricity, Gas and Water	Total
Austria	1.4 (4.9)	–	–	1.4 (4.9)	–	2.8 (9.8)	–	25.8 (90.2)	–	–	28.6
Belgium	–	–	170.7 (43.7)	–	97.9 (25.0)	268.6 (68.7)	11.9 (3.0)	105.9 (27.1)	4.4 (1.1)	–	390.8
Cyprus	102.4 (1.9)	108.6 (2)	605.4 (11.2)	162 (3.0)	1166.7 (21.5)	2145.1 (39.5)	107.3 (2.0)	3143.6 (57.9)	–	28.7 (0.5)	5424.7
Czech Republic	–	–	4.5 (2.7)	2.6 (1.6)	5.5 (3.3)	12.6 (7.6)	–	143.5 (86.7)	–	9.4 (5.7)	165.5
Denmark	–	–	5.3 (0.5)	1.0 (0.1)	2.0 (0.2)	8.3 (0.8)	–	1032.6 (99.2)	–	–	1040.9
Finland	–	–	29.8 (80.8)	–	–	29.8 (80.8)	–	7.1 (19.2)	–	–	36.9
France	8.0 (2.6)	–	122.2 (39.0)	–	2.5 (0.8)	132.7 (42.3)	–	176.7 (56.3)	0.3 (0.1)	3.8 (1.2)	313.5

Germany	4.2 (0.8)	–	129.0 (25.7)	2.2 (0.4)	18.1 (3.6)	153.5 (30.6)	–	334.1 (66.5)	–	14.8 (2.9)	502.4
Greece	–	–	–	–	1.3 (100)	1.3 (100)	–	–	–	–	1.3
Hungary	–	–	–	–	9.8 (99.3)	9.8 (99.3)	–	0.1 (0.7)	–	–	9.9
Ireland	0.3 (0.1)	–	56.0 (27.9)	–	0.7 (0.3)	57.0 (28.4)	–	143.6 (71.6)	–	–	200.6
Italy	0.2 (0.1)	7.1 (3.0)	17.3 (7.2)	–	39.3 (16.3)	63.9 (26.5)	–	174.7 (72.5)	–	2.2 (0.9)	240.9
Lithuania	–	–	0.4 (85.9)	–	0.1 (14.1)	0.5 (100)	–	–	–	–	0.5
Luxembourg	–	8.4 (1.6)	518.0 (97.1)	–	–	526.4 (98.7)	–	6.8 (1.3)	–	–	533.2
Malta	–	3.8 (15.6)	20.5 (84.4)	–	24.3 (100)	24.3 (100)	–	–	–	–	24.3
Netherlands	1.5	182 (0.8)	2517 (10.5)	12695 (53.0)	1544 (6.5)	16939.7 (70.8)	148.8 (0.6)	6041 (25.2)	11 (0.1)	795 (3.2)	23935
Poland	5.3 (12.1)	–	29.5 (67.2)	2.5 (5.7)	3.5 (8.0)	40.8 (93.0)	–	3.0 (7.0)	–	–	43.8
Portugal	–	–	–	–	0.1 (50.0)	0.1 (50.0)	–	0.1 (50.0)	–	–	0.2

(Table 3.4 Continued)

(Table 3.4 Continued)

EU Member States	Community, Social and Personal Services (A)	Construction (B)	Financial, Insurance, Real Estate and Business Services (C)	Transport, Storage and Communication Services (D)	Wholesale, Retail Trade, Restaurants and Hotels (E)	Total Services (A + E)	Agriculture, Hunting, Forestry, Fishing and Mining	Manufacturing	Miscellaneous	Electricity, Gas and Water	Total
Romania	–	–	1.7 (44.9)	–	1.3 (36.4)	3.0 (81.1)	0.4 (10.8)	0.3 (8.1)	–	–	3.7
Slovakia	–	–	–	–	–	0.00	–	0.3 (100)	–	–	0.3
Spain	–	156 (48.8)	0.8 (0.3)	–	2.9 (0.9)	159.7 (50.0)	–	159.5 (50.0)	–	–	319.2
Sweden	–	–	1.7 (26.3)	–	–	1.7 (26.3)	3.1 (48.3)	–	0.1 (1.0)	1.6 (24.3)	6.5
UK	596.1 (10.0)	15.7 (0.3)	957.3 (16.2)	1567 (26.5)	1333 (22.5)	4470 (75.5)	10.6 (0.2)	1150 (19.4)	289 (4.8)	3.7 (0.1)	5923.5
EU (23)	719.4 (1.8)	481.6 (1.2)	5187.1 (13.3)	14434.7 (36.9)	4228.7 (10.8)	25051.6 (64.0)	282.1 (0.7)	12648.7 (32.3)	304.8 (0.8)	859.2 (2.2)	39146.2

Source: Compiled and calculated from the RBI database on 'Overseas Indian Direct Investment' available at http://www.rbi.org.in/scripts/Data_Overseas_Investment.aspx (accessed on 18 July 2013).

Notes: 1. In Bulgaria, Estonia and Latvia and Slovenia, there were no Indian investments during this period. Croatia became a member on 1 July 2013; therefore, it is not included in the table.

2. Per cent share is given in parentheses.

For instance, in Poland, the UK and Netherlands, the services sector accounted for a major share—93, 75 and 71 per cent, respectively—of India's investment, whereas in France and Germany, Indian investment is mainly in the manufacturing sector.

Key Barriers to India–EU Trade and Investment

The discussion shows that bilateral trade and investment in services between India and the EU has increased over time. This has largely been facilitated by unilateral liberalisation, technological developments, changes in business models and establishment of services value chains. However, bilateral trade in services between these two economies has not realised its full potential. India's trade in services with the EU is less than the EU's bilateral services trade with China and Japan. In 2011, bilateral trade in services between India and the EU was valued at US$31 billion, whereas EU–China and EU–Japan trade in services were valued at US$45 billion and US$38.4 billion, respectively.[22] In 2011, India contributed 1.9 per cent and 2.2 per cent, respectively, to the EU's total exports and imports of services, compared to China's share of 4.3 per and 3.8 per cent, and Japan's share of 3.6 per cent and 3.3 per cent, respectively.[23] In 2011, India accounted for only 0.4 per cent in extra-EU FDI inflows compared to a 5 per cent share for Japan, 3.4 per cent for Singapore, 1.3 per cent for China and 1.2 per cent for Australia.[24]

Both India and the EU have certain restrictions that impede bilateral trade and investment flows. According to the OECD FDI Restrictiveness Index, India and the EU Member States impose some barriers to trade and investment in services, including restrictions on foreign equity

[22] Compiled from Eurostat, Table: EU International trade in services: Exports, imports and balance by partner zone', available at http://epp.eurostat.ec.europa.eu/tgm/table.do?tab= table&init=1&plugin=1&language=en&pcode=tec00082 (accessed on 22 September 2013). Values are converted from euro to US dollar. Exchange rate – for 2011, €1 = US$1.3943 (average). Extracted from historical exchange rates, Oanda currency converter, available at http://www.oanda.com/currency/historical-rates/

[23] Extracted from, WTO (2013), Table 1.2, p. 22.

[24] Calculated from Eurostat, Table: EU direct investment inward flows by extra EU investing country, available at http://epp.eurostat.ec.europa.eu/tgm/table.do?tab=table&in it=1&plugin=1&language=en&pcode=tec00048 (accessed on 31 July 2013).

participation and regulatory conditions on FDI inflows. Other restrictions include barriers to movement of service providers (Table 3.5).

- *Foreign Ownership and Investment Requirements*
  Limitations on foreign ownership constitute the most common form of restriction on services in India and most EU Member States. These restrictions include limits on foreign equity participation, local incorporation requirements and licensing requirements. In India, the FDI restrictions vary across different services sector (for details, see Table 3A.4 in Appendix). In several sectors where full foreign presence is allowed, it is subject to minimum capital requirements and other restrictions. For example, in construction and related engineering services, there is a minimum capital requirement (US$10 million for wholly owned subsidiaries and US$5 million for joint ventures with Indian partners); and a minimum lock-in period of three years (from the completion of minimum capitalisation before original investment) for repatriation of the amount. Among EU Member States, in Austria investment by non-EU nationals is limited to 49 per cent in professional services (including accountancy, legal, engineering and architectural services). In Hungary, a minimum of 26 per cent of the shares of a broadcasting company must be owned by Hungarian citizens and residents.[25] These restrictions impede the operation of Indian or European companies in each other's market and make it difficult to integrate operations across the value chain, thus causing fragmentation in the services market.
- *Multiple Regulators and Regulations*
  Both India and the EU have a quasi-federal governance structure. In India, services sectors such as education and health come under the state governments or are jointly regulated by the central and state governments. The multiplicity of regulators has led to the need to obtain multiple clearances. For example, there are around 13 regulatory bodies (including the All-India Council for Technical Education, the University Grants Commission and other

---

[25] For details, see OECD (2012a) and USTR (2013).

Table 3.5

*Scores for India and the Selected EU Member States on OECD's
FDI Restrictiveness Index, 2012*

Country	FDI Equity Restrictions	Screening	Key Personnel	Operational Restrictions	Total FDI Index
India	0.248	0.033	0.008	0.008	0.297
EU Member States					
Austria	0.090	0.009	0.000	0.007	0.106
France	0.027	0.000	0.005	0.012	0.045
Germany	0.017	0.000	0.000	0.006	0.023
Greece	0.032	0.004	0.002	0.001	0.039
Hungary	0.048	0.000	0.000	0.001	0.049
Italy	0.046	0.000	0.000	0.004	0.050
Netherlands	0.035	0.200	0.000	0.014	0.249
Poland	0.056	0.000	0.006	0.010	0.072
Spain	0.021	0.000	0.000	0.000	0.021
Sweden	0.028	0.027	0.000	0.003	0.059
UK	0.036	0.000	0.000	0.025	0.061

Source: Compiled from OECD FDI Regulatory Restrictiveness Index, available
at http://www.oecd.org/daf/internationalinvestment/investmentstatis-
ticsandanalysis/fdiregulatoryrestrictivenessindex.htm

Notes: 1. The index measures four types of restrictions:

   a. Foreign equity restrictions.
   b. Screening and prior approval requirements.
   c. Restrictions on employment of foreigners as key personnel such
      as foreign key personnel are not allowed, economic needs test,
      time-bound limit on employment of foreign key personnel and
      nationality or residency requirements for board of directors, and
      so on.
   d. Operational restrictions such as restrictions on the number of
      branches, capital repatriation and land ownership.

   2. In the Index, the values range between '0' and '1', in which '0' repre-
      sents no regulatory impediments to FDI in the country or the country
      is an *open economy* and '1' represents restrictions on foreign invest-
      ments. The Index includes 22 sectors in 55 countries (including 23
      EU Member States).

universities) to regulate higher education (Mukherjee, 2013), and the financial services sector is governed by around 60 Acts and related rules and regulations.[26] Similarly, in the EU, regulations are implemented at two levels of government—the EU level and the national or individual Member State level. All laws and regulations are passed by the European Parliament and implemented by individual Member States. In the EU, there are about 35,000 requirements in the services sector across 27 EU Member States. This multiplicity of laws and regulators creates regulatory overlaps, gaps and ambiguities.

- *Heterogeneity in Regulations in the EU*
  Unlike the case of goods, the EU has a non-harmonised market for services. There is heterogeneity in regulations in the EU and regulations vary across different Member States. The individual Member States retain considerable discretion in services regulations, implementation and enforcement, even in the presence of common regulations at the European Commission level. Services Directive (2006/123/EC) has undoubtedly reduced regulatory heterogeneity, but in highly regulated sectors, such as financial services and professional services, there is still regulatory heterogeneity.

- *Outdated/Absence of Governing Regulations in India*
  Several regulations in India are outdated and services such as e-commerce, cloud computing and courier services do not have governing regulation. A number of Bills including the Public Procurement Bill, 2012[27] are pending in Parliament.

- *Restrictions on Movement of Persons*
  Restrictions on visas and work permits and requirements on minimum experience, licensing and nationality/citizenship, among others, restrict the movement of persons between India and the EU. In India, for an employment visa, the foreign national should draw a salary of more than US$25,000 per annum (except for categories such as ethnic cooks, non-English language teachers,

---

[26] http://finmin.nic.in/press_room/2013/fm_speech_ICSI22052013.pdf (accessed on 22 September 2013).

[27] Details are available at http://164.100.24.219/BillsTexts/LSBillTexts/asintroduced/58_2012_LS_EN.pdf (accessed on 22 September 2013).

translators and staff working for embassies and high commissions in India). This minimum salary requirement impedes the entry of foreign semi-skilled workers into India. The other important barrier is the cumbersome and time-consuming visa process; it usually takes 55–60 days to get an Indian visa.

In the EU, work permits and visas are under the jurisdiction of different Member States and the policies vary across Member States. For example, while the Schengen visa permits business visitors from a third country like India to enter Member States that are signatories of the accord, the visa is granted only for a short period and the duration of stay varies across Member States. Moreover, service providers have to first enter the country that gives the visa and have to fulfil the requirements and conditions of that country. For example, in Germany, a short-term visa is granted on an individual/case-by-case basis and it varies between 10 days and 90 days. In the UK, along with other requirements,[28] citizens of several countries, including India, are required to get screened for tuberculosis.[29] In Ireland, there is a salary threshold of €30,000 for all work permits.[30]

There is a nationality requirement in several EU Member States. In France, only French nationals, nationals of EU Member States or nationals of countries with bilateral agreements are allowed to operate in certain sectors, such as private research institutions, insurance, forwarding agencies, retail, audio-visual and communications and telecommunications.[31] In several EU Member States including Austria, Belgium, the Czech Republic, Finland, France, Germany, Poland, Sweden, the Netherlands, Luxembourg, Greece and the UK, there are labour market and economic needs tests.

[28] (a) Not working during stay; (b) not registering a civil partnership during stay; (c) presenting evidence of sufficient money to fund stay; (d) showing proof of intention to leave the UK at the end of the visit and the ability to meet the cost of return/onward journey and (e) demonstrating evidence of suitable care arrangements and parental consent for stay in the UK if a person is under the age of 18.

[29] http://www.ukba.homeoffice.gov.uk/policyandlaw/immigrationlaw/immigrationrules/ (accessed on 30 July 2013).

[30] Quinn (2011) and http://www.citizensinformation.ie/en/employment/migrant_workers/employment_permits/work_permits.html (accessed on 30 July 2013).

[31] Invest in France (2012).

Denmark follows the Green Card scheme for allowing foreign professionals. It is based on a points system where language and adaptation skills earn points. Austria, Slovenia, the Czech Republic, Greece and Lithuania require knowledge of the language for permanent residence and citizenship (Goyal and Mukherjee, 2013), which is difficult for Indian service providers.

- *Cultural and Linguistic Barriers*
  Both the EU and India are multilingual and multicultural regions. The EU has 23 official languages and India has 22 official languages.[32] At the central or EU level, all official documents are published in all the languages and individual Member States publish documents in their local language. In India, all official documents are published in English. In the EU, a foreign company has to employ a legal national legal expert to interpret all laws and regulations of an individual Member State, while in India, European companies have to hire translators for English. This creates risks and uncertainties, and adds to the costs.

Despite numerous trade barriers, bilateral trade and investment between India and the EU has increased. Both Indian and European companies have established a large presence in each other's market. The EU market has become an important investment destination for Indian companies, especially for procuring technology, while India has created tremendous opportunities for European companies. India and the EU have been negotiating a Broad-based Trade and Investment Agreement since 2007 that aims to ease trade and investment barriers between the two sides.

The Way Forward

India and the EU have trade and investment complementarities, but these have not been fully explored. Although the EU is India's biggest economic partner, there are some areas of concern. The global financial crisis and the Eurozone crisis have adversely affected the EU economy and increased protectionism in the EU region. EU Member States such as

---

[32] These are Assamese, Bengali, Bodo, Dogri, English, Gujarati, Hindi, Kannada, Kashmiri, Konkani, Maithili, Malayalam, Manipuri, Marathi, Nepali, Oriya, Punjabi, Sanskrit, Santhali, Sindhi, Tamil and Telugu.

France are facing huge unemployment issues. Such economic conditions coupled with slow growth in domestic demand and falling productivity and competitiveness are major concerns for EU companies. While India can offer an attractive market and an alternative investment destination that can help EU companies diversify their risk, the slow pace of reforms in India, and the difficulties in doing business have affected bilateral trade and investment flows.

Bilateral trade and investment flows can increase if the existing barriers to trade and investment are addressed. Most of the barriers can be addressed through autonomous liberalisation in India and the EU Member States. In particular, India needs to remove restrictions on FDI in services and implement regulations that bring in operational certainty. The EU needs to harmonise the services market across Member States, especially with respect to the ease of movement for temporary service providers from third countries.

Some of the barriers can be addressed through inter-governmental agreements between India and EU Member States. For instance, India has bilateral social security agreements with only a few EU Member States;[33] these are Belgium, France, Denmark, Germany, Luxembourg and the Netherlands. Similar agreements have been finalised with Austria, the Czech Republic, Finland, Hungary, Portugal and Sweden, but are yet to be implemented.[34] India does not have any agreement nor is it negotiating one with Member States such as the UK. It is important to have such agreements with more EU Member States, but this is possible only through inter-government collaboration. As part of the India–EU BTIA, both economies can not only take commitments to bind the existing level of liberalisation, thereby guaranteeing operational certainty, but they can also streamline their operational procedures. For instance, the investment chapter in the India–EU BTIA can override the Bilateral Investment Protection Agreements or Bilateral Investment Treaty (BIT) that India has with individual EU Member States and there can be a common agreement that will enable business to have cross-country investments.

---

[33] Bilateral Social Security Agreements are designed to protect the interests of Indian workers posted in these countries for short-term assignments by exempting them from social security contributions under the host country legislation for a stipulated period.

[34] For details, see Ministry of Overseas Indian Affairs, available at http://www.moia. gov.in/services.aspx?ID1=285&id=m4&idp=81&mainid=73 (accessed on 31 July 2013).

A key hindrance in enhancing bilateral trade and investment flows between India and the EU is the lack of political will and pressure to sign the India–EU BTIA. The two economies have been negotiating this trade agreement for more than six years and recently their interests have shifted from the BTIA agreement to other agreements. While the EU is focusing on the US–EU Transatlantic Trade and Investment Partnership (TTIP) agreement, India has shifted its negotiating resources to the Regional Comprehensive Economic Partnership (RCEP), which includes ASEAN and six countries, namely Australia, China, India, Japan, Republic of Korea and New Zealand. If India is able to seal a comprehensive agreement with the EU, the gains in services are likely to be higher than what it can achieve under the RCEP because the EU is a larger trading partner for India in services than RCEP countries. Also, with China being a key player in the RCEP, the agreement will become complicated since China is also a large player in global trade in services (Fukunaga and Isono, 2013). Further, there are wide variations among RCEP members in terms of their approach to services liberalisation. Similarly, for the EU, there are greater benefits under the BTIA than the TTIP (Das, 2013; Hengel, 2013; Khandekar, 2013). The BTIA would give the EU preferential access to a large emerging market in Asia that has restrictions on market access in services, and companies from India and the EU could jointly explore third-country markets. If the BTIA is signed, companies from the EU would have a distinct advantage over their competitors from the US in the Indian market. In light of the huge potential benefits that can accrue to both sides from the India–EU BTIA that is currently under negotiation, industry, policy-makers and lobbying groups in both economies should focus on an early conclusion of this agreement and should aim to achieve substantial coverage of the services sector and depth in service sector commitments under the agreement.

Appendix

Table 3A.1

Share of Services in Total Trade—India and the EU (%)

Year	India			EU		
	Exports	*Imports*	*Trade*	*Exports*	*Imports*	*Trade*
1991	21.7	22.5	22.2	21.3	19.3	20.3
1992	20.1	22.2	21.3	22.2	20.6	21.4
2001	28.6	28.5	28.5	21.6	21.4	21.5
2002	28.3	27.1	27.7	22.1	21.8	22.0
2003	28.8	25.5	27.1	22.5	21.9	22.2
2004	33.3	26.3	29.5	22.9	21.6	22.3
2005	34.5	24.9	29.2	22.8	20.8	21.8
2006	36.4	24.8	30.0	22.6	20.1	21.4
2007	36.7	23.6	29.4	23.3	20.2	21.8
2008	36.0	23.8	29.1	23.4	20.1	21.8
2009	36.1	24.0	29.2	26.2	23.1	24.6
2010	35.4	25.1	29.5	24.7	21.4	23.0
2011	31.2	21.2	25.5	23.7	20.3	22.0
2012	33.6	20.5	25.9	24.1	20.7	22.4

Source: Calculated from UNCTAD Statistics on International Trade in Services, available at http://unctadstat.unctad.org/ReportFolders/reportFolders. aspx (accessed on 25 June 2013).

Notes: 1. Total trade including merchandise and services trade.

2. Due to the expansion of the EU, the data is calculated differently. From 1991 to 2003, the data is for EU-15; from 2004 to 2006, the data is for EU-25; and from 2007 to 2012, the data is for EU-27.

Table 3A.2
Trends in Services Trade for India and the EU (US$ billion)

	India				EU			
Year	*Exports*	*Imports*	*Total Trade*	*Trade Balance*	*Exports*	*Imports*	*Total Trade*	*Trade Balance*
1991	4.9	5.9	10.9	−1.0	406.4	380.6	787.0	25.8
1992	4.9	6.7	11.7	−1.8	453.6	434.1	887.7	19.6
2001	17.3	20.1	37.4	−2.8	637.6	622.2	1259.8	15.4
2002	19.5	21.0	40.5	−1.6	699.3	664.6	1363.9	34.8
2003	23.9	24.9	48.8	−1.0	851.2	800.8	1652.0	50.4
2004	38.3	35.6	73.9	2.6	1030.5	937.2	1967.7	93.3
2005	52.5	47.3	99.8	5.2	1188.5	1071.2	2259.8	117.3
2006	69.7	58.7	128.4	11.0	1330.5	1170.5	2501.0	160.0
2007	86.9	70.8	157.7	16.1	1627.7	1399.6	3027.3	228.1
2008	107.1	88.3	195.5	18.8	1806.1	1562.7	3368.8	243.4
2009	92.6	80.3	173.0	12.3	1631.4	1405.4	3036.9	226.0
2010	124.0	117.1	241.1	7.0	1690.7	1439.5	3130.1	251.2
2011	137.7	124.6	262.3	13.1	1890.6	1580.79	3471.5	309.7
2012	148.1	125.9	274.0	22.3	1834.4	1516.1	3350.5	318.3

Source: Compiled and calculated from UNCTAD Statistics on International Trade in Services, available at http://unctadstat.unctad.org/ReportFolders/reportFolders.aspx (accessed on 25 June 2013).

Note: Due to the expansion of the EU, the data is calculated differently. From 1981 to 2004, the data is for EU-15; for 2005 and 2006, the data is for EU-25; and from 2008 to 2012, the data is for EU-27.

Table 3A.3
Trends in FDI Inflows and Outflows for India and the EU (US$ billion and % share)

	FDI Inflows				FDI Outflows			
	India		EU		India		EU	
Year	*Value*	*% Share*	*Value*	*% Share*	*Value*	*% Share*	*Value*	*% Share*
1980	0.08	0.15	21.28	39.35	0.004	0.01	21.90	42.46
1990	0.24	0.11	97.31	46.91	0.01	0.00	130.57	54.07
2000	3.59	0.26	698.28	49.78	0.51	0.04	813.12	65.99

(Table 3A.3 Continued)

(Table 3A.3 Continued)

| | FDI Inflows | | | | FDI Outflows | | | |
| | India | | EU | | India | | EU | |
Year	Value	% Share	Value	% Share	Value	% Share	Value	% Share
2001	5.48	0.66	383.96	46.39	1.40	0.19	429.90	57.50
2005	7.62	0.78	496.07	50.49	2.99	0.34	606.52	68.76
2006	20.33	1.39	581.72	39.79	14.28	1.02	690.03	49.10
2007	25.35	1.29	850.53	43.15	17.23	0.79	1199.33	55.15
2008	42.55	2.44	487.97	27.98	19.40	1.02	906.20	47.43
2009	35.65	3.01	346.53	29.24	15.93	1.36	370.02	31.61
2010	24.64	1.98	304.69	24.50	14.63	1.11	407.25	30.77
2011	31.55	2.07	420.72	27.60	14.75	0.87	561.81	33.16

Source: Calculated and compiled from UNCTAD Database on Foreign Direct Investment, available at http://unctadstat.unctad.org/ReportFolders/ reportFolders.aspx (accessed on 19 August 2013).

Table 3A.4
FDI Limits on Services Sectors in India (as of June 2014)

FDI Limit	Sectors	Route
FDI is Prohibited	➢ Lottery, gambling and betting including casinos, chit funds	
	➢ Nidhi company, trading in transferable development rights (TDRs); manufacturing of cigars, cheroots, cigarillos and cigarettes, of tobacco, etc.	
	➢ Real estate or construction of farm houses	
	➢ Atomic energy	
74%	➢ Broadcasting carriage services including teleports, direct-to-home, multiple system cable networks, mobile TV and headend-in-the-sky (HITS)	Up to 49% through automatic route; beyond 49% through government route
	➢ Air transport services (non-scheduled air transport service)	
	➢ Ground handling services	
	➢ Banking private sector	
	➢ Satellites—establishment and operation	Government route

(Table 3A.4 Continued)

(Table 3A.4 Continued)

FDI Limit	Sectors	Route
51%	➢ Multi-brand retail trade	Government route
49%	➢ Cable networks (local cable operators)	Automatic route
	➢ Petroleum refining by public sector undertakings (PSU)	
	➢ Air transport services—domestic scheduled passenger airline	
	➢ Private security agencies	Government route
26%	➢ Insurance	Automatic route
	➢ Broadcasting services (terrestrial broadcasting FM radio and uplinking of news and current affairs TV channels)	Government route
	➢ Defence industry	
	➢ Print media (publishing of newspapers and periodicals dealing with news and current affairs and publication of Indian editions of foreign magazines dealing with news and current affairs)	
20%	➢ Banking services—public sector	Government route

Source: Compiled from DIPP (2014).
Note: Automatic Route of entry implies that there is no need to get approval from the Reserve Bank of India (the central bank) or the government; Government Route means that prior approval is needed from the Foreign Investment Promotion Board (FIPB) under the Department of Economic Affairs, Ministry of Finance.

PART II

4

Expanding Collaboration in Logistics: The BTIA and Beyond

Smita Miglani

Introduction

Logistics involve a wide set of activities dedicated to the transformation and distribution of goods, from raw material sourcing to final market distribution and related information flows between point of origin and point of end use. It covers various forms of freight transportation such as roads, railways, air and maritime; consolidation of cargo; and other services such as storage and warehousing, courier and express delivery, border clearance and payment. On average, logistics costs account for 7–8 per cent of the final cost of a finished product in developed countries, but is much higher (usually more than 10 per cent) in developing countries.[1]

Studies have shown that logistics infrastructure has a positive impact on economic growth in an economy (Liu, 2009; Yuan and Kuang, 2010)

---

[1] For instance, logistics cost as a percentage of GDP is about 13 per cent for India, 18 per cent for China and 17 per cent for Thailand.

and economic growth itself creates a need for logistics infrastructure (Yang, 2010; Yang and Zheng, 2011). Efficiency in logistics and trade facilitation systems is also seen to enhance industrial activity (Yu, 2007) and competitiveness (Navickas et al., 2011). For all these reasons, logistics has been an important part of the growth process and modernisation of developed economies like the US and the EU as it is for emerging economies like India and China.

This chapter focuses on trade and collaboration in logistics between India and the EU. In terms of their nature and level of advancement, the logistics markets of these two economies are quite different. The EU is a world leader in the provision of logistics services and has a well-organised and evolved infrastructure that is becoming saturated. On the other hand, the Indian logistics sector is underdeveloped and fragmented but growing at a fast pace. In addition to being interesting case studies in themselves, the trade complementarities and opportunities for joint collaboration between India and the EU are worth exploring.

In this context, it is important to note some of the recent developments in the logistics sector. The Indian government has announced the setting up of economic corridors, which will need state-of-the-art logistics facilities and there are tremendous opportunities for the EU companies to invest in these corridors. Already the UK government has expressed interest in Bangalore Mumbai Industrial Corridor (BMIC). The success of the 'Make in India' campaign of the prime minister depends on an efficient supply chain and India can learn from the EU's experience in setting up efficient supply chains. The Indian government is focusing on trade facilitation and ease of doing business and EU experience in these areas will be beneficial for India.

Logistics is an important area for trade negotiations in bilateral and multilateral agreements for India and the EU. The EU has been a demandeur in the World Trade Organization's (WTO) GATS negotiations[2] and in its bilateral trade and investment agreements to liberalise the sector (WTO, 2005a). India is a target market, which over the years has become

---

[2] GATS negotiations are based on a request-offer process where a country makes a bilateral request to its trading partners, who, after taking into account the requests from all countries, make an offer. The offers are multilateral, that is, all WTO members, whether the country has made a request or not, benefit from it. In the plurilateral request-offer process that began after the Hong Kong Ministerial, a group of countries—the demandeurs make a request to another group, the 'target' countries.

liberal in its FDI regime and continues to open up the sector. The EU is a proponent of the Trade Facilitation Agreement in the WTO, and recently India has agreed to accept the agreement. India is changing its trade facilitation regime in line with the WTO agreement. The proposed India–EU BTIA is expected to increase trade and investment flows between the two economies in the coming years and, hence, increase the demand for efficient logistics. The logistics sector has been recognised as a crucial sector under this agreement. Given the recent developments, it is likely that the India–EU BTIA will also have a chapter on trade facilitation focusing on cooperation between India and the EU. Against this backdrop, this chapter looks beyond the BTIA and analyses possibilities for India–EU collaboration in the sector.

Following an initial discussion of classification and coverage of logistics services, the chapter provides an overview of the logistics sectors in India and the EU. This is followed by a detailed analysis of India–EU trade and collaboration in logistics and the barriers in each market. Finally, suggestions are made on how to circumvent the existing barriers through international negotiations and reform measures.

Classification and Coverage of Logistics Services under WTO

WTO members use the Services Sectoral Classification List (MTN. GNS/W/120; also known as the W/120) as a guide for scheduling commitments in different sectors under GATS.[3] Logistics is not clearly defined as a distinct industry in the W/120 list and, therefore, countries have different views on the coverage and key segments to be liberalised under it. In this scenario, some countries have used a checklist approach[4] to negotiate logistics services in the WTO as shown in Table 4.1.

The checklist divides logistics services into three categories: core freight logistics services, related freight logistics services and non-core

---

[3] This document is based on the U.N. Provisional Central Product Classification (CPC).

[4] Communication from Australia, Canada, Chile, Djibouti, the European Communities, Hong Kong (China), Iceland, Japan, Korea, Lichtenstein, Mauritius, New Zealand, Nicaragua, Norway, Panama, Peru, Singapore, Switzerland, The Separate Customs Territory of Taiwan, Penguh, Kinmen and Matsu, and the United States. 18 February 2005, TN/S/W/34. For details, see Kaeser (2011).

Table 4.1

Scope of Logistics Services with CPC Codes and W/120 Classification

Group	Industries	CPC Code	Classification
Group I: Core freight logistics services	Cargo handling services	CPC 7411 CPC 7419	11.H
	Storage and warehousing services	CPC 742	11.H
	Transport agency services	CPC 748	11.H
	Other auxiliary services, including customs brokerage services	CPC 749	11.H
Group II: Freight transport services	Maritime transport services		11.A
	Rail transport services—freight transport	CPC 7112	11.E
	Road transport services—freight transport	CPC 7123	11.F
Group III: Related logistics services	Technical testing and analysis services	CPC 8676	1. F. E
	Management consulting and related services	CPC 865, 866	1.F.c, 1.F.d

Source: Compiled from WTO (2004), Freight Logistics Checklist, TN/S/W/20 and WTO (1991) MTN.GNS/W/120.

Note: The 1989 Provisional Central Product Classification (CPC Provisional) was used to draw up this list.

freight logistics services. Group I consists of core freight logistics services, defined as services essential to logistics operations; these services are covered in WTO negotiations under *Services auxiliary to all modes of transport*. Group II consists of freight transport services that are integral to logistics operations; these services are covered under *Transport Services*. Group III consists of related logistics services, defined as services desirable to build an enabling environment for logistics services.

The discussion in this chapter broadly follows the checklist classification. However, there are some deviations. For example, the IT aspects of logistics have been covered since they are linked with other services such as multimodal transport facilities and global supply chains. Postal and courier, distribution (wholesale trade, retail and commission agent services) and construction services are excluded. The inland waterways segment is also not covered since it is not an important mode of transportation in India and EU companies have a limited presence.

Overview of the Logistics Sector in India and the EU

This section compares logistics in India and the EU focusing on their size, evolution and significance for the domestic economy. The Indian logistics sector accounted for a turnover of US$90 billion in 2011. The sector was growing at around 15 per cent per annum until the recent slowdown of 2012 (Deloitte–ICC, 2012). In the EU, logistics is one of the biggest sectors and a key driver of all economic activity. In 2010, it accounted for a turnover of US$1,230 billion. Thus, the size of the EU logistics market is 13–14 times that of India. Compared to India, growth rates of freight transport in EU have not been very high in the past two decades. Freight volumes grew at just 1.2 per cent per annum between 1995 and 2009.[5]

Logistics is not recognised as a separate industry in India and there is no government mechanism providing disaggregated data on revenue, contribution to GDP and employment for the sector as a whole. According to the National Sample Survey Organization (NSSO), in 2011–2012, the transport and storage segments[6] together contributed about 6.7 per cent to Indian GDP (at factor cost and at 2004–2005 prices).[7] The share has increased over time from about 3 per cent in the 1950s. In the same year, the contribution to employment was 4.3 per cent of the total workforce.

In contrast, logistics accounted for 11 million jobs in the EU and represented 4.9 per cent of the economy in terms of value addition in 2012.[8]

---

[5] Freight volumes grew at 0.4 per cent per annum between 2000 and 2009. Source: http://www.eea.europa.eu/data-and-maps/figures/freight-transport-volume-billion-tkm (accessed on 3 June 2013).

[6] The NSSO classifies the transport sector under the category 'transport, storage and communications', in which 'transport' is divided in two sub-segments: 'railways' and 'transport by other means'.

[7] The contribution also increased over time. In the 1950s, the sector contributed about 3 per cent, in the 1980s the share increased to 5 per cent and then to 6.2 per cent in 2002–2003. Source: CSO data.

[8] http://europa.eu/rapid/pressReleasesAction.do?reference=IP/12/717&type=HTML#footnote-1 (accessed on 22 April 2013).

In 2008, the transport services sector in the EU-27 employed around 9.1 million persons, accounting for about 4.5 per cent of the total workforce. Around two-thirds of this workforce was employed in land transport (road, rail and inland waterways), 2 per cent in sea transport, 5 per cent in air transport and 27 per cent in warehousing and supporting activities (such as cargo handling, storage and warehousing) (European Commission Statistical Pocketbook, 2012).

In terms of sub-segments, in India roads account for the majority (about 60–65 per cent) of domestic freight movement; railways account for 30–33 per cent; maritime (coastal and inland) is close to 5 per cent[9] and the remainder is through air carriers. For international trade, shipping is the dominant mode of freight transport, accounting for about 90 per cent by volume (and 70 per cent by value).[10] For the EU, 77.5 per cent of inland freight is carried by roads, 16.5 per cent by railways and 5.9 per cent by inland waterways.[11] The volume of air freight is limited compared with the much higher volumes transported by other modes, but is growing over time.[12]

In India, while segments like railways and aviation are organised,[13] others like road transport and warehousing are largely fragmented and unorganised.[14] Moreover, only a few service providers specialise in providing 3PL/4PL services and reverse logistics but their number has been growing.[15] In contrast, logistics is an advanced industry in the EU in

[9] Inland water transportation is underdeveloped despite 14,000 kilometres of navigable rivers and canals.

[10] The rest of international trade is through air transport; less than 1 per cent is through land transport. Trade through roads and railways is only with neighbouring countries. For details, see Mukherjee and Miglani (2010).

[11] http://epp.eurostat.ec.europa.eu/statistics_explained/index.php/Freight_transport_statistics (accessed on 20 February 2013).

[12] http://epp.eurostat.ec.europa.eu/statistics_explained/index.php/Air_transport_statistics_at_regional_level (accessed on 7 May 2013).

[13] Corporatised in the case of the aviation sector; road transport and warehousing are comparatively non-corporatised.

[14] The road transport segment is dominated by small truck companies and individual truckers. Corporate is defined as 'of or relating to a corporation'.

[15] 3PL and 4PL stand for third-party logistics and fourth-party logistics, respectively. Reverse Logistics stands for all operations related to resources at least one step back in the supply chain for value addition, proper disposal or re-manufacturing. It is seen as the flow of goods from the point of consumption to the point of origin and also involves planning and managing (collection, disassembly and processing), efficient flow of/reuse of surplus inventory.

keeping with its status as a developed country. It has several integrated service providers that are organised and use highly advanced technology with a focus on cost reduction. Logistics has been at the heart of the EU single market integration and is directly linked to consumer, environment, energy, research and international trade policy.

The Indian and EU logistics sectors can be compared with their global competitors using the World Bank's Logistics Performance Index (LPI) and Doing Business indicators. The LPI, 2014 reveals a modest rank for India (46) among 160 countries, lagging behind the US (9) and the United Arab Emirates (UAE. 27), as well as behind China (28) and the entire EU-27 average (37).[16] India has been lagging behind especially because of low scores on parameters such as customs, infrastructure and international shipments. Similarly, the *Trading Across Borders* parameter in the *Doing Business* Index 2014 that ranks 189 economies puts India at a lower rank (132) than several other European countries.

India has a quasi-federal governance structure. Segments like railways, national highways, major ports, international shipping, civil aviation and inland waterways are under the jurisdiction of the central government, while others like state and rural roads, minor ports, coastal shipping and trucking are under state governments. In addition, there are some areas of joint jurisdiction (rural roads) where the state governments work in coordination with local/municipal bodies and the central government.[17] There is no single independent regulator for the entire logistics sector in India. There are some sector-specific regulators such as the Warehousing Development and Regulatory Authority (WDRA)[18] and the Directorate General of Civil Aviation (DGCA).[19] At the centre, multiple ministries are responsible for road transport, air transport and shipping. Railways and postal services remain public monopolies in India. In the EU, transport is a policy responsibility shared between the Union and Member

[16] In 2012, six of the top 10 logistic performers were EU countries.

[17] Apart from transport ministries and departments, several other ministries such as the Ministry of Finance, the Ministry of Environment and Forests and the Ministry of Consumer Affairs, as well as the Food and Public Distribution (which regulates inter-state movement of goods) regulate this sector.

[18] The WDRA regulates and ensures implementation of the provisions of the Warehousing (Development and Regulation) Act, 2007 for the development and regulation of warehouses and promotes orderly growth of the warehousing business.

[19] The DGCA regulates air transport services to/from/within India and enforces civil air regulations, air safety and airworthiness standards.

States. The European Commission (EC) creates framework conditions for the sector through its Directives (laws) that come into force when the national government takes steps to introduce and implement them within national laws.

In India, the logistics sector was liberalised in phases following the overall economic liberalisation process started in 1991 and has been characterised by the relaxation of FDI regulations, public–private partnership (PPP) models and tax concessions and other incentives to encourage private players. The government's aim has been to attract additional investment, improve the productivity/quality of services and infuse competitiveness in service provision. Today, there are only a few logistics segments that have restrictions on foreign investment (see Table 4A.1 in the Appendix). With relaxed FDI norms and high margins, private investment (both domestic and foreign) has increased. Between April 2000 and June 2012, FDI to India in ports, sea and air transport amounted to US$3,278.84 million (around 1.7 per cent of cumulative inflows).[20] If related activities such as construction and railway-related components are included, FDI inflows in this period amounted to about US$5,639.58 million. Transport is also among the major sector-wise overseas investments by Indian companies every year. According to data compiled by the Reserve Bank of India, *transport, communication and storage services* together accounted for 2.85 per cent of overseas investments between 2008–2009 and 2011–2012.[21]

At present, logistics in India is a complex chain of processes across multiple modes of transport and centred on manufacturing and retail in key industries such as automobiles and auto-components, IT, electronics, textiles and fast-moving consumer goods. Reforms in all segments are ongoing and are evolving with the growth and the changing needs of the economy. The entry of experienced international players and the increased economic activity have catalysed the emergence of new segments such as third party logistics/fourth party logistics (3PL/4PL), reverse logistics, express delivery services, cold chains and containerised cargo movement. IT is embedded in almost all stages of the supply

---

[20] FDI Statistics, DIPP, Ministry of Commerce and Industry, Government of India. Source: http://dipp.nic.in/ (accessed on 5 June 2013).

[21] April 2011 to 22 February 2012. Source: http://www.rbi.org.in/ (accessed on 5 June 2013).

process and is reducing the need for multiple agents. Companies are now developing end-to-end cargo management capabilities to establish asset ownership in parts of the cargo value chain. All these are likely to promote the development of an integrated logistics value chain in the coming years.

In the EU, liberalisation of trade and freight transport movements began with the Treaty of Rome and the formation of the European Economic Community in 1958. This provided for the establishment of a common transport policy in order to remove obstacles to free competition between transport operators from different Member States. However, despite treaty obligations, progress in integrating transport across the European Community was slow until the late 1980s because Member States retained their national control over transport. Rapid change happened with the inclusion of transport in the *Single European Act* of 1986 as part of plans to complete the single market since it made it easier for foreign transport providers to work across Member State borders.[22]

The EC published its first White Paper in 1992 on the future development of a common transport policy and its liberalisation. This objective was achieved in 2001 in all but the rail sector. Three Directives (2001/12/EC, 2001/13/EB and 2001/14/EB) on the development of the railway transport market and market liberalisation came into force on 15 March 2001. The second major policy document—the White Paper on European Transport Policy—was produced in 2001. It identified about 60 measures to enable the completion of integrated market areas of competition and tried to link all modes of transport, eliminate barriers, attract private investors, protect users of transportation and manage the globalisation of transport. The White Paper established the conditions in which transport market activities work easily on a Community basis. The focus was on removing barriers such as lack of fiscal and social harmonisation that led to distortions in competition. Thus, the focus is now on rebalancing all modes of transport and reducing the environmental impact of transportation. The Green Paper of the EU in 2006 continued to develop its transport policy, building on the existing policies and initiatives from the Lisbon Strategy. It also tried to find the correct balance between the economic, social and environmental dimensions of sustainable development. It aimed to launch a debate about a sustainable maritime policy for

---

[22] Full liberalisation of international road freight within the EU was completed by 1998.

the EU as part of its integrated market to facilitate trade traffic (Commission of the European Communities, 2006).

With globalisation and the enlargement of the EU, domestic and foreign trade volumes increased in the region. This created the need for an intermodal transport system across Member States.[23] A series of Directives and measures were adopted to promote intermodality in transport and sustainability in freight movement to establish reliable, cheaper, more efficient and environment-friendly networks in the region. For instance, the White Paper 2011 of the EC proposed initiatives to build a competitive transport system that would increase mobility, remove major barriers in key areas and stimulate growth and employment. These are expected to reduce Europe's dependence on imported oil and cut carbon emissions in transport by 60 per cent by 2050. The Logistics Action Plan 2007 promoted interoperability and actions in electronic information on freight, training and quality indicators, simplification of processes, urban transport and long-distance corridors (The Directives are listed in Table 4A.2 in the Appendix).

As a result of operating in increasingly complex and vast supply chain networks, several EU companies have become experienced and have expanded their operations across the globe. Good policies have also helped companies to diversify regionally. Today, several leading and technologically advanced companies in the logistics sector are of EU origin. Some top players are Deutsche Post DHL and DB Schenker AG (Germany) in diversified services and Maersk A/S (Denmark) and CMA-CGM (France) in sea freight services. As for inward and outward FDI from the EU, by the end of 2009, the transportation and storage sector accounted for US$40,853 million and US$64,915 million, respectively.

Regarding future growth potential in India, some industry associations and private consultancy organisations have tried to estimate the figures. Estimates vary but all studies show double-digit growth for the industry by 2030. The demand for human resource in the transportation, logistics and warehousing sectors of India will increase from 7.3 million in 2008 to about 25 million workers by 2022 (National Skill Development Corporation [NSDC], 2009). This will include higher demand for warehouse managers, truck drivers and coastal seafarers, among others. The government now places high importance on logistics as a support

---

[23] Intermodal transport is more efficient than road freight for longer journeys.

system for increasing trade flows and economic growth (Planning Commission, 2009, 2011). Private sector investments are being encouraged in several segments to generate revenue and improve service efficiencies and delivery standards. The industry has invested heavily in new intermodal infrastructure. At the same time, the government is making efforts to remove obstacles to growth such as poor infrastructure and regulatory and other barriers.[24]

Growth rates of the European logistics market are considered to be in range of around 5 per cent (SMI-PwC, 2010), which is lower than that for India. In the EU, the focus of logistics policy for the future is on developing sustainable and eco-friendly systems. However, there are certain areas of concern. As put forward in Eurostat (2011: 460), 'strains on transport infrastructure (congestion and delays), coupled with constraints over technical standards, interoperability and governance issues may slow down developments within the sector'. Costs incurred through congestion,[25] labour shortages and dependence on fossil fuels are also increasing. The identification of obstacles to efficient provision of logistics services is an ongoing process and efforts to combat worsening network congestion are recognised as crucial to decrease costs and environmental damage.

Bilateral Trade Flows between India and the EU

Both the EU and India are among the world's top exporters and importers of transportation services. In 2011, the EU-27 ranked first in the world for exports of transportation services, accounting for about 43.3 per cent (approximately US$372.5 billion), while India ranked 8th, with a share of 2 per cent (approximately US$17.5 billion). The EU-27 also ranked first in the world, accounting for 30.7 per cent share (approximately US$338.3 billion) for imports of transportation services, while India ranked fourth with a share of 5.2 per cent (approximately US$56.9 billion) in total global imports of such services. Globally, the EU and

[24] For details of recent initiatives in the sector, see Union Budget 2012 of the Government of India. http://indiabudget.nic.in/index.asp (accessed on 1 May 2013).

[25] Congestion costs Europe about one percent of GDP every year.

India are key players in logistics. The EU has a supplier and demandeur position, while India is a recipient and a target market. The EU has a positive trade balance in transportation services with the rest of the world, while India has a negative trade balance.

Logistics is a crucial segment of bilateral India–EU trade and investment. There are three dimensions to India–EU collaboration in these services: government–government, government–business and business–business collaboration in various segments (Box 4.1).

In 2004, India and the EU signed a Customs Cooperation Agreement to make customs procedures less complex and to facilitate trade in

---

Box 4.1: Key Areas of India–EU Collaboration

Government-to-Government

- Customs Co-operation Agreement (2004)
- Research in road transport and development under the India–EC S&T Agreement (2005)
- India–EC Maritime Transport Project (1998–2003)
- India–EU (negotiations on since June 2007)
- EU–India Civil Aviation project (2001–2006)
- Horizontal Aviation Agreement (2008)
- The Seventh Framework Programme (FP7) (2007–2013)
- Sectoral MoUs

Government-to-business

- PPP models in port and airport handling
- EU's Seventh Framework Programme for Research (FP7)

Business-to-business

- Freight forwarding
- Cargo handling and container leasing
- Express delivery and integrated logistics

Source: Compiled by the author.

accordance with international standards. The two sides also signed a Horizontal Aviation Agreement in September 2008 to restore legal certainty to the bilateral air services agreements between India and EU Member States.[26] A Maritime Agreement has also been under negotiation between the EU and India since 2003, in order to improve the conditions and legal framework under which maritime transport operations to and from India are carried out. This is expected to reduce delivery time and costs in the sector. The research and innovation activities of the EU have been grouped under the Framework Programme (FP) of the EU that was started in 1984. The Seventh Framework Programme (FP7) (2007–2013) is underway and has a strong focus on India. Collaborative research has been identified under nine priority areas in the FP7, one of which is transport (including aeronautics) with an allocation of US$5.33 billion.[27]

India and the EU have been negotiating a comprehensive BTIA since June 2007 in which logistics is recognised as a crucial sector. The European Community and its Member States have been a demandeur to liberalise the sector, while India has continually liberalised its logistics sector over the years and has been a target market for FDI. Table 4.2

Table 4.2
Trade in Transportation Services: EU 27 with India (in US$ million)

	2006	2007	2008	2009	2010	2011
Exports	3002.55	3626.52	3767.99	3161.14	4729.15	4811.98
Imports	1885.31	2042.64	2407.54	1967.28	2426.05	2578.99
Trade Balance	1094.70	1583.88	1360.44	1193.86	2303.10	2232.99

(Table 4.2 Continued)

[26] The agreement brings several provisions in the 26 bilateral air services agreements between EU Member States and India in line with EU law. It removes nationality restrictions in bilateral air services agreements between EU Member States and India and thereby allows any EU airline to operate flights between India and any EU Member State where it is established and where a bilateral agreement with India exists and traffic rights are available. The EC and India have also agreed on a Joint Action Plan that sets out the priorities and modalities for future technical cooperation in a broad range of aviation areas including aviation safety, security, airports and air traffic management, environment and economic regulation.

[27] This is equivalent to €4.1 billion. Source: http://ec.europa.eu/transport/themes/research/fp7/ (accessed on 20 May 2013). Currency conversion is based on average exchange rate data extracted from www.oanda.com: 1US$ = €0.7767 for fiscal year 2012–2013.

(Table 4.2 Continued)

	2006	2007	2008	2009	2010	2011
Percentage Share in Total						
Exports	31.05	28.71	31.89	26.17	32.93	34.3
Imports	24.72	22.01	22.4	20.14	21.11	20.6

Source: Eurostat Statistical Books, various issues. http://ec.europa.eu/eurostat/
publications/collections/statistical-books (last accessed on 13 August
2014).

shows that the EU's exports of transportation services to India increased
at a cumulative average growth rate (CAGR) of 12.24 per cent between
2006 and 2010, while its imports from India grew at 6.5 per cent during
this period. The trade balance has been in favour of the EU and has been
growing over the years.

Primary Survey

Since segment-wise data on bilateral trade between India and the EU
in logistics services is not available, a primary survey was carried out
to analyse the extent and nature of cross-border trade, investment and
collaboration between these two regions. This also helped to identify
barriers to free entry and operation in these markets.

The sampling frame is given in Table 4.3. The survey covered 21 logistics firms: 10 EU multinational companies with collaborations/tie-ups in

Table 4.3
Sampling Frame

Respondents	Number of Respondents
EU companies in India	10
Indian companies	11
Industry associations	5
Embassies of EU Member States in India and EC experts	4
Indian ministries/government departments	4
Total	34

Source: Compiled by the author.

India, eight Indian companies with offices and collaboration in the EU and three Indian companies planning to expand operations to the EU next year. Semi-structured questionnaires were used for the interviews. Information was also gathered through discussions and on-site visits with representatives of companies, industry associations, government bodies and embassies.

Since the sample size is small, a qualitative approach was used to analyse the information. The survey showed that the range of services provided by Indian and EU companies include third-party logistics, ground- and air-freight forwarding, logistics consulting, customs brokerage, air, ground and maritime freight transportation and storage and warehousing. However, while EU companies generally provide end-to-end logistics services, Indian companies have been contributing in a few segments, such as logistics consulting and the supply of seafarers. It was found that logistics services trade between the EU and India takes place primarily through Mode 1 (cross-border), Mode 3 (commercial presence) and Mode 4 (movement of natural persons).[28] Mode 1 involves the transportation of goods between India and EU by sea or air. Trade in Mode 3 is dominated by EU companies; it was found that Indian companies do not have large investments in the EU and operate there either through a network of agents/associates or through functional tie-ups. Trade in Mode 4 is dominated by India. It involves the cross-country temporary movement of professionals (consultants, managers, technicians, engineers, and so on) to provide logistics and transport services. Trade also takes place through Mode 2 (consumption abroad) where services

---

[28] As per the GATS, there are four modes of service delivery. Mode 1: Cross border supply implying supply from the territory of a Party into the territory of the other Party. In this case, trade in services takes place and this is equivalent to cross-border movement of goods. Mode 2: Consumption abroad implying consumption in the territory of a Party by the service consumer of the other Party. Mode 3: Commercial presence supply of service by a service supplier of a Party through commercial presence in the territory of the other Party). In this case the service supplier establishes a legal presence in the form of a joint venture/subsidiary/representative/branch office in the host country and starts supplying services. Mode 4: Presence/movement of natural persons—supply of service by a service supplier of a Party through presence of natural persons of a Party in the territory of the other Party. It covers people moving on employment contracts from a company in India to a company in a foreign country, employees of the same company who is posted to their foreign offices and people going to get business or for marketing. This definition covers only temporary movement and not citizenship, residence or employment on a permanent basis in the foreign country.

providers from the EU and India use each other's port and airport facilities. The survey found that the EU, being a region with a long history of economic advances and trade flows, is home to a large number of logistics companies. Over the years, several of them have acquired prominence in delivering high-quality and modernised services and have spread their operations to a number of countries beyond Europe. They have a large capital base, superior and specialised know-how, aggressive marketing and a global network. In contrast, the Indian logistics sector, traditionally being underdeveloped and fragmented, mainly has small- and medium-sized companies that have largely been confined to domestic operations and only recently have started venturing abroad.

The size of investments by EU companies in India is substantial and several of them have offices across India. Most of them are multinationals and provide integrated and door-to-door services including outsourcing and 3PL services. The survey found that they generally enter through joint ventures in order to gain local market knowledge and get assistance from their local partners in acquiring and setting up offices and establishing operations. Other common modes of entry are consortium and representative offices. Companies like DHL Express took the acquisition route, but about 75 per cent of EU companies set up wholly owned subsidiaries after initial entry.

EU companies view India, along with China, among their top business destinations.[29] In comparison, investment by Indian companies in the EU is not significant; they enter the EU primarily to meet the existing customer requirements. Two observations in this context are worth noting. First, Indian companies still possess limited knowledge about EU markets and, second, due to their smaller size and underdeveloped specialities, they prefer not to make large investments but have small tie-ups that involve minimal commitment and costs. Indian companies stated that they saw market potential in the emerging markets of Eastern Europe.

As of now, India's share in the EU logistics market is very low (less than 1 per cent). Indian companies stated that less than 5 per cent of their revenues were from operations in EU markets. In contrast, the EU's share in the Indian logistics industry is significant. In fact, EU firms like

---

[29] Several EU companies started operations in China before entering the Indian market and feel that China has a distinct advantage over India due to better infrastructure facilities.

DHL and Maersk Line dominate and are counted among the top-ranking players in the Indian supply chain industry.[30]

The strengths of local companies in India are their local knowledge, experience with procedures and handling government, flexibility, strong customer base and lower costs of operation. Their weaknesses are their small financial base and lack of competitiveness on a global scale. In contrast, the strengths of the EU companies are their large capital base, wide global network and access to the latest technologies.[31] Their weaknesses are lack of local market knowledge and not being able to get through procedures in India.

Areas for Future Collaboration between India and the EU

At an annual economic growth rate of 7.5 per cent, it is estimated that India's freight traffic is likely to more than double from the current levels by the year 2020.[32] The EU companies are optimistic about their growth prospects in India and most of them predict a very high growth rate. They foresee tremendous opportunities to invest in economic corridors and supply chain in the next 5–10 years. As infrastructure like economic corridors develops, there will be scope for new services like toll traffic management, green channelling and parking management. Investment is already shifting from provision of infrastructure to carriage, i.e. facilitating the movement of cargo and passengers using newly created infrastructure. The scope for collaboration on investment in integrated logistics services is increasing. Cooperation in environment-friendly fuel technologies and lighter, safer and cost-competitive engines and battery-operated cars can also be mutually beneficial. Indian and European companies can have joint R&D programmes for fuel-efficient technologies. Sharing information on technical standards would benefit companies from both India and the EU.

---

[30] DHL has a 60 per cent market share in India and Maersk Lines, with P&O, accounts for nearly 30 per cent share of all incoming and outgoing containers in the country.

[31] All EU firms also have investment offices and networks in other developing country markets such as China, Malaysia, Thailand and the Middle East.

[32] http://indiagovernance.gov.in/files/Logistics_Infrastructure.pdf (accessed on 12 September 2013).

The EU companies also pointed out that they expect high growth in India due to the growth of e-commerce business. EU logistics service providers such as Deutsche Post DHL are among the key players in the Indian e-commerce segment.

The sector where the EU appears to have a key strategic interest in the Indian market is maritime services. Indian seafarers are recognised and sought after by the companies that were interviewed. Some respondents recommended that the Indian government and Indian companies could analyse the technology and processes being implemented in the EU, for instance, at sea ports and in freight loading/unloading, and learn how to replicate these in the Indian market. Table 4.4 shows the top three opportunity factors and respondents' views on how they perceive the Indian/EU markets.

Among Indian companies, there is not much enthusiasm as of now in establishing greater presence in Europe through Mode 3. The key reasons cited were lack of knowledge about the market and the ongoing economic recession in the region. In addition, Indian companies are not large enough or advanced enough in operating standards to compete with established companies in the EU. However, access to global networks and clientele and exposure to international best practices were important to them. They said that they could also explore possibilities of providing software planning, management and consultancy services in *advanced trucking* and construction projects. The Indian government could take the initiative in studying the EU market and learn from their models of seamless transport, green channelling and customs risk management system.

Table 4.4
Top Three Opportunity Factors

Indian Companies for EU Market	EU Companies for Indian Market
• Better network and access to global clientele	• Greater access to the unsaturated Indian market, including trucking and 3PL
• Exposure to international business practices and technical procedures	• Potential in Indian market is huge as Indian consumer is moving towards express delivery modes
• Global connectivity	• India can serve as a hub for South Asia

Source: Compiled by the author.

Barriers in the Logistics Sector in India and the EU

The information on barriers to logistics trade between India and the EU is based on an analysis of secondary information and the primary survey. To start with, average logistics costs in India amount to around 13 per cent of GDP, which are much higher in developed countries such as the US (9 per cent), Europe (10 per cent) and Japan (11 per cent) (Deloitte, 2009; NSDC, 2009). Transportation is the most important segment, accounting for about 62 per cent of logistics costs.

Barriers in logistics services mainly arise from bottlenecks in infrastructure and complexities in policies and the regulatory environment. For India, various studies have reviewed the inefficiencies that impact the productivity, performance and revenue of companies in logistics (Deloitte, 2009; Planning Commission, 2009). In the World Bank's Doing Business Report 2014,[33] which ranks 189 countries, on *trading across borders* India has a much lower rank (132) than China (74) and the simple average for EU-27 (43). The World Bank's Logistics Performance Index (LPI), 2014 gives India a rank of 54, reflecting weaknesses in customs, infrastructure, international shipments, logistics competence, tracking and tracing, and timeliness. Some European countries have high ranks: Germany (1), the Netherlands (2), France (13), Denmark (17) and Spain (18).[34]

Overall, the EU is far ahead of India on several parameters such as infrastructure and customs and has made great strides in establishing a liberalised and efficient market in logistics. However, its transport sector continues to present various legal barriers to market entry. Administrative, technical and regulatory barriers also exist.[35]

The trade barriers between India and the EU are listed in terms of specific problems as well as Mode 3 (commercial presence) and Mode 4 (movement of natural persons).

---

[33] For details, see World Bank–International Finance Corporation (2011).

[34] For details, see http://lpi.worldbank.org/ (accessed on 7 June 2013).

[35] The EU transport policy has developed progressively towards an integrated policymaking mechanism. Since the first White Paper appeared in 1992, the general trend has been to facilitate the movements of goods and services within a single market. This process was based not only on dismantling internal barriers but also on integrating national markets.

Barriers in the EU

This section covers various barriers in the EU logistics sector that impact trade and investment activity in the region. These mainly relate to infrastructure and the policy and regulatory environment. They have been compiled from the primary survey and are confirmed by other sources such as the Office of the United States Trade Representative (USTR).

Infrastructure Bottlenecks

- The availability and quality of infrastructure varies across Member States and is particularly low in the Eastern Europe (Bulgaria, Greece, Poland, Romania and Slovenia), where renovation and upgrading of an otherwise extensive railway infrastructure is a challenge. The quality of port infrastructure is poor in Bulgaria, Italy, Poland, Romania and the Slovak Republic. On air transport infrastructure, Bulgaria, Lithuania, Poland, Romania and the Slovak Republic fare poorly. In inland waterways, significant bottlenecks need to be removed in Bulgaria and Hungary, which would improve efficiencies in the entire EU transport network.

Complex Regulatory Environment

- Indian companies pointed out that the accounting standards and fiscal disclosure requirements in the EU are very strict and complex. According to Beke (2010), Indian companies are not prepared to follow the EU accounting and disclosure standards because it is expensive in terms of training manpower and investing in software.
- The regulatory burden has been high in Greece, France, Hungary and Italy as well as in emerging economies such as Slovenia and the Slovak Republic in the road freight sector. This is due to the increasing burden of taxation and duties that constrain the entry of new players.
- In the maritime sector, some Indian companies pointed to the cumbersome regulations for advance declaration of cargo at EU ports that make the loading of cargo a hassle.

Incomplete Liberalisation

- Administrative, technical and regulatory barriers limit the free market access of private operators and competition in rail transport.

In several cases, the incumbents still own or operate services or facilities (such as marshalling yards), which hampers free competition by private operators. Rail liberalisation is delayed in Lithuania, Greece, Latvia, Luxembourg, Spain and Ireland. There is also incomplete separation of infrastructure management from operations (Cefic, 2012).

Discriminatory Policies

- Prospective non-EU investors in Greece's maritime and air transport sectors are required to obtain licences and other approvals that are not required of Greek or other EU investors.
- The EU Utilities Directive (2004/17), covering purchases in the transportation sector, requires open, competitive bidding procedures, but discriminates against bids with less than 50 per cent EU content that are not covered by an international or reciprocal bilateral agreement. The EU content requirement applies to foreign suppliers of goods and services.

Barriers in Government Procurement—Lack of Transparency and Corruption[36]

- There is corruption and lack of transparency in the government procurement markets of some EU Member States such as Italy, Lithuania and Bulgaria. This creates obstacles for firms that bid on public procurement. Slovenia and Portugal have short timeframes for bid preparation, and there is lack of clarity in the tendering documentation and opacity in the bid evaluation process. There are preferences for EU, especially local firms. In addition, the requirement to have bid documents in the local language creates problems for Indian companies.

Mode 4 Barriers

- An examination of the schedules of commitments in EU's Revised Offer (WTO, 2005b) under the WTO shows that most Member States (such as UK, Germany, France, Denmark and Greece) made no binding commitments on the movement of natural persons to supply services in logistics segments such as cargo handling services, storage and warehouse services and maritime

---

[36] Compiled from USTR (2012).

services. This is true of both the market access and national treatment commitments. In addition, the horizontal commitments of
the EC Schedule impose stringent conditions that may not be easily met by people from developing countries like India. These
include residency requirements, specific educational degrees or
technical qualifications and membership in specific associations.

Barriers in India

Infrastructure Bottlenecks

- In India, with growing economic activities, significant demand–
  supply gaps have emerged in transport services in road, waterways and airline networks.

  First, domestic freight movement is heavily skewed in favour of
  the road sector. Nearly 60 per cent of cargo is moved by roads
  compared with about 37 per cent in the US and 22 per cent in
  China. Moreover, the national highways, which constitute only
  about 2 per cent of road network, have to carry nearly 40 per
  cent of the freight load of the country, causing road congestion.
  Underdeveloped infrastructure in shipping and aviation and the
  Indian Railways' policy of subsidising passenger tariff by freight
  tariff has led to the road sector becoming over-burdened. Inadequate road network coverage and the poor quality of roads along
  several stretches hamper logistics operations in the country. The
  road sector also suffers from issues of access and congestion of
  traffic. In the railways, there is freight congestion along most
  high-density corridors.

  In sea transport, the lack of facilities at ports such as Paradip and
  Mangalore allows only small vessels to enter. There are problems like lack of deep water routes and insufficient dredging and
  berthing capabilities which make it possible to handle only about
  5,500 TEUs in one ship, whereas ports in China and Europe facilitate around 13,000 TEUs per ship. This causes companies to use
  smaller ships, which increases costs to end users.

- Congestion at major ports creates a backlog in the clearance process. Ships may have to wait for up to four days to offload cargo,
  which increases time and cost for shipping lines and customers.

Coastal shipping is characterised by inadequate port and land infrastructure (such as inadequate depth at ports) that hamper large-scale use for freight movement. Lack of hinterland connectivity is also a problem.

- Airport infrastructure is also weak in terms of handling cargo; it lacks an integrated system of handling cargo at terminals, often causing chaos in the clearance process. Most airports do not have round-the-clock custom facilities. A company pointed out that Singapore uses Roll in and Roll out (RoRo), which handles about eight cars per minute, whereas in India it is three cars in 10 minutes.

- There is a lack of adequate cold storage facilities and warehouses in the country. Moreover, according to Deloitte–ICC (2012), 80–85 per cent of warehouses are traditional with sizes of less than 10,000 square feet. Several of these are not equipped with cemented roofs, efficient security systems, racking facilities or a consistent electricity supply. Their owners are private sector players with limited capital for investment.[37] The lack of land availability at affordable rates in several cities such as Delhi and Mumbai is also a cause for concern.

Inter-state Variations in Laws

- There are variations in the laws across states in India. For instance, one company said that the registration of a Multiple Trailer Single Horse under which a trailer and the engine can be registered separately is allowed in states like Maharashtra but not in others like Delhi and Haryana. This hampers efficient use of engines and trailers. The varied rules and regulations impede the process, with bribes being common to move the cargo faster.

Lack of Chain Control

- The logistics sector is fragmented and hence a company lacks control over the entire supply chain. Large multi-modal logistics parks and integrated logistics services have not developed due to

---

[37] The large warehousing owners are mainly government agencies such as the Central Warehousing Corporation (CWC) and State Warehousing Corporations (SWCs), whose focus is the storage of food grains.

various barriers such as delay in implementation of single goods and services tax (GST).

Government Procurement Market

- There are problems in the public procurement markets due to lack of competition and transparency. In India, procurements are carried out through three channels of tender invitation: Open Tender Enquiry (OTE), Limited Tender Enquiry (LTE) and Single Tender Enquiry (STE). LTE is recommended when a pool of vendors has been established, while STE is recommended only in exceptional circumstances like national calamities or other emergencies. The choice between these can significantly impact participation level in the tender. Organisations often (unknowingly or on purpose) fail to use the OTE and tend to depend on the LTE. According to Malhotra (2012), there are numerous cases where the prescribed rules and guidelines are not followed and the OTE channel is ignored. There are also bureaucratic hassles and complex procedures.

Technology-related Barriers

- The logistics sector is hampered by low rates of technology adoption and automation in areas such as vehicle tracking and warehouse management. In the railways, most terminals (goods sheds) used for freight loading/unloading are antiquated due to lack of investment.

  Lack of standardisation in equipment is another problem. Most ports/airports lack testing facilities for key products like textiles. There is also a shortage of officers to coordinate the testing process. Laboratories are located far from the ports like those in Mumbai, which acts as a barrier to the fast clearance of goods.

Lack of Coordination in Infrastructure Planning

- Numerous industry players stated that there is little coordination among the various bodies of the government in creating infrastructure. For instance, when one government department is planning additional port capacity for container handling, little thought is given to evacuation logistics by another department (Deloitte–ICC, 2012). Work needs to be integrated to reduce high transaction costs prevalent in the economy.

Fragmentation and Domination of Small Players

- There is a high level of fragmentation in the industry. This is especially true of the trucking segment where nearly 70 per cent of the owners own between one and five trucks. Intense competition among operators has led to several problems, such as low margins and the limited capacity of operators to invest in trucks, tracking and safety equipment. This has also led to a trend of overloading and inefficiencies in the segment.
- Fragmentation is a problem in warehousing, particularly in industrial sector. This is partly due to multiple and differential state-level tax regime in India. As a result, owners have set up multiple warehouses at various locations to minimise intra-state movements and associated taxes. This is highly inefficient and adds to inventory carrying costs.

Skill-related Barriers

- There is a lack of skilled workforce in different segments of the logistics sector (NSDC 2009). There is need for improved technology skills and driving skills including safety procedures and multi-operational skills (such as maintaining delivery records and negotiating and handling queries) in India.

Customs Procedures

- USTR (2012) and USTR (2013) report concerns about India's customs valuation criteria in import transactions. India's valuation procedures allow its customs officials to reject the declared transaction value of an import when a sale is deemed to involve a lower price than the ordinary competitive price. India's customs valuation methodologies do not reflect actual transaction values and raise the cost of exporting to India beyond applied tariff rates. India does not assess the basic customs duty, additional duty and special additional duty separately on the customs value of a given imported product. Instead, the additional duty is assessed on the sum of the actual (or transaction) value and the basic customs duty, while the special additional duty is assessed on the sum of the actual (or transaction) value, the basic customs duty and the additional duty. This can result in importers paying higher duties than they should be liable for based on the actual value of their imported product.

- India's customs officials require extensive documentation. There are complications due to India's complex tariff structure and multiple exemptions, which may vary by product, user or intended use. Physical inspections by customs, multiple documentation requirements and bribes cause unnecessary processing delays and problems for traders.

Constraints on Inter-state Movement of Goods

- Trucks in India have to pass through multiple checkpoints and stop at state borders to pay toll taxes and octroi, for inspections, and so on. An estimate of the time taken at checkpoints shows that for a journey of 2,150 kilometres between Kolkata and Mumbai, a truck had to stop at 26 checkpoints for as much as 32 hours (Deloitte–ICC, 2012).
- State taxes such as sales tax, excise and octroi toll have to be paid at the entry of every state border. A lot of time gets wasted in paying these different taxes at different locations.

High Tariff Rates

- The Indian Railways follows a policy of subsidising passenger tariff by freight tariff. This has resulted in a sharp increase in railway freight rates over the years, and they are among the highest in the world. Rail freight rates in India are nearly four times of those in the US.[38]

Other Problems

- Ports in India suffer from long turnaround times for ships. The Jawaharlal Nehru Port Trust (JNPT) has more than double the turnaround time of Colombo and Singapore ports because of congestion at berths and the slow pace of unloading cargo.[39]
- Companies complained that terminal handling agencies have to pay higher charges to port authorities for handling a larger number of ships; this acts as a disincentive to expanding operations

---

[38] The movement of freight traffic is frequently subordinated to passenger traffic on the railway network. This results in a freight train taking as long as 6–8 days for a journey of 2,000 kilometres. Also, there are delays in transit time for freight trains on several routes (Deloitte–ICC, 2012).

[39] For details, see CRISIL (2012).

and adds to their cost of operation. As a result, companies are shifting their cargo from ports regulated by the Tariff Authority for Major Ports (TAMP) to other ports.

- The amount of cargo traffic handled at Indian ports is still modest. In 2010–2011, the highest volume of cargo traffic handled by any port in India was 82 million tonnes (Kandla) and the major ports combined handled about 569.91 million tonnes; in the same year, Rotterdam port in Europe handled about 430 million tonnes of traffic.
- Pilferage at sea ports (mainly at the customs level) and a deliberate slowing of the clearing process were also mentioned by several companies.

Barriers Related to Mode 3 and Mode 4

- There is a cabotage restriction on the movement of foreign registered ships, which prohibits them from moving cargo from one Indian port to another Indian port. This wastes time and adds to the costs of companies. One company in the survey mentioned that Vallarpadam Port in Kochi (Kerala) was designed as a hub in southern India, but due to the cabotage restriction, only 15–20 per cent of the potential is utilised.
- In its WTO Revised Offer of 2005, India offered to allow entry of natural persons only to technical and managerial personnel.[40] India did not offer to take commitments in the specific category of services related to logistics such as services related to management consulting, technical testing and analysis services and in air transport services.

Addressing Barriers through International Negotiations

In the WTO's Doha Round of Negotiations and in its bilateral trade agreements, the European Communities have been a demandeur to liberalise various segments of the logistics sector in emerging economies.

[40] WTO (2005c).

It also made significant commitments in its WTO Revised Offer in the year 2005. India has improved its commitments compared to the Uruguay Round, but compared with the EU, it did not make substantial commitments in its WTO Revised Offer that year. At present, India's FDI regime is far more liberal and it is in a position to undertake greater commitments in almost all segments of logistics. These can be offered under the ongoing negotiations for a proposed BTIA between India and the EU.

The EU appears to have a key strategic interest in the Indian market in cargo reservation, inland transport and cabotage. However, there seems to be limited scope for further liberalisation in inland transport since both India and the EC have imposed a cabotage condition and the coastal areas of India are considered sensitive for security reasons. India has no clear policy on the development of inland transport, which makes it difficult to take international commitments.

Since the Indian and the EU maritime sectors are fairly open and there are no major FDI restrictions, they can bind the existing regime. Greater harmonisation of port policies across EU Member States, centralised and harmonised recognition procedures for Indian seafarers and cooperation in port management and training can be raised in the BTIA.

At present, India and the EU are negotiating a bilateral maritime agreement. The focus of the agreement is on enhancing market access and the right to establishment and non-discriminatory access to auxiliary services. Non-discriminatory access to port facilities in EU Member States and India will be mutually beneficial. India and the EU in their respective Revised Offer submitted to the WTO made additional commitments that give non-discriminatory access to port facilities; similar commitments should be made under the India–EU BTIA. Companies operating in the EU are treated as EU companies if they have a wholly owned subsidiary. Since India has no restrictions on the form of operations, Indian companies would benefit if such restrictions were removed in the EU. Additionally, increasing transparency, facilitating visa and work permits and cooperating in areas like safety, security, combating terrorism and training can benefit both India and the EU.

If one examines the interests of the two economies by the four modes of trade, namely Mode 1, Mode 2, Mode 3 and Mode 4; the EU companies would like a liberal Mode 3 regime to invest in India. However, Indian companies too have an interest in Mode 3 liberalisation. From the EU, India should request full commitments for Mode 3 in services such as engineering and integrated engineering services and technical testing and analysis services. In road freight, India can offer full market access and national treatment commitments in Mode 3, since foreign service suppliers are already providing these services in India. In rail freight, Mode 3 could be encouraged for segments like warehousing and dedicated freight corridors (DFCs) where FDI is already permitted. India can also offer binding commitments in warehousing in exchange for commitments in other areas of export interest. Commitments can also be sought in Mode 1 in road freight to gain from trade in transport management software systems. India can also seek assistance from the EU in developing its DFCs. In services auxiliary to all modes of transport, India can ask the EU for binding commitments in Modes 1 and 3. India can offer to bind the existing regime (India has autonomously opened up all subsectors under services auxiliary to all modes of transport) and also offer commitments in Modes 1 and 2 in maritime auxiliary services in exchange for reciprocal commitments from the EU.

As outsourcing logistics functions become increasingly common, companies in Europe are likely to seek innovative and cost-effective solutions to their IT needs in the sector. This will open up opportunities for Indian companies to provide logistics and related services in Europe. Since India has substantial offensive interests in Mode 1 and Mode 4 for IT-enabled logistics services, it can ask for greater commitments in these categories in exchange for Mode 3 commitments in freight logistics from the EU.

Mode 4 in road freight is kept unbound by all EU Member States. The definitions of intra-corporate transfers are narrow and restrict activities that can be undertaken by foreign professionals, especially managers. This issue can be raised by India in the BTIA.

The EU is a major proponent of Trade Facilitation Agreement in the WTO and trade facilitation is a key objective in its bilateral agreements. Recently, India has agreed to be a part of the WTO's Trade Facilitation agreement and the country is initiating several reforms to improve trade facilitation and ease of doing business. Trade facilitation is likely to be a key component of the India–EU BTIA and India can learn from EU's experiences of developing an efficient and seamless supply chain. The support for trade facilitation in India and EU provides huge opportunities for future collaboration and sharing of information. Companies in both economies will benefit if there are more partnerships and collaborations. While India can be the gateway for the EU companies to establish presence in the South Asian Association for Regional Cooperation (SAARC) region, collaboration with Indian companies can help EU companies to access their skilled workforce and provide services at competitive rates in third country markets.

Policy Recommendations and the Way Forward

This chapter has analysed the opportunities, prospects and constraints on trade, investment and collaboration between India and the EU in the logistics sector.

It found that Indian and EU companies have complementarities and there are several areas where they can collaborate to benefit from each other's expertise. Over the next decade, significant investments are likely to be made in the Indian logistics sector that would offer opportunities for private participation. There is scope for increased collaboration in maritime auxiliary services, port and warehouse management (especially cold storage), 3PL/4PL and clean-fuel technology transfers. There is scope to benefit from the technological and R&D capabilities of EU companies and even enter into PPP arrangements in skills training of the workforce. India can also learn from the EU's experience in creating a single market for transport and logistics, which will lead to a competitive business environment.

There are various barriers between India and the EU that need to be removed to enhance efficiency and India–EU trade in the sector. For instance, both India and the EU suffer from congestion in transport infrastructure such as roads. There are also some reform requirements common to all modes such as capacity addition, manpower training, developing a common window system and simplifying bureaucratic procedures. While the EU has started developing an intermodal freight transport system, multimodal transportation in India has a long way to go. However, the recent push towards integrated transport, development of economic corridors and green channelling in India will speed up the process of multimodal transport. The EU needs to ensure a more harmonised logistics market and fair competition, and India needs to remove procedural bottlenecks and develop an integrated transport policy. Already the new central government of India has integrated a number of transport ministries and this is a step in the right direction.

Although India has not made any commitments under the GATS for logistics services such as road freight, cargo holding, storage and warehousing and transport agency services, it has autonomously opened up most subsectors, and FDI of up to 100 per cent is allowed through the automatic route. India can offer to bind these commitments with reciprocal commitments from the EU and also ask for harmonised recognition procedures for professionals through Mode 4 in the road freight and maritime sectors. India has also agreed to sign the WTO's Trade Facilitation Agreement which has the potential to reform domestic customs practices and decrease time and costs of the movement of goods.

There are several problems in the logistics sector that cannot be addressed in the BTIA, but require domestic reform measures in both India and the EU to improve efficiency levels, attract investments and increase trade volumes. The most common recommendation made during the primary survey of companies was to focus on infrastructure development in India. For instance, the freight forwarders stated that airport infrastructure should have sufficient clearance facilities to make sure that goods are cleared on time. For sea connectivity, the development of minor ports and expansion of existing capacities of major ports is required. The need for infrastructure development offers opportunities for EU companies to invest in India.

To develop a balanced multi-modal logistics infrastructure, a National Integrated Logistics Policy is needed in India. This would entail developing long-distance corridors, medium-distance connectors and last mile interfaces. A shift is required from a road-focused network to a balanced multi-modal network that leverages railways and waterways to transport heavy throughput over long distances. To ensure non-stop movement of carriers by road at state borders, computerised networking between state tax authorities is needed.[41] The respondents stated that for the logistics industry to benefit from the implementation of GST in terms of reduced domestic transport costs, a well-connected network between various state authorities is needed. Lack of coordination between state authorities on issues such as approvals for land acquisition and environment clearances often causes delays and financial losses in transport projects. Development of an efficient transport network needs efficient coordination between the central and state governments and across different departments of the state governments. Areas where reforms are required pertain to administration and governance: improving system efficiency by streamlining customs and approvals, transparency, greater coordination in government procedures and labour reforms. India is already proposing to have green channels and efficient clearances in road transport corridors. The country can learn from the experiences of EU Member States in developing such green channels.

Another recommendation concerns the non-existence of an efficient port community system in India. This is an electronic platform or association of key stakeholders that connects the multiple systems operated by a variety of organisations that make up a seaport or airport community. Members come from port authorities, shipping companies, customs and municipal authorities, and the platform is organised and used by firms in the port community. Such communities exist in the EU.[42] If such communities are formed in India, they would help streamline processes in and around ports and create the backbone of a single window system.

When asked about reforms in the EU, Indian companies stated that they did not possess in-depth knowledge about the entire EU market and were still exploring it. However, they stated that the European Commission is working towards creating a fully integrated transport network in the region. Several Member States would benefit from lowering barriers to market entry and reducing regulatory burdens in transport markets. This is especially true in the case of Germany, France, Italy, Spain and Austria, which are large and/or transit countries.

---

[41] Some respondents mentioned that poor infrastructure opened up possibilities for corruption by officers as well.

[42] Port Community Systems (PCSs) have a long tradition in Europe. The first to be established in ports in Germany, France and the UK began to operate in the late 1970s or early 1980s. Countries such as the Netherlands and Spain started their PCSs in the 1990s or at the turn of the century.

Appendix

Table 4A.1

Logistics Segments with Restrictive FDI in India

Sector	FDI Policy
Air Transport (Airlines)	• Up to 49% FDI allowed (100% for non-resident Indian (NRI)) in scheduled air transport service/domestic scheduled passenger airlines through the automatic route.
	• FDI up to 74% and investment by NRIs up to 100% allowed in non-scheduled air transport services (automatic up to 49%; government route beyond 49% and up to 74%).
	Foreign airlines are allowed to invest in Indian companies, operating scheduled and non-scheduled air transport services, up to the limit of 49% of their paid-up capital under the government approval route.[a]
	• FDI up to 74% and investment by NRIs up to 100% allowed in ground handling services (automatic up to 49%; government route beyond 49% and up to 74%).
Railways	With effect from August 2014, 100% FDI is allowed in construction, operation and maintenance of certain railway infrastructure.

Source: DIPP, Government of India.

Notes: 1. The above policy is not applicable to Air India.

2. Air Transport Services includes domestic scheduled passenger airlines, non-scheduled air transport services, helicopter and seaplane services.

[a]Includes both FDI and foreign institutional investment (FII).

Table 4A.2
Legislative Measures in the EU Logistics Sector

Objective	Legislative Steps/Measures	Main Proposals for Action
Common/ Competitive Transport systems	• Treaty of Rome 1958	Development of several strategically significant trans-national corridors
	• Trans-European Network or TEN (T) programme through the Maastricht Treaty	
	• White Paper 2011: Roadmap to a Single European Transport Area—Towards a competitive and resource-efficient transport system	Proposed initiatives to build a competitive transport system that will increase mobility, remove major barriers in key areas and fuel growth and employment. These are expected to reduce Europe's dependence on imported oil and cut carbon emissions in transport by 60% by 2050. By 2050, some key goals proposed are:
		• No more conventionally fuelled cars in cities.
		• 40% use of sustainable low-carbon fuels in aviation; at least 40% reduction in shipping emissions.
		• A 50% shift of medium-distance intercity passenger and freight journeys from road to rail and waterborne transport.
Intermodal Transport System	• Council Directive 92/106/EEC on establishment of common rules for certain types of combined transport of goods between Member States.	Member States take the necessary measures to ensure that motor vehicle taxes applicable to road vehicles routed in combined transport are reduced or reimbursed.

	Communication COM (97) 243 on Intermodality and Intermodal Freight Transport.

Establishment of integrated infrastructure and transport means:

- Intensify intermodal design of the trans-European transport networks
- Enhance design and functions of intermodal transfer points
- Harmonise standards for transport means

Establish interoperable and interconnected operations through:

- Integration of freight freeways in an intermodal context
- Develop common charging and pricing principles
- Harmonise competition rules and state aid regimes on intermodal basis

Establish mode-independent services and regulations through:

- Harmonisation and standardisation of procedures and EDI
- Research and demonstration
- Benchmarking
- Intermodal statistics

Sustainable Transport Policy

Communication COM (2001) 370 White Paper on *European transport policy for 2010: time to decide*—supplemented by mid-term review: Communication to the Council and European Parliament, titled *Keep Europe moving—sustainable mobility for our continent* (COM (2006) 314).

Measures to combat emissions from transport and stated that the Commission would encourage the development of a market for *clean vehicles*.

(Table 4A.2 Continued)

(Table 4A.2 Continued)

Objective	Legislative Steps/Measures	Main Proposals for Action
	• Regulation (EC) No 1382/2003 of the European Parliament and of the Council on granting of Community financial assistance to improve the environmental performance of freight transport system (Marco Polo Programme).	The EC may grant financial aid for projects related to the logistics market that contribute to reducing congestion in road freight transport system or improving the environmental performance of the transport system by optimising transport to and from intermodal transport chains in EU Member States.
Enhancing supply chain security	• Council Directive 2005/65/EC to introduce Community measures to enhance port security in the face of threats of security incidents. • Communication COM (2006) 79 to provide greater protection for all European freight transport against possible terrorist attacks.	• Common basic rules on port security measures and an implementation mechanism for these rules. • Establishing appropriate compliance monitoring mechanisms. • Establishment of a mandatory system requiring Member States to create a security (*secure operator*) quality label for operators in the supply chain meeting European minimum security levels, thus allowing mutual recognition of the label on the internal market; • Introduces a voluntary scheme under which operators in the supply chain increase their security performance in exchange for incentives; • Makes operators in the supply chain responsible for their security performance in European freight transport;

	• Allows *secure operators* to benefit from facilitations where security controls are carried out and to distinguish themselves positively from other competitors in the area of security, giving them a commercial and competitive advantage.
• Freight Transport Logistics Action Plan 2007	The EC proposed a series of measures to promote freight transport logistics, make rail freight more competitive, create a framework for European ports to attract investment for their modernisation, and put maritime freight transport on equal footing with other transport modes.
Intelligent Transport Systems	• Deployment of European Satellite Navigation systems—European Geostationary Navigation Overlay Service (EGNOS) and Galileo

Source: Compiled by the author.

5

Trade and Collaboration in Energy Services

Smita Miglani

Introduction

Energy plays a vital and pervasive role in all economies of the present world. It is seen as a strong determinant of the quality of living and an important driver of economic development[1] and international trade. This is even truer of large economies such as the EU and India.

The energy market broadly comprises four main players: energy consumers, producers or generators, equipment suppliers and service suppliers. It is often difficult to distinguish between energy goods and services when companies are vertically integrated and simultaneously perform all energy-related activities, namely production, transmission and distribution. In such a case, products like oil and solid fuels which can be easily stored are considered as goods, while the value added to energy goods is classified under energy services. Energy services, thus, include all services related to energy production, distribution and transmission

[1] In fact, energy availability and consumption have become so important that 'energy consumed per capita' is one of the key indicators of the modernisation and progress of a country. Provision of energy services in an adequate, affordable and reliable way is considered essential for economic welfare, eradication of poverty, infrastructure development, growth of health services, commerce, communication and other economic activities.

such as geological mapping of exploration and production (E&P) sites, drilling, technical testing, marketing, transportation, distribution, energy efficiency, maintenance, consulting, auditing, network maintenance, and metering and billing, among others. These can be rendered across all segments of energy—primary (fossil fuel) and secondary (i.e. electricity)—and across renewable and non-renewable energy.[2] Electricity, however, has characteristics of both goods and services.[3]

Enhancing energy production and attaining high-efficiency standards have emerged as key areas of concern for both India and the EU in recent years. Over 80 per cent of their energy consumption is based on fossil fuels; and they are both net importers of these resources. The use of both renewable and non-renewable energy is increasing in these regions and competition is seen as one way to promote efficiencies. For all these reasons, energy services are a crucial component for both India and the EU in their international trade engagements.

This chapter analyses the nature and potential of energy services sectors in India and the EU, the prospects for enhancing mutual trade and investment and key constraints on the same. The assessment is based on secondary research of the sector as well as discussions with stakeholders. It concludes with a discussion on addressing barriers through international negotiations and the way forward for collaboration between India and the EU.

Classification and Coverage of Energy Services under GATS

Energy services were not negotiated as a separate sector during the Uruguay Round of WTO negotiations (1986–1994). During that Round, it was decided that the production of primary and secondary energy should be covered under the General Agreement on Tariffs and Trade (GATT), and transmission and distribution of energy services should be subject to

[2] For details, see Mukherjee and Goswami (2009).

[3] Electricity may be considered as a good in the sense that it is manufactured through the process of materially transforming fuels into electrons, and a service in the sense that it cannot be stored and must be produced and consumed simultaneously.

GATS rules. The WTO member countries drew up the 'WTO Services Sectoral Classification List' (MTN.GNS/W/120) based on the United Nations Central Product Classifications (UNCPC) for negotiations. However, 'energy services' was not covered as a separate comprehensive category in the W/120 and the majority of global energy services are not covered by specific commitments under GATS. Important energy services (transport, distribution, construction, consulting, engineering, and so on) are covered by the respective horizontal categories, while some energy-related services are listed as separate subsectors.[4] Under each broad category, there is a corresponding CPC number for energy services. For instance, CPC 632 relates to non-food retail services under which CPC 63297 covers retail sales of fuel oil, bottled gas, coal and wood. After the Uruguay Round, the coverage of energy services in the UNCPC has undergone changes in line with developments in this sector. For instance, in CPC Version 1.0, new services such as electricity distribution services (69110) and gas distribution services through mains (69120) have been included.

Thus, energy services do not constitute a separate economic sector, but cut across several other services sectors such as construction and environmental services. Complexities of classification under the GATS mean that a country has to take a cautious stand during its negotiations and scheduling of commitments at the international level, and also because the sector is continually evolving. From the beginning of the Doha Round, several WTO members including the EU raised concerns about inadequate classification and provided alternative classifications. The European Commission (EC) Communication (S/CSS/W/60) of 23 March 2001 focuses on several sectors/subsectors in which it would like WTO members to undertake commitments, and highlights its own interest in liberalising trade in energy services. Nuclear materials are excluded from the EC's bilateral negotiations since they are sensitive.

---

[4] For instance, services incidental to mining and services incidental to energy distribution are classified under 'Other Business Services', and pipeline transportation is covered under 'Transport Services'. One of the reasons for the poor coverage of energy services in the W/120 is that the UNCPC, from which it is drawn, does not list energy services as a separate category.

The EC recognises the need for regulating this sector to achieve public policy goals and emphasises the establishment of a transparent, objective and pro-competitive regulatory framework.

For the analysis in this chapter, we use the W/120 classification in the GATS framework, which is shown in Table 5.1.

Table 5.1
Coverage of Energy Services

W/120	CPC No.	Description
1.A.e	8672	Engineering services
1.A.f	8673	Integrated engineering services
1.C.a	85103	Research and experimental development services on natural sciences and engineering and technology for casting, metal, machinery, electricity, communications, vessels, aircraft, civil engineering, construction, information, etc.
1.F.c	865	Management consulting services
1.F.d	866	Services related to management consulting
1.F.e	8676 (partial)	Technical testing and analysis services
1.F.h	883	Services incidental to mining
	5115	Site preparation work for mining
1.F.j	887	Services incidental to energy distribution
1.F.m	8675 (partial)	Related scientific and technical consulting services
1.F.n	8861–8866 (partial)	Maintenance and repair of fabricated metal products, machinery and equipment, and electrical machinery (excluding maritime vessels, aircraft or other transport equipment)
3.B	5134–5136	Construction work for civil engineering for long-distance pipelines, for local pipelines, for constructions for mining
3.E	518	Renting services related to equipment for construction or demolition of buildings or civil engineering works with operator
4.A	62113	Commission Agents Services—sales on a fee or contract basis of fuels

(Table 5.1 Continued)

(Table 5.1 Continued)

W/120	CPC No.	Description
4.B	62271	Wholesale trade services of solid, liquid and gaseous fuels and related products (excluding electricity and town gas)
4.C	63297	Retail services of fuel oil, bottled gas, coal and woods
11.G.a	7131	Pipeline transportation of fuels

Source: Compiled from W/120 and Collective Request in Energy Services. (http://commerce.nic.in/wto_sub/services/Plurilateral%20Request%20 on%20Energy%20Services.pdf accessed on 15 September 2013).

Note: 'Services incidental to mining' covers services such as drilling services, derrick building, repair and dismantling services, and oil and gas well casings cementing services, rendered on a fee or contract basis at oil and gas fields.

Overview of the Energy Sector in India and the EU

As with all major economies of the world, energy is an important ingredient of growth and development in India. High and rapid economic growth in the past few years has created high demand for energy and India has emerged as both a major energy producer and consumer on the world map. Its share in world's total energy reserves, production and consumption as compared with EU countries is shown in Table 5.2.[5]

In 2012, coal accounted for the majority—about 56 per cent—of India's primary fuel consumption (Figure 5.1). In the same year, oil and gas together comprised about 40 per cent of India's primary energy consumption; in contrast, the corresponding share for the EU was about 63 per cent.

India accounts for only about 1 per cent of the world's total uranium reserves (World Nuclear Association, 2008). Due to lack of raw material, it has not been able to use nuclear energy extensively to generate electricity. In 2011, India ranked fifteenth in the world in nuclear energy

[5] Like the EU, India has a shortage of fossil fuels, which constitute a major proportion of its import basket.

Table 5.2
India Energy Statistics by Source in 2012 (% of world total)

Fuel	Reserves	Production	Consumption
Coal	7.0 (6.5)	6.0 (4.3)	8.0 (7.9)
Oil	0.3 (0.4)	1.0 (1.8)	4.2 (14.8)
Natural Gas	0.7 (0.9)	1.2 (4.4)	1.6 (13.4)
Nuclear	–	–	1.3 (35.7)
Hydroelectricity	–	–	3.1 (8.9)
Other Renewable[a]			4.6 (40.0)

Source: Compiled from BP (2013).
Notes: The corresponding figures for the EU are given in parentheses.
[a]These include wind, geothermal, solar, biomass and waste.

Figure 5.1
Primary Energy Consumption by Fuel in India and the EU (2012)
(in mtoe [million tonnes of oil equivalent] and %)

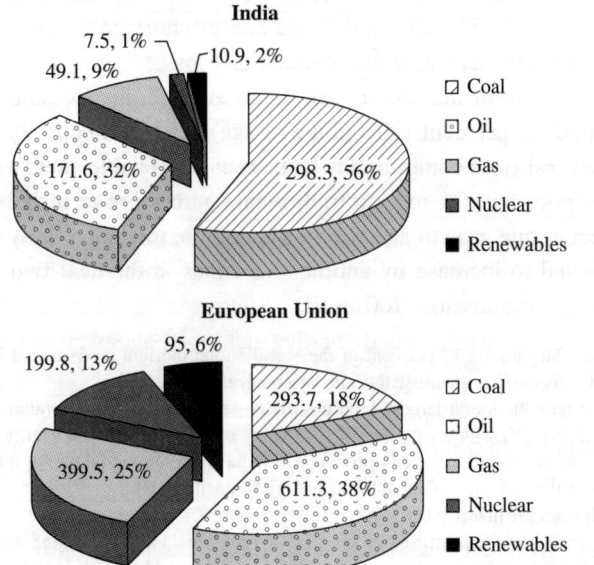

Source: Compiled from Primary Energy: Consumption by fuel, BP (2013).
Note: In BP Statistical Review, primary energy comprises only commercially traded fuels. It excludes fuels such as wood, peat and animal waste, wind, geothermal and solar power generation.

consumption (EU ranked first). The share of nuclear energy was only about 1.3 per cent in India's primary energy consumption as against 12 per cent in the EU.[6] However, India is abundantly endowed with sources of renewable energy such as solar, wind, hydro and bio-energy and has significant potential for generation of electricity from these sources. These resources are environment-friendly and create employment opportunities in rural areas.[7] India is the world's seventh largest hydroelectricity-consuming country, while EU is the fifth largest. Biomass along with dung cakes accounts for almost one-third of India's total primary energy consumption (Planning Commission, 2006).

Electricity is a key input for India's economic growth and its installed capacity increased from 1,362 MW in 1947 to about 2,54,049 MW in 2014. Thermal electricity accounts for around 70 per cent of total electricity generation, followed by hydroelectricity (around 16 per cent). The share of nuclear (2 per cent) and other renewables (12.5 per cent) is much lower in India than for the EU. However, its current per capita electricity consumption at 778.71 kWh[8] is only about one-fourth the global average.[9] There is an average energy shortage of around 10 per cent. Aggregate technical and commercial losses[10] pose a grave threat to the viability of the sector, which, on average, incurs annual losses of around 25 per cent (all-India average) of total electricity generation. Several rural communities lack access to reliable energy services and the poor have to rely on traditional sources for their daily needs. With economic growth and rise in population, total electricity demand is expected to increase by another 3.5 times in the next two decades (Planning Commission, 2002).

---

[6] India has around 12 per cent of the world's total thorium reserves and is actively developing technology to utilise thorium as a nuclear fuel.

[7] It is now the fourth largest wind electricity generator in the world (after Germany, Spain and the US) with a total installed capacity of 6270 MW. Wind energy generates around 3 per cent of all electricity produced in India and a substantial part of this is under private initiatives. Source: Global Wind Energy Council (2007).

[8] Kilowatt per hour.

[9] http://www.eksporttilindien.um.dk/NR/rdonlyres/340EA029-3355-430E-9E66-6A2AF16CF2AC/0/EnergysectorinIndia.pdf (accessed on 4 March 2013) and http://www.ficci.com/Sedocument/20218/Power-Report2013.pdf (accessed on 2 February 2014).

[10] Technical losses are mainly due to inadequate investments over the years for system improvement work, resulting in unplanned extensions of distribution lines, overloading of system elements (transformers and conductors) and lack of adequate reactive power support. Commercial losses are mainly due to low metering efficiency, theft and pilferage.

Figure 5.1 shows that for the EU, about 80 per cent of energy use is based on fossil fuels—oil, gas and coal. Oil is the most important energy source for the chemical and transport industry, while natural gas is important for power generation and heating appliances in houses.[11] In spite of low reserves of oil and gas, the EU is a major player in the world's energy market and is the second largest consumer of energy in the world.[12] The UK is the leading energy-producing country, accounting for nearly 30 per cent of the EU's annual energy production. Other major energy-producing countries are Germany, the Netherlands and Poland. The leading energy-consuming countries are Germany, France and the UK, which together account for about 48 per cent of total energy consumed.

There is wide variation across EU Member States in terms of reserves, production and consumption of energy. Some small Member States such as Malta, Cyprus, Slovenia, Latvia Estonia and Luxembourg have negligible reserves of energy resources and account for less than 1 per cent of the EU's production and consumption. There are also differences in endowments of fossil fuels, degree of exploitation of resources and Member States' domestic policies.

Coal is an important source of energy consumption in the EU. However, its production and consumption differs across Member States. Oil is the most important primary fuel for several Member States. The UK is the largest oil-producing country, accounting for about 68 per cent of EU's total annual oil production, and Germany is the leading oil-consuming country, accounting for about 16 per cent of its oil consumption (BP, 2011). EU Member States are dependent on oil imports, but their source countries vary. For instance, while Germany and Poland rely mainly on Russia, France meets its requirements from the Middle East, North Africa, the North Sea and Russia (Geden et al., 2006). After oil, natural gas is the most important primary fuel.[13] Most natural gas produced in the EU comes from North Sea gas fields that are shared by the UK and the Netherlands.

In 2012, the EU's share in nuclear energy accounted for about 35.7 per cent in the world consumption. It contributes to around one-third of

[11] http://www.eusustel.be/public/documents_publ/The%20European%20Union_final.pdf (accessed on 9 April 2013).

[12] http://www.eurunion.org/eu/index.php?option=com_content&task=view&id=2403 (accessed on 9 April 2013).

[13] http://ec.europa.eu/dgs/energy_transport/state_aid/doc/com_2007_0253_en.pdf (accessed on 15 March 2013).

the Union's electricity production and, at present, it represents the largest source of carbon-free energy in Europe (Commission of the European Communities, 2006).

Renewable energy accounts for a significant share of the EU's energy production, and the EU as a whole and individual Member States are focusing on renewable energy due to concerns related to global warming, inadequate domestic supply of hydrocarbons, energy security, high prices of fossil fuel and environment-friendly technologies, among others. The volume of renewable energy produced within the EU-27 increased overall by 60.2 per cent between 1999 and 2009, equivalent to an average increase of 4.8 per cent per annum. Among renewable energies, the most important source in the EU was biomass and waste, accounting for about 68 per cent of primary renewables production in 2009, followed by hydropower (19 per cent of the total). Although its level of production remains relatively low, there was a particularly rapid expansion in the output of wind energy, which accounted for 7.7 per cent of the EU's renewable energy produced in 2009. The largest producer of renewable energy within the EU in 2009 was Germany, with an 18.7 per cent share of the EU-27 total, followed by France (13.2 per cent), Sweden (10.7 per cent) and Italy (9.9 per cent). There were considerable differences in the renewable energy mix across Member States, reflecting to a large degree natural endowments and climatic conditions.[14]

External dependence on energy is a key concern for the Indian government. Table 5.3 gives projections by the Planning Commission for India's primary commercial energy requirements until 2016–2017. It shows that imports account for a large proportion of the energy requirements of India. Given the shortage of fossil fuels, India, like the EU, is focusing on renewable energy and issues of demand-side management, energy security and efficiency and sustainable development. In the next two decades, the main challenge is to provide access to cost-effective energy services. The development goal of providing access to convenient energy needs a significant increase in services supplied. The challenge lies in expanding access to basic energy services for a large number of energy-poor while also keeping it environmentally sustainable.

[14] For statistical data on sustainable development in areas of climate change and energy for the EU, see http://epp.eurostat.ec.europa.eu/statistics_explained/index.php/Sustainable_development_-_Climate_change_and_energy (accessed on 15 March 2013).

Table 5.3

Projected Primary Commercial Energy Requirements for India (in mtoe)

	2010–2011[a]	2016–2017[b]
Oil	164.32 (76.4%)	204.80 (80.5%)
Natural gas and LNG	57.99 (19%)	87.22 (28.4%)
Coal	272.86 (19.8%)	406.78 (22.1%)
Lignite	9.52	14.00
Hydro	10.31 (4.6%)	14.85 (3.5%)
Nuclear	6.86	9.14
Renewables	0.95	1.29
Total Energy	522.81 (36.53%)	738.07 (37.95%)

Source: Planning Commission Statistics.

Notes: Parentheses show proportion of imports in energy requirement.
[a]Provisional data.
[b]On the assumption that annual demand/growth would be 6.5 per cent, up to 2016–2017. These figures include use of oil and gas feedstock for fertiliser and other non-energy usage.

Given the gap between demand and supply of energy, the EU, like India, is a net importer of energy and in the past five years on an average, it imported about 50 per cent of its energy needs. The domestic resources of the EU (especially in oil and gas) are limited. Coal is mainly available in central and eastern European countries such as Poland, Germany and the Czech Republic (BP, 2008). Energy imports represent 6 per cent of total imports; 45 per cent of oil imports are from the Middle East and 40 per cent of natural gas is imported from Russia.[15] Energy demand has been rising every year by about 1–2 per cent (European Commission, 2006a). However, energy intensity[16] in the Union is falling. It fell by 1.6 per cent per annum between 1990 and 2009.[17]

[15] http://europa.eu/scadplus/leg/en/lvb/l27037.htm (accessed on 12 March 2013).

[16] The energy intensity of an economy is a measure of the amount of energy needed to produce one unit of economic output. A reduction in energy intensity means that less energy is needed to produce the same output and is thus related to energy efficiency. The indicator presented here is calculated as the ratio of gross inland energy consumption (in tonnes of oil equivalent) to GDP (in constant 1995 euro).

[17] http://forum.eionet.europa.eu/nrc-energy/library/ener17_final/download/1/ENER17_final.doc (accessed on 10 September 2013).

The EU depends on imports for more than 50 per cent of its energy needs and is susceptible to energy price fluctuations in the global market. The external dependence on energy is an important issue in political debate and energy security and plays a crucial role in the EU's international engagements (Directorate General for Energy and Transport, 2004). The EU leads the world in energy demand management and in the development of low-carbon technologies. Although it is already the world's most energy-efficient region, it has the potential to go much further. This is recognised by the EC. The 2005 EC Green Paper on Energy Efficiency (European Commission, 2005a) stated that up to 20 per cent of EU's energy use could be saved between 2005 and 2020 by improving efficiency. From time to time, the EC identifies bottlenecks that prevent the use of cost-effective technologies such as lack of appropriate incentives, information and financing mechanisms. Measures to overcome these bottlenecks are proposed at all levels—EU, national, regional and local.

For India, data from the 66th Round of the National Sample Survey Organisation (NSSO), Government of India conducted during July 2009–June 2010 reveals that the energy sector employed about 800,000 people.[18] In terms of contribution to the GDP, NSSO statistics are compiled for select subsectors; hence, it is difficult to give an exact estimate for the entire energy sector. However, in 2009–2010, mining and quarrying and electricity, gas and water supply together contributed about US$38,145 million to GDP (about 4.3 per cent share) at 2004–2005 prices. As regards the EU, in 2007, the total number of employees in the energy sector was 1.6 million.[19] Though an exact estimate for the entire energy sector is not available, the electricity sector alone was worth around 5 per cent of EU GDP in the year 2008.[20]

The governance structure in the sector reflects India's quasi-federal set-up. Different ministries of the central government, namely the Ministry of Coal, the Ministry of Petroleum and Natural Gas, the

[18] As per the four-digit classification under NIC 2004, the subsectors included in this figure are mining of coal and lignite; extraction of peat; extraction of crude petroleum and natural gas; and service activities incidental to oil and gas extraction, excluding surveying; and electricity, gas, steam and hot water supply.

[19] As per the National Income Accounts Statistics from the CSO, the combined share of electricity, gas and water supply in total employment was 1.1 per cent and remained unchanged between 1999–2000 and 2009–2010.

[20] By end-2010, the EU renewable energy industry employed over 1.1 million people (European Commission 2011, 2012a).

Ministry of New and Renewable Energy, the Ministry of Power and the Department of Atomic Energy play a crucial role in policy formulation. Under them there are various public sector undertakings (PSUs), technical and research institutions, organisations and agencies (under the purview of nodal ministries or autonomous) and state-level nodal agencies (to formulate and implement policies at state levels). In the EU, energy is a policy responsibility shared between the EU and Member States. The EC creates appropriate framework conditions for the sector through its Directives (laws) that come into force in any country when the national government takes steps to introduce and implement them within national laws.

Market Structure and Liberalisation of Indian Energy Sector

Over the years, the energy sector of India has undergone substantial changes. In the past, due to its public good characteristics, energy-related services were mostly supplied by state-owned monopolies and involvement of the private sector was limited. However, since the 1990s, the sector has undergone substantial reforms and liberalisation as also in the case of the EU, and now private players have an important role in the development of this sector. Privatisation has led to the emergence of global players in energy services and enhanced global trade in the sector.

Coal, a sector of prime importance for the economy (for thermal power generation), was nationalised in the post-independence period. In the 1990s, private players were allowed in captive mining for electricity generation, coal washing and other industrial end-uses. Deregulation of coal prices began in 1996 and the Colliery Control Order in the year 2000 fully deregulated the coal pricing regime under which the government PSU, Coal India Limited (CIL), was allowed to fix prices in relation to market prices and revise them from time to time. India's total coal production is falling short of demand, and there is a paucity of funds with the nationalised sector for investment and expansion. Various recommendations have been made to encourage private participation and improve productivity and efficiency.[21] Development of appropriate

---

[21] For instance, the Shankar Committee Report of the Expert Committee on Road Map for Coal Sector Reforms (Part I, December 2005 and Part II, October 2007) and the Ashok Chawla Committee on Allocation of Natural Resources (May 2011).

technology and reforms in the sector have been emphasised from time to time to increase competition. These include the amendment of the Coal Mine Nationalisation Act (1972) in the year 2014 to allow specialised private-sector-owned mining companies to enter the sector, allow coal to be traded in real time and set up electronic exchanges to discover its present and future prices as well as to monitor sales and set up a coal sector regulator. India has been facing shortage of coal leading to import of coal by some large companies. In December 2014, the Lok Sabha passed the Coal Mines (Special Provisions) Bill, 2014, which allows private investors to invest in the erstwhile nationalised coal mines. This is likely to help in sustaining current levels of employment in these mines and power generation.

The oil and gas sectors were also nationalised in the post-independence period. After nationalisation, production showed an upward trend but started to decline in the 1980s. At the same time, there was a steady increase in consumption demand for oil and gas. This created the need to expedite exploration efforts and develop and manage newer reserves. A series of measures followed which encouraged private/foreign players to participate in the sector. In the 1980s, the government started to offer different sedimentary basins to foreign oil companies for E&P. To generate additional investment and upgrade technology, in 1997, the government introduced the New Exploration Licensing Policy (NELP). Under this policy, off-shore and on-shore exploration blocks were offered to private/foreign companies. So far, nine rounds of the NELP have been completed. Various other incentives, such as seven years of income tax holiday from the commencement of commercial production and the abolition of customs duties on import of equipment for exploration operations, were given to encourage investment. EU companies such as Cairn Energy (Scotland), British Gas (UK), British Petroleum (UK) and Premier Oil (UK), ENI (Italy) and Geopetrol (France) have been awarded blocks.[22] The government has recently deregulated diesel prices, marking them to the market and global prices.

India started focusing on renewable energy after the oil shocks of the 1970s. The early programmes were initiated with a target-oriented supply-push approach and were driven by direct subsidies from the

[22] http://petroleum.nic.in/speeches/08-01-2008.doc (accessed on 15 March 2013).

government. In the 1990s, there were changes in the regulatory structure and policy and there was a shift from financial to fiscal incentives and renewable energy programmes that focused on commercialisation and greater involvement of the private sector. By the end of the 1990s, more than 80 per cent of energy from renewables was generated by the private sector (Guru, 2002). At present, foreign investment and technology transfer is encouraged through various policy initiatives. In the recent past, the government has been giving greater importance to the development of India's huge hydro potential[23] to meet its ever-increasing power demands. The Indian government's focus has shifted to solar energy and foreign companies are encouraged to invest in this sector. Many foreign companies such as Morgan Stanley (US) are likely to make big investments in India in this sector.

The Indian electricity sector is covered under the concurrent list and is administered by both the central and state governments.[24] The Constitution has, however, given supremacy to the central legislation. The transmission network across the country has been demarcated by the central government into five separate regions that form regional grids. The sector was brought under government control after independence and after the 1990s it was progressively liberalised. To expand generation capacity, the central government opened electricity generation for foreign/private investment and encouraged the establishment of Independent Power Producer projects to attract additional capital in the sector. Concessions such as 100 per cent ownership, long-term purchase agreements and assured profits were also offered. In June 2003, the Electricity Act was enacted,[25] which provided a framework for a more competitive, transparent and commercially driven power sector. It recognised power trading as a distinct activity, provided open access[26] to the transmission

[23] It is estimated that about 69 percent of India's total hydro potential remains untapped.

[24] See Table 5B.1 in Appendix B for the regulators and some key regulations/programmes in the Indian energy sector.

[25] With its coming into force, the Indian Electricity Act, 1910, Electricity (Supply) Act, 1948 and Electricity Regulatory Commissions Act, 1998 were repealed.

[26] The Electricity Act, 2003 aims to create a competitive electricity market in India through open access. As a first step in the process, a generating company is permitted to sell a portion of the power it generates to any distribution licensee in the country. In the second stage, the generating company will be able to sell power directly to bulk consumers, bypassing the distribution company.

and distribution network, allowed third-party sales and introduced the concept of trading bulk electricity.

FDI up to 100 per cent has been allowed in generation, transmission, distribution and electricity trading subject to the provisions of this Act. Private entities were permitted to establish, operate and maintain power generation plants and enter into long-term power purchase agreements with the State Electricity Boards (SEBs). Provisions of 100 per cent FDI along with fiscal incentives such as zero customs duty on the import of capital goods for mega power projects and an income tax holiday for generating plants for 10 years will make India an attractive destination for foreign investors. The per capita electricity consumption in India has been increasing. FDI norms are continually being relaxed and up to 100 per cent FDI is allowed in most segments now. Table 5A.1 in Appendix A gives an overview of FDI regulations in the energy sector.

Ensuring continuous power supply is one of the key reform agenda of the government. The current power minister[27] declared that by 2019, the entire country will get 24×7 power supply in states like Gujarat, Rajasthan, Madhya Pradesh and Chhattisgarh. The focus for this will be on renewable sources of energy and this opens new opportunities for the EU-based companies to invest in India. The government is undertaking reforms to encourage investments and, therefore, potential for foreign investments in this segment is likely to increase manifolds.

Overall, reforms in the electricity sector have restructured the vertically integrated market structure into a competitive one. Market efficiency has improved; mobility and the number of players have increased. Regulations have contributed to the creation of a competitive market place that in future will bring an open market in the electricity sector.

Market Structure and Liberalisation of the EU Energy Sector

Like India, the energy markets of EU member countries have also undergone rapid changes over the past two decades. These changes are not in isolation but in line with the worldwide trend towards liberalisation, restructuring and privatisation. Before the 1980s, energy generation,

---

[27] The current power minister (December 2014) is Shri Piyush Goyal.

grid expansion and selling were undertaken predominantly by public-owned vertically integrated monopolies or oligopolies that were granted exclusive rights. They mainly catered to the domestic market in a non-competitive environment and government intervention was limited to subsidies, price setting and volume limits. This resulted in monopoly profits and monopoly-induced inefficiencies. The liberalisation process began in the 1990s. Given the scarcity of fossil fuels, increasing demand pressures and the need to increase supply efficiency, the liberalisation process focused on improving efficiency and transparency in a market where private and public generators and retailers compete on a regulated and unbundled system of energy infrastructure. It was envisaged that exposing large parts of the energy supply chain to competitive pressures would reduce prices and, thus, benefit users in the long term.

Much of the liberalisation process across Member States has been due to initiatives undertaken at the EU level. These pertain to common characteristics such as unbundling, independent regulators, public service provisions and security of supply in each Member State.[28]

Given that the EU is a net importer of energy, this sector has been accorded central importance in the supranational and national policy framework. All energy policy decision-makers at the EU level (Commission, Parliament and Council), have emphasised that 'energy policy must form part of the general aims of the Community's economic policy based on market integration, deregulation, limited public intervention (to safeguard the public interest and welfare), sustainable development, consumer protection and economic and social cohesion' European Commission (1995:2). However, beyond these general aims, energy policy must pursue particular aims in the energy sector that reconcile competitiveness, security of supply and protection of the environment.[29]

Overall, the reforms were pursued at two parallel levels. First, under the EU Electricity and Gas Directives, member countries were required to take at least a minimum number of steps by certain key dates towards liberalisation of their national markets. Second, the EC promoted efforts to improve interfaces between national markets by improving cross-border trading rules and expanding cross-border transmission links.

[28] http://www.euractiv.com (accessed on 4 April 2013).
[29] http://www.europarl.europa.eu/factsheets/4_12_0_en.htm (accessed on 1 April 2013).

The aim of these policies was to enable companies to compete with national incumbents, competitive pressure being such that operators are able to realise productivity gains and/or decrease margins via economies of scale. Realising the need for efficient and flexible functioning of renewable markets, important Directives in these segments have been initiated since 2001.

A series of Directives were passed to set up a policy framework and a timeframe for Member States to work towards creating a competitive internal market to enable efficient use of scarce resources. The European Directives (approved by the EC in the second half of the 1990s) designed a common framework for energy markets built on certain objectives and principles. Member States were allowed some flexibility in implementing the intended outcomes and they could develop their own plans in line with these Directives. Some of these (such as the electricity and gas Directives) directly impact the functioning and outcomes of EU energy markets, while others such as those on internal services market integration or recognition of professional qualifications indirectly influence the energy sector (see Table 5B.1 in Appendix B).[30]

Market integration and liberalisation in the coal sector began in the 1950s as it was seen as a necessary component of an open market for steel. The opening up of the gas sector followed the liberalisation of the coal and oil sectors. Like India, restructuring of electricity and gas markets across EU Member States began in the early 1990s. The extent of liberalisation varied across countries and the 1990s saw the governments of several EU Member States reducing their shares in prominent petroleum companies. British Petroleum (UK), ENI (Italy), Repsol (Spain), Total (France), ELF (France) and Mazeikiu Naftu (Lithuania) underwent a transition from being state-owned to becoming publicly listed companies.[31]

The liberalisation process consisted of two phases. In the first phase, the EC made efforts to ensure competitive market conditions in the distribution of gas and electricity sectors. Council Directive 90/377/EEC (June 1990) was adopted to improve transparency in gas and electricity

---

[30] Some major Directives in the sector are summarised in Table 5B.1 in Appendix B.

[31] A company that is owned by the public through shares listed on a stock exchange and traded on the open market (widely acceptable to all investors/consumers). It can raise capital through sale of stocks and convertible bonds.

prices charged to industrial end users (amended by Commission Directive 93/87/EEC of October 1993). The importance of establishing an efficient internal energy market in the EU was recognised in Council Directive 91/296/EEC (May 1991) on the transit of natural gas through grids that aimed at making trade between different EU Members more efficient. Greater integration of the market and efficient and transparent energy practices were encouraged by Directive 94/22/EC on conditions for granting and using authorisations for prospection, exploration and production of hydrocarbons.[32] This Directive complemented Directive 90/531/EEC on procurement procedures of entities operating in the water, energy, transport and telecommunications sectors (repealed and replaced by Directive 93/38/EEC, which was further repealed and replaced by Directive 2004/17/EC). The second phase of the EU's deregulation programme introduced more comprehensive regulatory measures to establish common rules for an internal energy market. Directive 98/30/EC (June 1998) laid down a set of common rules and procedures on the organisation and functioning of the natural gas sector. The Directive of 1998 (98/30/EC) was replaced by Directive 2003/55/EC for gas, which came into operation at the same time as Directive 2003/54/EC for electricity. Both Directives were concerned with common rules for internal markets of natural gas and electricity. Gas Directive 2003/55/EC sought to achieve full opening of the gas markets while maintaining high standards of public service and a universal-service obligation. A two-phase timetable was laid for fully opening the gas markets— Phase I which came into force on 1 July 2004 opened the non-residential market, while Phase II which came into effect on 1 July 2007 aimed to fully open the market.

The Directives were adhered to by Member States according to their individual country situations and levels of political autonomy. The UK was one of the early countries to liberalise. Italy, the Netherlands, Austria, Belgium, the Czech Republic, Denmark, Germany, Ireland and Spain also opened their gas markets to competition for all consumers and households before 1 July 2007. France, Bulgaria, Hungary, Poland, Romania,

---

[32] All Member States (except Luxembourg and Finland, which are exempt from transposition because they do not have any potential hydrocarbon resources) have transposed Directive 94/22/EC into national law. http://europa.eu/scadplus/leg/en/lvb/l27007.htm (accessed on 14 March 2013).

Slovakia, Slovenia, Lithuania, Luxembourg, Sweden and Estonia did so on 1 July 2007, while Finland, Latvia, Greece and Portugal were granted derogations[33] on gas market opening (Europa Press Release, 2007). It was believed that the internal market would give smaller companies easier access to the energy market and ensure sufficient investments in power plants and transmission networks that would, in turn, reduce interruptions in supplies (Europa Press Release, 2007).

On its part, the EC is continuously trying to further liberalise the market by ensuring implementation and enforcement of market opening Directives and taking steps to break the vertically integrated players. On 19 September 2007 the EC adopted a third package of legislative proposals to further its energy policy objectives.[34] Under this, the EC proposed two options to EU Member States to complete liberalisation of the gas and electricity sectors. The first option was legal disintegration of supply and production activities from network operations (*ownership unbundling*). The second option was to allow energy supply firms to maintain ownership of their transmission assets but leave their management to an Independent System Operator (ISO) for taking investment and commercial decisions.[35] The EC stated that *ownership unbundling* was the preferred option. It would ensure non-discriminatory access to energy grids by smaller firms wishing to compete in markets dominated by vertically integrated energy companies (such as EdF in France and E.ON Ruhrgas AG in Germany). Subsequently, however, France, Germany, Austria, Bulgaria, Greece, Luxembourg, Latvia and the Slovak Republic opposed the EC's proposals and outlined a *third option* (regulated unbundling) for liberalisation. This states that fair competition can be achieved without full ownership unbundling or the ISO option

[33] Derogation is a provision in an EU legislative measure that allows for all or part of the legal measure to be applied differently, or not at all, to individuals, groups or organisations.

[34] It was mentioned that shortcomings in the gas and electricity markets included lack of adequate rules on transparency and access to market information and that vertically integrated incumbent companies effectively remain dominant in their national markets, leading Member States to implement regulated prices. For details, see http://europa.eu/rapid/pressReleasesAction.do?reference=SPEECH/07/562&format=HTML&aged=1&language=EN&guiLanguage=en (accessed on 12 March 2013).

[35] Proposal for a Regulation of the European Parliament and of the Council establishing an Agency for the Cooperation of Energy Regulators. http://eur-lex.europa.eu/LexUriServ/LexUriServ.do?uri=CELEX: 52007PC0530:EN:NOT (accessed on 5 April 2013).

and national regulatory authorities could request Transmission System Operators (TSOs) to legally invest in grid and infrastructure upgrades (if safeguards for the independence, management and investment decisions of TSOs are taken into consideration).[36]

Effective regulation is perceived to be necessary in ensuring fair competition practices after privatisation at the EC level. Under the provisions of the Gas Directives, regulators now hold a minimum set of powers in every Member State. At the EU level, the European Regulators' Group for Electricity and Gas (ERGEG) was set up in 2003 as an Advisory Group of independent national regulatory bodies to assist the EC in consolidating the internal market for electricity and gas. Development of the Trans-European Energy network (TEN-E) was considered a prerequisite for internal market integration, diversification of energy supplies and sustainable development.[37] In 2003, the EC (Commission of the European Communities, 2003) also emphasised the importance of increased interconnection for reduction of inter-country price differences and associated benefits to customers. In the year 2009, with the adoption of Directive 2009/72/EC and Directive 2009/73/EC, new rules were introduced on unbundling for transmission system operators and distribution system operators.

The structure of EU's energy industry has changed considerably today. Deregulation and privatisation increased competition in the international market, expanding companies' efforts in exploration and exploitation of oil fields both inside and outside the EU. It also led to several mergers and acquisitions in this sector.[38] Harmonisation of the EU internal market is still in progress and the extent to which the Directives have been implemented in member countries varies. There is still a varying degree of legal and ownership unbundling within the EU. There is the absence of a coherent approach, meaning that the pan-EU playing field for energy giants is competitive but not completely in level. Moreover, there is also the issue

[36] http://renewenergy.wordpress.com/2008/02/03/eight-eu-states-oppose-unbundling-table-third-way/ (accessed on 5 April 2013).

[37] The Trans-European Energy network (TEN-E) is part of the Trans-European Networks (TENs) programme (including transport, energy and telecommunications) that aims to provide high-quality infrastructure-supporting links between EU Member States and with other European countries. It is due to be completed by 2020.

[38] http://www.eurofound.europa.eu/eiro/2004/05/feature/pl0405104f.htm (accessed on 12 March 2013).

of a trade-off between the internal market, climate policy and securities of supplies policy. The development of grid infrastructure at the same time as an enabler for creating the internal market is also pending.

The EU has also adopted a framework for energy end-use efficiency and energy services. This includes an indicative energy savings target for Member States, obligations on national public authorities for energy savings and energy-efficient procurement and measures to promote energy efficiency and energy services. The European Energy End-Use Efficiency and Energy Services Directive (2006/32/EC), also known as the Energy Services Directive (repealing Council Directive 93/76/EEC) was passed to establish frameworks (institutional, financial and legal) to eliminate market barriers and imperfections that prevent efficient end-use of energy. This Directive requires Member States to achieve a 9 per cent reduction in final energy use by 2016 and applies to distribution and retail sale of energy and the delivery of measures to improve end-use energy efficiency.[39] The EU's European Energy Service Initiative (EESI) promotes the development and implementation of innovative projects in energy service contracting and contributes to establishing efficient energy service markets in Europe.[40] The ESCO business is fast evolving in the region as its has become very important for the implementation of the EU's vision for energy-efficient buildings. A significant push is underway in the EU to make new buildings and major renovation *nearly zero energy* by 2021.

As a result of all these measures, in the post-liberalisation period the EU companies have expanded operations across the US, Asia, Africa and the Middle East and developed core competencies in local and neighbouring markets.[41] They have grown through mergers and acquisitions, and acquired the latest technical know-how and best management practices

[39] It requires the government to place an obligation on energy suppliers to provide and promote fuel efficiency improvement measures and/or fuel efficiency audits to their customers, but also allows the government to adopt either a mandatory or voluntary approach.

[40] At the local and regional levels, the EESI supports development and consulting by national online advice centres, training for local authorities, enterprises and disseminators and provision of advice for implementation and further development of the ESC in pilot projects.

[41] They have benefited from expanding their presence in tightly adjacent markets of Europe. Given their geographical, cultural and linguistic proximity, these markets were easier to operate, but there were technical and regulatory barriers to cross-border trade. After removal of these barriers, operation within the EU became easier and efficiency improved through competition.

over the years. Four European companies were listed in the global ranking of the top 20 companies in 250 global energy companies in 2012.[42]

Bilateral Trade Flows and Collaboration between India and the EU

Both India and the EU have liberalised their energy sectors and are important players in global trade in energy services. They have similar resource endowments, but in energy services they have trade complementarities. For instance, India wants foreign investment and the latest technical know-how, which EU companies possess. EU companies, on the other hand, are exploring investment opportunities in developing countries. In fact, EU companies are one of the major foreign investors in the Indian energy sector. From April 2000 to March 2013, the share of the energy sector (including petroleum, power, non-conventional and coal production) was US$15,831.70 million (8.18 per cent) in total FDI inflows.[43]

Energy and climate change are areas of major significance for India and the EU. Both sides recognise the need to work towards achieving safe, secure, affordable and sustainable energy supplies. Joint efforts in the development of more efficient, cleaner and alternative energy chains have been taken in the past. In the India–EU Strategic Partnership Joint Action Plan of September 2005.

India and the EU agreed to launch an India–EU Initiative on Clean Development and Climate Change. This included:

- Identifying and developing ways of widening access and overcoming barriers to dissemination of such technologies in India and the EU;
- Increasing funding and promoting public–private partnerships for R&D of cleaner technologies;
- Promoting adaptive research and development to suit the resource endowment of both parties;
- Reducing the price gap between clean and less efficient technologies via economies of scale.

---

[42] The ranking is provided by Platts, a division of The McGraw-Hill Companies. http://top250.platts.com/Top250Rankings (accessed on 5 March 2013).

[43] DIPP.

It was decided that India and the EU would take steps to encourage and promote sustainable patterns of consumption and production to lessen the adverse impacts of climate change. India and the EU also agreed to strengthen the implementation of the Clean Development Mechanism (CDM) to promote cooperation between India and the EU and encourage companies to engage in such projects. They also agreed to cooperate on improving adaptation to climate change and to integrate adaptation concerns into sustainable development strategies. Both sides agreed to cooperate to enhance the scientific, technical and institutional capacity to predict climate change and its socio-economic impacts.

Efforts have been made at the government level to promote India–EU trade in energy services. At the 5th India–EU Summit in Hague, the energy sector was recognised as a key area for cooperation. An India–EU Energy Panel was set up in 2005 as a formal instrument of cooperation to coordinate joint efforts and matters of mutual interest. The Energy Panel decided to set up Working Groups in the following areas:

1. Energy efficiency and renewable energies
2. Coal and clean coal conversion technologies
3. Fusion energy, including India's membership in hi-tech civilian thermonuclear projects

Both sides agreed to cooperate closely in the areas of promoting energy efficiency and energy conservation; development of affordable clean energy technologies; identifying new technologies in new, renewable, conventional/non-conventional energy sources; and in oil and gas. This was with a view to promoting security of supplies and stability in prices; technology and expertise in the exchange of energy between different grid systems and the development of energy markets; development of hydrogen and fuel cells; and methane recovery and use.

There is significant scope for collaboration in R&D in this sector. Since 1984, the research and innovation activities of the EU have been grouped under the Framework Programme (FP) that allows researchers from a third country to participate in EU research projects funded by the EC. Under the Seventh Euratom Framework Programme (2007–2013), fusion energy research, nuclear fission and radiation protection have an allocation of €2.8 billion. In 2001, the EU and India signed a Science and

Technology (S&T) Agreement; the two economies agreed to strengthen co-operation in areas such as new and renewable energy. There are several initiatives between the Indian government and the EU Member States such as India and France signed the Indo–France Nuclear Cooperation Agreement on civil nuclear co-operation in the year 2008. With this agreement, India and France could also co-operate in other areas such as nuclear safety, radiation and environment protection and nuclear fuel cycle management.

Primary Survey

There are hardly any studies on India–EU bilateral trade in energy. Moreover, disaggregated data on bilateral trade in energy services is not available. To fill this lacuna, understand the trade and investment patterns and identify the trade barriers, a primary survey was conducted. A total of 38 respondents in India participated in the survey. These included 12 EU companies in India, 10 Indian companies and industry associations, government bodies and embassies from both sides.

Presence of EU Companies in India

The survey revealed that the EU companies are major foreign investors in the Indian energy sector. The EU companies usually get their projects through competitive bidding. They apply to advertisements and tenders floated by the government and other nodal agencies. However, most EU companies were unwilling to disclose their investment plans. They are spread across all segments of energy. Several of them are large established MNCs and have been operating in India for decades. For instance, in the E&P segment, there are large EU multinationals such as Cairn Energy (UK), Hardy Oil and Gas plc (UK), Premier Oil India (a subsidiary of Premier Oil Plc, UK) and ENI India (headquarters in Italy, but this is the wholly owned subsidiary of the UK company). There are also companies in fuelling and terminalling services, mostly through joint ventures. For instance, Indian Oiltanking Infrastructure and Energy Services Limited (IOT) is a joint venture of Oiltanking GmbH (Germany) and Indian Oil Corporation Limited (IOCL) where the German partner has a 50 per cent equity stake to build and operate terminalling services for petroleum products. Indian Oil Skytanking Ltd (IOSL) is a joint venture company formed by Indian Oil Corporation Ltd, IOT and Skytanking Holdings GmbH of Germany, with equal participation. The company designs, finances, constructs and operates aviation fuel farm facilities and into plane fuelling services. The joint venture company of Shell B.V (Netherlands) with the Mangalore Refinery and Petrochemicals Limited (MRPL), known as Shell MRPL Aviation Fuels and Services Private Limited, has supplied aviation turbine fuel to 12 Indian airports in the past. Shell has one of the largest FDI inflows in this sector (around US$1 billion) and operates through multiple subsidiary companies across a range of products and services.

In the gas segment, SHV Energy (known as Super Gas in India) of Dutch origin has been involved in the trade and distribution of LPG cylinders since 1996 and now operates in 17 Indian states.[44] Gaz de France (France) has a 10 per cent stake in Petronet LNG Limited and is involved in developing facilities for import and re-gasification of LNG at Dahej (Gujarat) and Kochi (Kerala). In April 2012, GDF Suez SA agreed to collaborate with GAIL (India) Limited to set up India's first floating terminal on India's east coast to import LNG.[45] BG India (a subsidiary of BG Group plc, UK) has a 30 per cent share in two offshore fields, namely Tapti and Panna/Mukta, a 65 per cent controlling stake in Gujarat Gas Company Limited and a 49.7 per cent stake in Mahanagar Gas Limited. In 2009, BG India Energy Solutions Private Limited (BGIES), a wholly owned subsidiary of BG Group, commenced midstream gas marketing operations in India to undertake wholesale marketing and distribution of natural gas. BG Group also has a 65.12 per cent controlling stake in Gujarat Gas Company Limited (GGCL), which is India's largest private sector natural gas distribution company in sales volume. Elf Gas India Limited (a subsidiary of Total) imports LPG and operates its storage facility at Mangalore. The French major Alstom's subsidiary, Alstom T&D India, also has a well-established electricity transmission business in the country.

---

[44] In 2010, it even acquired 100 per cent shares of Caltex Gas India Private Ltd. (CGIPL) of the US-based Chevron Group, engaged in import, storage, bottling and marketing of LPG.

[45] GDF Suez will hold a 26 per cent stake in the import terminal.

There are also several EU consultancy companies that either provide consultancy services to the government, companies and international organisations in India or have partnered with Indian companies. For instance, Wardell Armstrong (UK) has provided modern coal technologies to companies in India. Rock Mechanics Technology (UK), a leading supplier of rock mechanics consultancy and geotechnical services, has undertaken projects in India where it has provided services related to roof control management systems and stress measurement services in coal mines. IT Power India Private Limited (UK) offers consultancy services in renewable technology and management solutions. Wartsila India Limited (Finland) provides solutions for captive power plants; its areas of expertise are electrical and automation services and engine and propulsion services. Some energy-related consultancies are closely linked to environment consultancies and have opened up or plan to open R&D/technology centres in India. One example is Shell Technology India Private Limited in Bangalore that delivers advanced technical studies and services for Shell activities in India and abroad. Some Indian software companies also have collaboration with EU companies; for instance, Infosys has teamed up with Alstom Power Services (France) to set up an R&D centre in Bangalore to provide engineering solutions.

Some companies have diversified their range of operations beyond their traditional work areas in India. For instance, Électricité de France (EdF) provides consultancy services to Indian firms and the government, rather than power generation, which is their core expertise.

Subsidiaries of EU companies in India are exploring opportunities to export to the EU. For instance, Vestas RRB India Limited, a subsidiary of Vestas Wind System (Denmark), imports raw materials from the EU and is exploring possibilities of exporting there.

All EU companies hire their workforce locally. These are mostly skilled workers, but sometimes technical personnel are sent from the parent company in the EU to train Indian personnel. Likewise, Indians are also sent aboard to acquire training. The number of employees and conditions of employment vary depending on the requirements. Some large companies such as Enercon India Limited (Germany) and Alstom Transmission and Distribution (T&D) India that conduct the business of installing wind energy converters have employed more than 3,500 people in India. Others such as Fugro (Survey) India Private Limited

(Netherlands) have 180 engineers and scientists, and IT Power India Limited has around 30 employees (mostly engineers). ENI (Italy) has 20 direct employees and employs up to 600 people through contractors during exploration operations. Companies have hired European experts (reservoir engineers, geophysics specialists, petroleum engineers, geologists, and so on) for specialised services. Most of them are employed on a contractual basis for about one to three years.

Indian Companies in the EU

Only a few Indian companies were found to have operations in the EU. Suzlon Energy Limited, one of the world's major players in alternative energy with a global market share of 6 per cent, has a presence in more than 40 locations around the world including Denmark, Italy, Portugal and Greece. It offers total wind power solutions including consultancy, manufacturing, operations and maintenance support services. Suzlon has a large clientele in Europe in countries such as Italy, Portugal, Spain and Romania and has benefited from collaborating with EU companies and hires locally in the EU-27. Lanco Solar International Limited, an integrated solar value chain developer/service provider and a subsidiary of Lanco Infratech, has operations and experts based in six European countries (with headquarters in London). Acquisitions of local firms by Indian companies have helped them with local market knowledge and in hiring local skills. For instance, Essar Energy acquired Stanlow refinery in the UK in July 2011. Among consultancy companies, Engineers India Limited (EIL) has an office in London that provides third-party inspection services and procurement services for equipment manufacturing locations in Europe. Tata Consultancy Services (TCS), which has IT operations in several EU countries, provides consultancy services to Scotia Gas Networks (UK). NTPC also provides services such as conducting feasibility studies and engineering, planning and training in coal, oil- and gas-fired power plants in the EU, including France and Sweden.

Only a few Indian companies currently export services to the EU. However, some of them have some form of collaboration with EU companies either in India or in third-country markets and have found the collaboration fruitful. For instance, Hindustan Petroleum Corporation Limited (HPCL) has a 50–50 joint venture (known as South Asia LPG Corporation Private Limited or SALPG) with Total Fina Elf (France) to build an underground storage facility for LPG at Visakhapatnam and a joint venture with Colas SA (France) known as Hindustan Colas (HINCOL). It also has long-term licence agreements with EU companies such as M/S Axens (France) for a DHDS unit and M/s Porner (Austria) for a bitumen blowing unit. RPG Transmission Limited has collaboration with Rolls Royce Power Engineering Plc (UK) in the power transmission segment. Oil India Limited (OIL) has signed production-sharing contracts with Polish Oil and Gas Co. (POGC) and Geoenpro Petroleum for E&P in oil and gas sector. It has also partnered with the Spanish oil and gas company, Repsol S.A, for E&P in two oil blocks in Venezuela. The project involves exploitation of extra-heavy crude, setting up upgraders and marketing products. ONGC has signed MoUs with ENI (Italy) for joint operatorship in the upstream oil and gas sector in India and abroad, and with Shell (Netherlands) for technical collaboration in surface coal gasification. Bharat Petroleum Corporation Limited (BPCL) has a joint venture with Encore for oil well drilling operations in the North Sea; the skilled workforce was supplied by Encore for seismic studies in drilling and exploration. Gujarat State Petroleum Corporation Limited (GSPC) has collaborated with Fugro Robertson Limited (Netherlands) and Schlumberger Oilfield Services (France) for seismic survey and weather forecasting. Most collaboration is done on a project-to-project basis, mainly due to the nature of the energy business.

The reasons for the limited presence of Indian companies in the EU include the enormous opportunities they see domestically or in other countries of South Asia and Africa, the saturated EU market and the need for huge investments, the similar resource endowments, barriers to entry and operation in the EU and the fact that they have not explored the market as part of their international business plans.

It was pointed out that EU companies are technologically advanced and have strong R&D teams, managerial expertise and financial base. Their weaknesses, however, are high processing and manpower costs, which are the strengths of Indian companies. This way, Indian and European companies have trade complementarities. Respondents also pointed out that the BTIA negotiations have been going on since 2007, but companies had been collaborating before that. The PSUs have benefitted from collaboration with EU companies and said that the Indian government should facilitate such collaborations in the domestic market and encourage PSUs to form consortia with EU companies in third-country markets.

Areas for Future Collaboration

This section identifies some areas in each of the energy segments where there is potential for trade and investment collaboration or technology transfers between India and the EU. Primarily, EU companies are world leaders in E&P and renewables, and collaborations in these segments are likely to benefit Indian companies, both in India as well as in third-country markets.

In the oil and gas segment, several European companies have long experience of operating in the North Sea region and can provide knowledge to Indian companies in areas such as deep water E&P technology, gas hydrates exploitation, IOR/EOR, geophysical and geological data development and environmental assessment impact studies for shale gas exploration. India also has a resource crunch of geoscientists, petroleum engineers, drillers, and so on where training by EU companies has been beneficial in the past and can be explored further.

From the Indian side, there is scope for technology transfer in the lubricants segment, oil processing technologies, underwater pipelines and refinery maintenance (where Indian companies have an edge).

In the coal sector, India and the EU can collaborate in clean coal technologies, liquefaction of coal (UK and Germany have experience in this area), development of underground coal gasification (UCG) and coal-bed methane (CBM), underground mining technologies and joint R&D.

Companies pointed out that there is scope for investing in renewable energy services, especially the solar segment. EU companies such as Enercon India Limited (Germany), Conergy Renewable Energy Limited (Germany), Sun Technics Energy Systems (Germany), Bosch Rexroth Limited (Germany), the Juwi Group (Germany), Abakus Solar AG (Germany) and Mita-Teknik (Denmark) are present in India. These companies have set up small teams to explore opportunities in off-grid, micro-grid and rooftop applications to serve their clients. EU Member States such as Germany, the UK and Denmark possess technologies such as installing wind turbines in the sea that are useful for Indian companies. Collaboration in rural electrification is likely to benefit India. There is scope for collaboration in biofuels (such as bagasse-based plants) and hydro-electricity.

The reasons for European companies' interest in the Indian market include an unsaturated market and the industry's flexibility in adopting new technologies. They also pointed out that Indian entrepreneurs have local market knowledge and understand local governance systems, making collaboration with them useful to operate in the Indian market.[46] Indian companies, on the other hand, except for certain segments such as renewables, did not show much interest in expanding operations in the EU. They stated that as the EU internal market for services, in general, and energy, in particular, becomes more integrated, operational hurdles are likely to fall. However, as of now, they do not find significant scope for revenue generation there compared with opportunities in African countries, the Middle East, South Asia and even North America.

Barriers in the Energy Sector

This section focuses on the various barriers to the entry and operation of energy services players in the EU and India. These have been compiled from the primary survey and confirmed through secondary sources.

European Union

- *Barriers Related to Government Procurement*

  In 2004, the EU adopted a revised Utilities Directive (2004/17) that covered purchases in the energy (gas and heat) and some other services sectors. This Directive requires open, competitive bidding procedures, but discriminates against bids with less than 50 per cent EU content not covered by an international or reciprocal bilateral agreement. This requirement applies to foreign suppliers of goods and services (USTR, 2012) and Indians are at a disadvantage in the bidding process.

  In the government procurement markets of Ireland and Lithuania, lengthy procedures for budgetary decisions delay procurements, and suppliers often have difficulty in obtaining information about the basis for a tender award. There are also complaints

---

[46] They rated Gujarat and Rajasthan as favourable states for EU companies due to the single window clearance and better governance in these states.

about significant delays in finalising contracts and commencing work. There is lack of transparency in the public procurement process in Bulgaria, Italy, Hungary, Slovenia and Lithuania (see USTR, 2012).

There is a strong pro-EU bias in government contract awards in Austria. Although Austria's power utilities are in majority government-owned, under an EC ruling (2008/585/EC), they are exempt from having to issue public tenders for power generation projects. In Portugal, there are complaints of the Portuguese government favouring EU firms. In Spain, companies in the energy efficiency sector have reported being shut out of tenders for public projects due to bid design that favoured Spanish companies.

In Slovenia, there are short timeframes for bid preparation, lack of clarity in tendering documentation and opacity in the bid evaluation process. One specific complaint involves the quasi-judicial National Revision Commission (NRC), which reviews all disputed public procurement cases favouring the EU, and especially Slovenian firms under its *national interest* standard.

In Greece, prospective non-EU investors in the mining sector are required to obtain licences and other approvals that are not required of Greek or other EU investors. For example, non-EU investors need special approval from the Greek cabinet for exploitation of mines. Greek authorities consider local content and export performance criteria when evaluating applications for tax and investment incentives, although these are not prerequisites for approving investments.

- *Regulatory Constraints—Discriminatory Policies and Complex Regime*

  In Italy, the government in May 2011 announced a new incentive scheme for photovoltaic solar energy production that reduced previous, guaranteed feed-in tariff rates and included a new bonus of 10 per cent above the normal incentive rate for projects with at least 60 per cent EU content. This discriminates against some foreign investors.

  In July 2012, the Italian government announced an incentive scheme for photovoltaic solar energy production that is incentivised in favour of plants built with the EU-made components. All made-in-EU photovoltaic plants smaller than 12 kW are eligible for a premium over the normal incentivised feed-in-tariff (FiT).[47] For other plants, their ability to obtain the FiT is based on a ranking, the criteria for which includes whether they use components produced in the EU. For PV plants larger than 12 kW, those built with made-in-EU components qualify for a higher rank and have a better opportunity of getting both the incentivised tariff and premium (USTR, 2013).

In Romania and Spain, there is uncertainty and a lack of predictability in the legal and regulatory systems that impede foreign investments. In Romania, tax laws change frequently, and several companies experience long delays in receiving VAT refunds to which they are legally entitled. Deadlines for processing and payment of refunds as stipulated by law are sometimes not respected.

- *Incomplete Liberalisation*
  Energy market liberalisation in the EU has been difficult and is likely to remain so. While some countries, notably the UK, have created fully competitive markets within their own borders, other countries have concentrated on developing *national champions* to compete in an expected Europe-wide energy marketplace. For instance, in the Italian energy sector, the government undertook liberalisation reforms and established an Independent Regulatory Agency (IRA), but did not accord sufficient capacity to the competition authority, Autorità. The conflict of interest resulting from 30 per cent public stake in ENI SpA and ENEL SpA has kept the liberalisation process incomplete, and created a conflict of interest within a state that is both a shareholder and the regulator.

The level of liberalisation of European electricity markets remains low, while large incumbents, high market concentration, subsidies to fossil fuels and nuclear energy and regulated prices are common. Subsidies in some markets enable companies to lower their costs, which places non-subsidised firms at a comparative disadvantage.[48]

---

[47] Feed-in Tariffs are financial incentive to encourage uptake of renewable electricity-generating technologies. Countries such as the UK and Italy have these schemes for incentivising renewable energy companies. For details see http://www.energysavingtrust.org.uk/domestic/content/feed-tariff-scheme (accessed on 29 December 2014).

[48] For details, see EWEA (2012) and Buchan (2012).

- *Fiscal Regime and Fiscal Disclosure Requirements*
  Some companies pointed out that the accounting standards and fiscal disclosure requirements in the EU are very strict and complex. Currently, Indian companies are not prepared to follow their accounting and disclosure standards because this is expensive in terms of training manpower and investment in software.[49]

India

- *Monopoly-induced Inefficiencies*
  Despite liberalisation, the sector continues to be dominated by the public sector or PSUs and faces monopoly-induced inefficiencies. Price preference and subsidies (on LPG and kerosene) are given to PSUs, which results in a non-competitive business environment. Within PSUs, there is a lack of corporate governance, the decision-making process is long and cumbersome, and many of them, despite being overstaffed, do not have the required skills.
- *Multiple Governance Bodies*
  The multiplicity of ministries has resulted in multiple regulations. Since different subsegments of energy come under different ministries, they are often regulated separately rather than in an integrated manner. Moreover, several subsectors, such as mining, are regulated by both central and state governments. All of these create conflicts of interest and delays in decision-making and result in requirements of multiple clearances. For example, in the oil and gas sector, companies require more than 70 clearances for exploration and over 20 clearances for marketing. Since the sector is highly regulated, there are bureaucratic delays in getting approvals. For example, it takes 4–5 months to get an installation certificate for solar projects.

  It takes a long time to initiate regulatory reforms. For instance, it took four years to ratify the PNGRB Act, 2006. The Coal Mines Nationalisation (Amendment) Bill, 2000 is still pending

---

[49] For details, see Beke (2010).

in Parliament. The lack of coordination between planning and implementing agencies, lack of a comprehensive energy policy and weak corporate governance are also barriers.

- *Tax-related Problems*

    There are differences in state-level taxes and duties including value added taxes, wheeling[50] charges and buy-back of power. For example, 30 per cent VAT is imposed on high-speed diesel in Maharashtra compared to 8 per cent in Punjab. The lack of uniformity in taxes has resulted in variation in petroleum products prices in states. The proposed solution for this variation in taxation is a single Goods and Services Tax (GST).

- *Resource and Infrastructure Bottlenecks*

    Uncertainty of coal supplies: There are problems and uncertainties for independent power producers (IPPs) in securing coal supplies. Coal India Limited, the state-owned coal producer, entered into fuel-supply agreements (FSAs) with 48 new projects in 2012, albeit with a very low penalty (0.01 per cent) for non-supply. Several IPPs that are hard-pressed for domestic coal have signed FSAs because the penalty clause is very low.

    High cost of borrowing in India: Most private sector projects tend to source the debt portion of their funds in overseas markets because of the substantially higher nominal interest rates in India. Financial institutions are more willing to fund projects that are backed by state guarantees. Aggressive bidding has made funding more challenging since margins have become thin or non-existent. With low tariff rates, the high borrowing costs create risks for developers. Renewable energy companies find themselves competing with the coal or other conventional energy sectors when they borrow from Indian banks.

- *Skill-related Problems*

    Although India has an abundance of high-skilled manpower, there is a shortage of specific skills, especially specialists and engineers. Therefore, Indian companies often depend on foreign geologists and other specialists.

---

[50] Transfer of electricity between utility companies, especially through networks of one company on behalf of others.

- *Other Concerns*
  Local content requirement: There is a local content requirement
  of 30 per cent under the National Solar Mission. This is a deter-
  rent to companies that want to set up a wholly owned subsidiary
  in India.[51]

Addressing Barriers through International Negotiations

Maintaining a high rate of economic growth, reducing external dependence on fuel supplies and attaining energy efficiency are key concerns
for both India and the EU. With liberalisation, energy services have
become a key component of India's trade in services and FDI inflows.

India has progressively liberalised this sector since the early 1990s
and, at present, there are only a few market access barriers. In the
Revised Offer submitted by India to the WTO in August 2005, there was
substantial improvement in commitments in terms of sectoral coverage
and modes of delivery in various segments. The regulatory regime is
continually evolving and the sector is undergoing reforms. However, India
still lacks the standing of a global player and needs foreign investment,
technical know-how and best management practices.

The EU started liberalising the energy market at the same time as India
but is now an important global player and investor. The survey found
that collaboration with EU companies would not only make the domestic
industry globally competitive, but also enable Indian companies to enhance
their know-how and establish a presence in third-country markets.

The EU market is yet to be fully harmonised and Indian and other
foreign companies are facing various barriers in Member States, several
of which are regulatory. Although the EU's Revised Offer has various
restrictions, the EU is the coordinator of plurilateral requests in energy
and it seems to have an offensive interest. On the other hand, India seems
to have a defensive position in the WTO.

An analysis of India's Revised Offer shows that since the sector has
been unilaterally liberalised, it will not be difficult for India to accede

[51] For details, see USTR (2013).

to the EU's demands in most subsectors. In the Revised Offer, India has already offered to bind the unilateral regime for engineering services (CPC 8672), integrated engineering services (CPC 8673), R&D services on natural science and engineering (CPC 85013), management consulting services (CPC 86509), services related to management consulting (CPC 86601), technical testing and analysis services (CPC 8676 partial), services incidental to energy distribution (CPC 887), construction work for civil engineering for long-distance pipelines, local pipelines and mining (CPC 5134–5136) and renting services related to equipment for construction or demolition of buildings or civil engineering works with operator (CPC 518). Although no commitments were made in subsectors such as services incidental to mining and site preparation work for mining and related scientific and technical consulting services, these subsectors are unilaterally open otherwise. It may be difficult for India to undertake commitments in Mode 1 in pipeline transportation services for security and sensitivity reasons. Also, the EU's commitment in this subsector is limited. India can bargain for greater market access and removal of discriminatory barriers, especially in Modes 1 and 4 with the EU.

Indian companies pointed out that they need foreign technology and finance in subsectors such as services incidental to mining and the government may consider scheduling it subject to the existing regulations. In scientific and technical consultancy, India with its strong knowledge base can be an R&D centre for EU companies.

Survey participants agreed that energy should be a key chapter covered in the BTIA and that it should focus on renewables, energy-efficient technologies to reduce carbon emissions, technological assistance and technology transfers, human resource management, training, IT related to this sector, project management and R&D. Due to the cross-cutting nature of energy services and the absence of a clear definition, it is important for India to carefully undertake commitments in this sector so that they are synchronised with commitments in other sectors. The EU may want to link the sector with sustainable development, climate change issues, and so on.

Mode 4 is an important mode of trade in this subsector. Indian professionals face various market access barriers related to national treatment and domestic regulations in EU Member States. EU Members have scheduled hardly any sector-specific Mode 4 commitments and the horizontal offers are restricted to business visitors and intra-corporate transferees. India has the potential to offer consultancy services in the energy sector. These are largely offered on a project-by-project basis and often do not require physical presence. India should ask the EU to undertake commitments in CSS and IP delinked from commercial presence in subsectors in which India has an export interest. It should also push for removal of residency requirements that the service provider should be a natural person. In order to enhance the EU's attractiveness and foster careers in R&D, on 12 October 2005 the Council adopted Directive 05/71/EC on Scientific Visas[52] that prescribes specific procedures for admitting third-country nationals for scientific research.[53] Different EU Member States are offering flexibilities to scientific researchers from a third country subject to certain conditions. During the negotiations, India should push for greater market access for Indian scientists. However, it may be difficult for India to sign a mutual recognition agreement (MRA) with the EU in professions such as engineering, since the domestic EU market for this profession is yet to be harmonised.

India has a comparative advantage in providing consultancy services. Mode 1 in the Revised Offer of the EU is full of restrictions and the levels of commitments differ across the Member States. For instance, Portugal and Italy have kept Mode 1 unbound for engineering and integrated engineering services. Countries such as Austria and Hungary have kept Mode 1 unbound for R&D services, while newer members such as the Czech Republic, Cyprus and the Slovak Republic have kept Mode 1 unbound across technical testing and analysis services and advisory and consulting service related to mining. India should push for the removal of such barriers in the BTIA since Indian companies have the potential to enter the EU in these areas.

The EU's commitments in subsectors such as R&D for natural science, technical testing and analysis services, and related scientific and technical consulting services are extremely limited. India should push to

---

[52] Scientific visas are fast-track visa and work permit arrangements for third-country researchers, aimed at easing researchers' legal and administrative procedures and requirements with respect to travel and residence. Details in http://www.eu-delegation.org.eg/en/ Scientific%20Visa.pdf and http://ec.europa.eu/research/researchers ineurope/documents/ media_fact_sheet_scientvisa_en.pdf (accessed on 26 February 2013).

[53] This Directive provides a common definition of researchers.

broaden the coverage of commitments. In the EU, different modes of entry such as wholly owned subsidiary and branches are treated differently; the company is treated as an EU company if it is a wholly owned subsidiary. Since energy services are often delivered on a project-by-project basis, establishing a presence in the EU is expensive and companies often need to enter the market through other modes such as branches and representative offices. However, this adversely affects the Indian companies. Ceratin flexibilities can be given to the Indian companies under the India-EU BTIA. Apart from this, Indian companies face other barriers in the EU. Some of these such as real estate restrictions, restrictions on import of machineries and local content requirements which have been imposed by EU Member Countries to reduce an influx from countries like China can be discussed bilaterally. Stakeholders pointed out that an MRA in technical standards of equipment in the electricity sector would facilitate bilateral trade.

Conclusion and the Way Forward

India and the EU have similar energy resource endowments, but they have trade complementarities in energy services. In order to tackle its increasing energy demand, international fuel supply volatility and global warming concerns, India needs to ensure energy security for itself. For this, it needs foreign investment, the latest technical know-how and experience of best practices in management in areas such as coal, E&P and renewable energy that EU companies possess. EU companies, on the other hand, are financially strong and are exploring investment opportunities in the unsaturated energy markets of developing countries such as India.

Energy efficiency is one of the key priorities of the Indian government. The same was reflected during the UN Climate Change Conference in December 2014. As a result, the government is trying to upgrade to the right technology and sources of energy supply. This opens a vast variety of opportunities for the EU companies in this sector to invest in India. Additionally, investments in renewable sources of energy for power generation are a segment with opportunities for the EU companies to invest. As the current government is promoting this, reforms are likely and, therefore, there is potential for the EU companies.

Mode 3 is an important mode of trade in the sector and EU companies have emerged as major foreign investors in India. Currently, only a few Indian energy companies have operations in the EU due to the latter's saturated markets, untapped opportunities in domestic and other international markets and barriers to trade in the EU. High market concentration has been a major cause of worry since it adversely impacts trade through both Modes 1 and 3. Some Indian companies have world-class expertise in subsectors such as petroleum refining and wind-power generation. With specialisation catching up, these companies have shown an interest in exploring the possibilities of investing in EU markets in the near future.

The EU is a major proponent of multilateral liberalisation of energy services. Although its energy sector has undergone significant liberalisation in the past two decades, the EU market is yet to be harmonised. Indian and other foreign companies face various barriers in the EU region, several of which are regulatory. The EU Member States are at various levels of liberalisation and barriers to market entry are more prominent in East Europe. Moreover, most energy services trade remains intra-EU and this chapter has highlighted various market access and discriminatory barriers for Indian players that need to be addressed during the negotiations. In Modes 1 and 3, there is significant scope for removal of barriers.

Indian companies pointed out that since a major part of the sector is unilaterally liberalised and EU companies already operate in India, they do not anticipate any major threats from further liberalisation under the BTIA. The BTIA should facilitate know-how exchanges and business-to-business collaboration and enhance opportunities for small and medium enterprise (SME) collaboration and investment by EU financial intermediaries in India. Indian companies can gain from the experience of EU companies in unbundling, privatisation and restructuring, and learn from their global best practices. India's medium to long-term goal of establishing a national grid can benefit from the TEN-E programme of the EU. The EU's experience in opening up the energy market and encouraging competition and efficiency can be re-used through collaboration and technology transfers for India and for joint India-EU partnership in third-country markets.

Appendix A

Table 5A.1

Energy Segments with Restrictive FDI in India

S. No.	Services Sector	FDI Limit	Route	Other Conditions
1.	Atomic Energy	Not allowed		
2.	Services incidental to energy distribution Power Exchanges registered under the Central Electricity Regulatory Commission (Power Market) Regulations, 2010	49% (FDI & FII)[a]	Government route (for FDI); Automatic (for FII)	Subject to provisions of the existing law, Electricity Act, 2003
3.	Petroleum refining by Public Sector Undertakings (PSU), without any disinvestment or dilution of domestic equity in the existing PSUs.	Allowed up to 49%	Government route	No conditions

Source: Compiled by the author from various publications of DIPP, Government of India.

Notes: [a]Foreign investment is subject to an FDI limit of 26 per cent and an FII limit of 23 per cent of the paid-up capital.

Appendix B

Table 5B.1
Important Directives in the EU Energy Services Sector

Gas	Directive 2003/55/EC (26 June 2003) concerning common rules for the internal market in natural gas (repealing Directive 98/30/EC)
	Council Directive 2004/67/EC (26 April 2004) concerning measures to safeguard security of natural gas supply
Electricity	Directive 2003/54/EC (26 June 2003) concerning common rules for the internal market in electricity (repealing Directive 96/92/EC)
	Directive 2005/89/EC (18 January 2006) concerning measures to safeguard security of electricity supply and infrastructure investment.
Renewables/ Efficiency Directives	Council Directive 92/42/EEC (21 May 1992) on efficiency requirements for new hot-water boilers fired with liquid or gaseous fuels. Amendment: Proposal for a Directive on establishing framework for setting eco-design requirements for energy-using products and amending Council Directive 92/42/EEC (presented by EC)
	Directive 2001/77/EC (27 September 2001) on the promotion of electricity produced from renewable energy sources (RES-E) in the internal electricity market
	Directive 2003/30/EC (8 May 2003) on promotion of use of biofuels or other renewable fuels for transport
	Directive 2004/8/EC (11 February 2004) on the promotion of co-generation based on useful heat demand in the internal energy market and amending Directive 92/42/EEC
	Directive 2012/27/EU (25 October 2012) on energy efficiency.
Nuclear	Directive 96/29/EURATOM of 13 May 1996

Other Directives

Directive 2006/123/EC (12 December 2006) On Services in the Internal Market

Council Directive 2006/67/EC (24 July 2006) Imposing an Obligation on Member States to Maintain Minimum Stocks of Crude Oil and/or Petroleum Products

(Table 5B.1 Continued)

(Table 5B.1 Continued)

Directive 2002/91/EC (16 December 2002) On the Energy Performance of Buildings

Directive 2005/36/EC (7 September 2005) On the Recognition of Professional Qualifications.[54]

Directive 2004/18/EC (31 March 2004) On Co-Ordination of Procedures for the Award of Public Works Contracts, Public Supply Contracts, and Public Service Contracts (The Public Sector Directive)

Source: Compiled by the author.

---

[54] Since this Directive replaces Council Directive 89/48/EEC on the general system for recognition of professional qualifications, it affects the profession of engineering only in Member States where it is regulated.

6
Trade and Investment in IT and IT-enabled Services

Divya Satija

Over the past few decades, international off-shoring of production and services has grown considerably due to technological developments, globalisation, changes in business models and liberalisation of domestic markets. Despite the global slowdown, the global sourcing market grew from around US$106 billion to about US$130 billion between 2010 and 2012 (NASSCOM, 2013).

Today, the information technology (IT)/IT-enabled services (ITeS) sector provides a great business advantage (Lacity and Willcocks, 2001). Multinational companies from developed countries have been outsourcing back-office operations such as payroll, and core operations such as financial analysis to skilled but low-cost suppliers in other countries such as India (Wunsch-Vincent and McIntosh, 2004). In return, host countries have benefitted in terms of higher employment opportunities, skill and technological upgrading and higher capital inflows and trade flows (Ghibutiu and Dumitriu, 2008).

A substantial part of the IT/ITeS off-shoring is sent to India. In 2014, the IT-Business Process Management (BPM) sector had 38 per cent share in total services exports from India (NASSCOM, 2014). The major destination for India's exports of computer software and services is the US, which had a share of 55 per cent in 2009–2010. However,

EU countries, particularly the UK, the Netherlands and Hungary, came next with a share of 22.87 per cent.[1] Although this is partly because of the lower costs in India, the EU is also off-shoring IT/ITeS work because it faces a labour shortage due to its ageing population (European Commission, 2006b). There are other areas of bilateral trade and investment complementarities. The EU is ahead of India in IT technology and research and development (R&D). In the past few years, a number of Indian multinationals in this sector have bought EU companies and this has enabled them to acquire technology. With access to technology and research, India can leap ahead in the value chain. The complementarities between India and the EU have contributed to the growing bilateral trade and investment in the IT/ITeS sector.

At the same time, trade and investment between the India and the EU can be further enhanced. The EU Member States are coming out of the Eurozone crisis and there is need for investment in services such as risk management system for financial services which will require use of IT. The new government in India is focused on improving ease of doing business through implementation of IT and e-governance platform. In the Union Budget of July 2014, the government announced that all central government departments and ministries will integrate their services with the eBiz platform as a part of the prime minister's 'Digital India' campaign. This platform aims to create a business and investor-friendly ecosystem in India by making all business- and investment-related clearances and compliances available on a 24×7 single portal, with an integrated payment gateway. These offer tremendous opportunity for investment in the IT sector. India can learn from the EU's experiences of creating the e-biz platform. The recently launched 'Digital India' campaign has three core components: these include creation of digital infrastructure, delivering services digitally and digital literacy. It is based on the public–private partnership model. The government is in the process of initiating a number of allied reforms such as privacy and data protection law to facilitate digitalisation. All these will offer opportunity for investments and collaborations.

As of date, there are several barriers to movement of IT professionals. If barriers to movement of professionals are removed, then low-cost

---

[1] Electronics and Computer Software Promotion Council, India, Statistical Year Book (2009–2010).

skilled Indian professionals can help to meet the manpower shortage in some EU Member States as well as increase the export earnings of Indian companies. It will also promote knowledge interface and cooperation. Companies from India and the EU can also leverage their mutual strengths to access third-country markets.

Against this backdrop, we first analyse the bilateral trade and investment flows in the IT/ITeS sector between India and the EU in order to identify areas for collaboration between the two economies and the barriers to trade and investment flows. To better understand the issues involved, we conducted a survey to gather the views of stakeholders.

Definition and Coverage of the Sector

There is no universal definition of the IT/ITeS sector. Like any other services sector, the IT/ITeS sector can be classified either based on the country's definition or the UNCPC. In the Services Sectoral Classification (MTN.GNS/W/120), the IT/ITeS sector comes under computer and related services, which includes: (a) consultancy services related to the installation of computer hardware, (b) software implementation services, (c) data processing services and (d) database services and maintenance and repair services.[2] This classification is used during the World Trade Organization (WTO) negotiations. In India and the EU, the National Industrial Classification (NIC) 2008 and the NACE Version 2, respectively, are used to classify the IT/ITeS sector (see Chapter 2). There are no differences between the two classifications.

In India, most of the disaggregated data on the IT/ITeS sector is collected regularly by the National Association of Software and Services Companies (NASSCOM) and the Electronics and Computer Software Export Promotion Council (ESC). Even the ministries and government departments refer to these sources of data. Eurostat provides disaggregated data for the information and communication technologies sector of the EU at regular intervals. However, there are some discrepancies in the

---

[2] Due to the evolving nature of the services sector, the CPC has been revised frequently and the current CPC 1.1 provides a relatively comprehensive schedule. According to CPC Version 1.1, IT/BPO services are broadly covered under CPC 83 (Other Professional, Business and Technical services), CPC 84 (Telecommunication services; information retrieval and supply services) and CPC 85 (Support services).

definition, method of data collection and construction of indices across the sources.

Recent Trends and Developments

IT/ITeS is one of the fastest growing services sectors in India. The revenue of this sector increased from US$8 billion in 2000–2001 to US$101 billion in 2012 (NASSCOM, 2013). According to an estimate (Ministry of Communication and Information Technology, 2011), the IT/ITeS sector is expected to generate revenue of US$225 billion by 2020. It is a major contributor to the GDP, increasing from less than 2 per cent in 2000–2001 to 8 per cent in 2012–2013 (NASSCOM, 2013). Although the information and communications technology services sector in the EU has been growing and value addition in the information and communications technology services sector was around US$602.29 billion,[3] its contribution to gross domestic product (GDP) is lower than India's. The information and communications technology services sector accounted for 3.7 per cent of the EU's GDP in 2009.[4]

The IT/ITeS sector drives as well as supports technology adoption. Technology has changed the global landscape, leading to higher use of IT services in order to establish greater interconnectivity, lessen the need for physical movement of professionals and reduce delivery times. The growing need for IT has facilitated innovation and, as a result, R&D expenditure in the IT/ITeS sector across both economies has increased. According to NASSCOM (2012), in India, the expenditure on engineering research and development (ER&D) grew by 2.2 per cent in 2011 (NASSCOM, 2012). ER&D is driven by the convergence of technologies, which enables a single device to perform multiple functions. With the availability of skilled engineers, India is emerging as a leading ER&D offshore destination, and ER&D exports from India amounted to US$11.4 billion during 2012–2013 (NASSCOM, 2012). The majority of the exports are directed to North America and Europe. Although

---

[3] Exchange rate: 1€ = US$1.3942, period average for the time period 1 January 2009 to 31 December 2009, available at http://www.oanda.com/currency/historical-rates/ (accessed date 7 June 2013).

[4] Joint Research Centre, Information Society Unit, available at http://is.jrc.ec.europa.eu/pages/ISG/PREDICT/2da/1a.html (last accessed on 14 August 2015).

adversely impacted by the global slowdown,[5] R&D spending in the EU on information and communications technology services revived and increased by 2.2 per cent in 2009, and business R&D in the information and communications technology industry accounted for 1.7 per cent of the GDP (European Commission, 2012c).

The IT/ITeS sector in India has matured from merely providing services to partnering with their customers, which enables customers to expand their operations across different geographies. The domestic market is evolving from a captive market structure to third-party transformational outsourcing relationships. This implies that rather than merely running isolated processes for customers in the form of contracting out IT hardware and IT facilities, business process outsourcings (BPOs) have been engaging more deeply to identify and transform core business processes to add greater market value in the creation and delivery of end products and services. It yields hybrid IT services in which telecommunications, computer technology and software converge with content-oriented industries such as broadcasting and publishing. As a result, the use of IT services is dominant across the majority of sectors. Sectors such as banking, financial services and insurance, telecommunications, manufacturing, retail, healthcare, travel and transportation, construction and utilities, media, publishing and entertainment and education have increased their adoption of IT services. The Indian government has also increased its IT adoption in order to deliver government services. The information and communications technology industry in the EU has also evolved since the emergence of the Internet in the late 1980s. As in India, there has been a convergence across different services such as telecommunications and broadcasting (Veugelers, 2012).

Since the IT/ITeS sector is skill-intensive, it offers enormous potential for employment generation and skill development. The IT/ITeS sector in India employed around 40,000 people in the late 1990s, which increased continuously to an estimated figure of 2 million in 2008 (NASSCOM, 2008), 2.77 million in 2012 (NASSCOM, 2012) and is expected to reach 3 million during 2012–2013 (NASSCOM, 2013). In comparison, 2.7 million people or 1.25 per cent of the EU workforce in 2011 was employed in the information and communications technology sector (including computer programming, consultancy and related services).

[5] For details, see European Commission (2011b).

According to the Global Services Location Index of AT Kearney (2011), in terms of industry activity, India once again topped the chart on three indicators: BPO services, voice services and IT outsourcing services. In terms of people skills and availability, India ranks second with the highest score for size and availability of the labour force and education. In contrast, EU Member States recorded low scores for size and availability of the labour force: the UK (0.55), France (0.53), Germany (0.31) and Spain (0.40).[6]

The availability of skilled workers along with a large unsaturated market and government support in the form of export promotion schemes and incentives has had a positive impact on foreign direct investment (FDI) flows to this sector in India. Between April 2000 and March 2013, cumulative FDI inflows in the computer services sector (including hardware and software) amounted to US$11.69 billion, which accounted for about 6 per cent of total cumulative FDI inflows.[7] The global slowdown and the Eurozone crisis, among other factors, had a negative effect on FDI inflows. As a result, FDI in this sector exhibits a fluctuating trend between 2006–2007 and 2010–2011; it declined after the global slowdown, but then increased from 2011–2012 to 2012–2013.

In the EU, FDI inflows in the information and communication services sector made up 4.58 per cent of the total FDI inflows in the services sector in 2008.[8] The UK among all Member States is a prominent destination for both inbound and outbound FDIs in this sector. Factors such as its conducive business environment and well-developed infrastructure, its position as Europe's largest e-commerce market and its English-speaking resource base make it an attractive investment destination for Indian companies (Chanda, 2009). Indian IT firms such as Tata Consultancy Services (TCS) Limited, Wipro Limited and Infosys Limited are not only key players in this sector in India, but also have a significant global presence especially in the US and the EU. The UK has one of the largest presence of Indian IT companies such as HCL Technologies

---

[6] This index included 50 countries that were evaluated on 43 measures across three major categories—financial attractiveness, people skills and availability and business environment available at http://www.atkearney.com/index.php/Publications/offshoring-opportunities-amid-economic-turbulence-the-at-kearney-global-services-location-index-gsli-2011.html (accessed on 1 June 2015).

[7] DIPP (2013a).

[8] Calculated from Eurostat, Balance of Payment Statistics.

Limited, Infosys Limited, TCS Limited, Birlasoft UK Ltd. and Wipro Limited.

What is common to India and the EU is that the sector is dominated by SMEs. Various entrepreneurs have invested in start-ups that provide specialised services since this involves low initial investment while promising high returns. The Indian IT/ITeS sector consists of over 5,000 enterprises that offer services across different verticals, most of which are SMEs. In the EU, SMEs represented 99.4 per cent of the enterprises and accounted for 69 per cent of the employment and 58 per cent of the total turnover in 2006 for computer services and related activities (NACE 72) (ECORYS, 2009). However, the size of EU software companies is, in most cases, considerably smaller than that of their US or Japanese counterparts.

Another common feature in both economies is that IT firms are clustered around a few select regions. In India, the IT/ITeS sector is concentrated in a few states and some cities within those states. Initially, the sector developed in Mumbai (Maharashtra) and Bangalore (Karnataka), mainly after Texas Instruments[9] was established in the mid-1980s. Delhi and the neighbouring regions of Noida and Gurgaon developed as popular IT/ITeS locations simultaneously with cities such as Chennai (Tamil Nadu) and Hyderabad (Andhra Pradesh). These regions have witnessed an upsurge of multinational corporations such as Capgemini and Accenture, helped by the availability of skilled manpower and the high-speed data communication links and built-up space provided in software technology parks (STPs; Kumar and Joseph, 2005). Today, Bengaluru is known as the Silicon Valley of India. When operating costs started increasing in Tier I cities, companies started to relocate to Tier II and Tier III cities and the preference for these cities is growing.

In the EU, the majority of the information and communications technology services sector turnover is generated in the EU-15[10] with Spain, Italy, France, Germany and the UK accounting for approximately 70 per cent of the total turnover. In terms of employment generation, the

[9] Texas Instruments India Ltd. started by setting up a research facility in Bangalore in August 1985 and became the first global technology company to establish a presence in India.

[10] The number of member countries in the European Union prior to the accession of 10 candidate countries on 1 May 2004. The EU-15 comprises Austria, Belgium, Denmark, Finland, France, Germany, Greece, Ireland, Italy, Luxembourg, the Netherlands, Portugal, Spain, Sweden, and the United Kingdom.

sector is concentrated in and around large cities and high-tech countries that cover the south of the UK, Benelux, Denmark and Stockholm and the French region of Ile-de-France, the western region of Germany and the north of Italy. There are also important clusters in Madrid, Ireland and Finland, and emerging outsourcing destinations in Northern Ireland, Romania, Bulgaria, the Czech Republic and Poland. Various US, Chinese and Indian information and communications technology services multinationals have been establishing R&D, software development and services units in EU-10[11] and EU-15 countries. According to the AT Kearney Index (2011), Tier II cities are emerging as attractive investment destinations. The ranks of Member States such as Poland (24th), Estonia (11th), Latvia (13th) and Lithuania (14th) have improved considerably in the services location index.[12]

Governance Structure and Regulations

The Indian government adopted a pro-liberalisation stance towards the IT/ITeS sector after the 1991 reforms. The sector has benefitted considerably from the liberalisation of the telecommunications sector, reduction in import duties on equipment, relaxation of industrial licensing norms and allowing 100 per cent FDI in the sector through the automatic route. To promote exports, the government announced a few schemes such as STP scheme, special economic zones (SEZs) and export-oriented units (EOUs) under which tax exemptions are given for exports.

In the EU, too, there are hardly any market access restrictions to investment in IT/ITeS services. Both economies have offered to liberalise investments in services in their respective WTO Revised Offers.[13] India offered to allow 100 per cent FDI under the automatic route in data processing, software development, computer consultancy services, software supply services, business and management consultancy services, market research services, technical testing and analysis services. Indian government regulations do not distinguish between domestic and foreign

---

[11] Nations that joined the EU in 2004: the Czech Republic, Cyprus, Estonia, Hungary, Latvia, Lithuania, Malta, Poland, Slovak Republic and Slovenia. Nations that joined in 2007: Bulgaria and Romania.

[12] AT Kearney (2011).

[13] For details see WTO (2005b and c).

players. In the EU, there are some distinctions between EU and non-EU companies based on their modes of operation.

In terms of regulations, the Indian IT/ITeS sector is governed and regulated at the centre by the Department of Information Technology (DIT), under the Ministry of Communications and Information Technology. The sector is regulated under two Acts: the Information Technology (Amendment) Act, 2008 (which is an amended version of the Information Technology Act, 2000) and the Semiconductor Integrated Circuits Layout Design Act, 2000. Other acts such as the Copyright Act, 1957 and its various amendments govern the Intellectual Property Rights (IPR) of computer software. Since the sector is highly integrated, the policies of other government departments such as the Ministry of Commerce and Industry (offers export incentives), Department of Telecommunications (DoT), the Telecom Regulatory Authority of India (TRAI) and the Ministry of Finance (which looks after taxation) impact this sector.

The services market in the EU is not harmonised. However, various Directives have been implemented to regulate the information and communications technology sector. The Services Directive (discussed in Chapter 2) aims to integrate the services market; however, this Directive only regulates computer programming and consultancy services, and excludes other services under the information and communications technology services sector.[14]

Some regulations that affect IT/ITeS trade are discussed below.

- *Data Protection Regulations in India and the EU*
  A key issue that affects trade flows in the IT/ITeS sector is data security. Data protection regulations play a key role in the outsourcing of services, contracting of foreign firms and employment creation in this sector.

  Data protection in India is governed under the Information Technology (Amendment) Act, 2008. This Act provides legal recognition for transactions carried out through electronic data interchange and other means of electronic communication (commonly referred to as electronic commerce) that involves the use of alternatives to paper-based methods of communication and storage of information.

---

[14] For details, see Section on Definition and Coverage of the Sector.

This Act was amended in April 2011 and a new set of rules, the Information Technology (Reasonable security practices and procedures and sensitive personal data or information) Rules, 2011, were transposed to the Act. The Rules provide for the introduction of digital signatures, allowing public–private partnership in e-governance delivery of services, and so on. To address concerns about data protection and privacy, and to bring the Indian regulatory regime in line with global regulations, more stringent provisions have been provided for data protection in the new Rules. Some of these are listed below:

(i)   Sensitive personal data or information to be handled with reasonable security practices and procedures.
(ii) Gradation of severity of computer-related offences, committed dishonestly or fraudulently and punishment thereof.
(iii) Introduction of additional section for breach of confidentiality with intent to cause injury to a subscriber.

Regulations governing data security are crucial across the EU. To provide a regulatory framework to guarantee secure and free exchange of data across the national borders of EU Member States, the *Data Protection Directive* (95/46/EC) or the EU Directive on the protection of individuals with regard to the processing of personal data and on the free movement of such data was formulated. It restricts the transfer of personal data to locations outside the EU unless the importing country ensures adequate data protection under domestic regulations or international commitments. The Directive establishes strict guidelines for processing personal information based on the guidelines for the protection of privacy and trans-border flows of personal data adopted by the Organisation of Economic Co-operation and Development (OECD).[15]

[15] It requires companies that process the data to appoint a data controller who must register with government authorities. The data controller must notify the government authorities before processing any data. This notification includes informing the individual of the purpose of the processing, providing a description of the data subject and of the recipients to whom the data might be disclosed, proposed transfers to third countries and a description to ensure that basic security requirements have been met. It also requires a government authority to oversee data processing activities. Individual EU Member Countries are required to establish an independent public authority, namely, Data Protection Commissions, to supervise the protection of personal data by investigating and monitoring data processing activities and intervening in these activities where required.

This is an overarching Directive and has been complemented by new legal instruments that are Directives on data protection specific to different sectors. One such Directive is the Data Protection Directive in the electronics communication sector—Privacy and Electronics Communication Directive 2002/58/EC—that principally concerns the processing of personal data relating to the delivery of communications services.

Each EU Member State drafts its own privacy regulation to meet the requirements of the Data Protection Directive. Hence, each Member State has different regulations under the same Directive.

Some Directives that govern data privacy in the information and communications technology services sector are given below:

(i)   Directive 2000/31/EC on certain legal aspects of information society services, in particular electronic commerce, in the Internal Market or *Directive on Electronic Commerce*.

(ii) Directive 2002/20/EC on the authorisation of electronic communications networks and services or *Authorisation Directive*.

(iii) Directive 2002/58/EC concerning the processing of personal data and the protection of privacy in the electronic communications sector or *Directive on Privacy and Electronic Communications*.

(iv) Directive on legal protection of designs (98/71/EC), Directive on the enforcement of IPR (2004/48/EC) and the Directive on harmonising certain aspects of copyright and related rights in the information society or the Copyright Directive (2001/29/EC) govern the protection of IPR.

Since the regulations on data protection impact trade, investment and collaboration, they are discussed later in this chapter.

• *Labour Mobility and Labour Market Regulations*
Since the IT/ITeS sector is highly labour intensive, cross-country labour mobility is crucial to enhance trade in this sector. In the EU, work permits and visas are under the purview of individual Member States, which restricts the mobility of foreign workers.

Unlike in the EU, the movement of foreign nationals from one state to another is not restricted in India. Hence, the EU's services sector is relatively more restrictive than India's. In India, foreign nationals in the IT/ITeS sector are treated as professionals and a work permit is granted based on a valid working contract and an income of US$25,000 and above. Once a visa for stay of over 180 days is granted, the foreign national can enter India and has to register at the Foreigner's Regional Registration Office (FRRO) within 14 days of entry into India. Each state has its FRRO and, hence, expatriates can register in the state where they will be working.[16] A foreign national employed in India by an Indian company has to be paid in the local currency by the employer. On 30 September 2009, the Reserve Bank of India issued a notification that a foreign citizen who is resident in India and employed with an Indian company is allowed to remit the entire salary received in India in Indian rupees to any foreign currency account in a bank outside India as long as the foreign citizen pays income tax on the entire salary accrued in India.

A professional in India has to abide by labour market regulations. The Industrial Employment (Standing Orders) Act, 1946 formulated by the Labour and Employment Department under the Ministry of Labour and Employment is the main Act that protects the interests of labour in India. In the past, the IT/ITeS sector was largely exempt from this Act so that companies could have the flexibility to hire and fire employees. However, given that the sector is highly labour intensive and employs millions of people, the government recently felt that there is need to protect the interests of employees, and in 2012 the Labour and Employment Department rejected the exemption to the Act. The IT/ITeS sector will now be regulated under the Act, which requires employers to define and inform workers about the terms and conditions of employment on their premises. This could lead to greater interference by workers and disturbances by trade unions.

[16] http://www.realestatemumbai.com/Expatriates/FRRO-Foreigners-Regional-Registration-Office.aspx (accessed on 1 June 2015).

It is likely to hurt this industry unlike the manufacturing sector, which heavily relies on contract labour.

At the state level, West Bengal and Karnataka have implemented state-specific labour regulations to facilitate the growth of the IT/ITES sector. For example, in West Bengal IT/ITeS companies are treated as public utilities and are exempted from strikes. Certain exemptions allow employees to work 24×7 and 365 days a year. By an amendment in the Karnataka Shops and Commercial Establishments Act, 1961, from the year 2002, female IT employees are allowed to work in the night shifts.

Regulating labour mobility in the EU is a Member State subject and each Member State imposes different conditions on labour movement. This restricts the movement of non-EU professionals/nationals within the EU. Over the years, some measures have been taken at the EU level to facilitate intra-EU mobility, some of which have implications for foreign nationals.

(i)   Non-EU nationals entering the EU for a short term for business purposes can obtain a Schengen Visa (SV) to stay and work in certain EU Member States[17] for up to 90 days. They can also visit countries in the Schengen territory that are signatories of the Schengen Accord.

(ii)   The *Blue Card Directive* (2009/50/EC)[18] allows a high-skilled third-country national to enter, re-enter and reside for more than three months in the territory of a Member State of the EU. The objective of the Directive is to meet

---

[17] The signatories to the Schengen Accord are Austria, Belgium, the Czech Republic, Denmark, Estonia, Finland, France, Germany, Greece, Hungary, Iceland, Italy, Latvia, Lithuania, Luxembourg, Malta, the Netherlands, Norway, Poland, Portugal, Slovakia, Slovenia, Spain, Sweden and Switzerland.

[18] The EU Blue Card entitles holders to reside and work in the territory of an EU Member State. It is not a substitute for a visa, but those who hold the EU Blue Card can enter, re-enter and stay in the issuing Member State and pass through other Member States; work in the sector concerned; and enjoy equal treatment with nationals as regards, for example, working conditions, social security, pensions, recognition of diplomas, education and vocational training. The Directive was adopted by the EU Council on 25 May 2009 and came into force on 19 June 2009. The Directive determines common criteria for applicants and requires Member States to transpose its provisions into their national legislation by 19 June 2011.

the growing shortage of high-skilled labour in the EU. The decision on an EU Blue Card application is taken within 90 days of the application being submitted. Once the EU Blue Card is granted to a non-EU national with a job offer, it authorises uniform entry and residence in an EU Member State. It provides access to the EU labour market and residence rights. EU Blue Card holders enjoy equal treatment with nationals of the Member State, issuing it for working conditions, social security, pensions, and so on. After 18 months of legal residence in the first Member State, Blue Card holders and their family may move to another Member State for the purpose of highly qualified employment subject to the approval of the relevant authority in the second Member State. The EU Blue Card is valid for one to four years, with the possibility of renewal. A Blue Card may also be issued or renewed for shorter periods in order to cover the duration of the work contract plus three months. The EU Blue Card is issued by the relevant authorities of the participating Member States.

(iii) The EU *Single Permit Directive* (2011/98/EU) seeks to establish a simplified and harmonised procedure for non-EU nationals in order to obtain a work and residence permit in EU Member States. It defines a common set of rights awarded to migrants in order to address the gaps between third-country workers and EU citizens. It involves a single application procedure when non-EU nationals apply for work or stay in a Member State. The Directive applies to two main categories of non-EU nationals. The first category covers non-EU nationals who apply to reside in a Member State to work. The second group includes those who have already been admitted to a Member State for the purpose of work or purposes other than work and who are allowed to work, such as family members of migrant workers, students and scientific researchers.

Since the EU labour mobility legislations are not harmonised, certain Member State legislations affect labour mobility. Most countries of the EU-15 have bilateral agreements with the individual new Member States that allow specific labour migration (seasonal work, contingents for specific industries, and so on) or temporarily limit this migration.

• *Public Procurement*

The government is a key user of IT/ITeS and, therefore, public procurement regulations play a key role in enhancing trade in this sector. Public procurement in India is governed by the General Financial Rules, 2005, which attracts departmental action only in the case of violation. The Indian government is in the process of initiating a comprehensive Public Procurement Bill that would allow transparency in public procurement. In the EU, public procurement is governed under Directive 2008/C 91/02 on the application of Community law on Public Procurement and Concessions to Institutionalised PPP (IPPP) or *Directive on Public Procurement*.[19] The EU is a member of the plurilateral Government Procurement Agreement (GPA) under the WTO and in terms of regulations has a more robust domestic regulation than India. India has observer status in the GPA.

Global and Bilateral Trade

Trade data on India's IT/ITeS sector is provided by different sources, such as NASSCOM, the Reserve Bank of India (RBI) and the United Nations Conference on Trade and Development (UNCTAD). There is slight heterogeneity in the data, but all sources confirm that since 2005, computer and information services account for the highest share in

---

[19] At the Community level, there are no specific rules governing the founding of IPPP. However, in the field of public procurement and concessions, the principle of equal treatment and the specific expressions of that principle, namely, the prohibition of discrimination on grounds of nationality and Articles 43 EC on freedom of establishment and 49 EC on freedom to provide services, are to be applied in cases where a public authority entrusts the supply of economic activities to a third party. More specifically, the principles arising from Article 43 EC and Article 49 EC include not only non-discrimination and equality of treatment, but also transparency, mutual recognition and proportionality. For cases that are covered by the Directives on the co-ordination of procedures for the award of public contracts ('the Public Procurement Directives'), detailed provisions apply. For details, see http://eur-lex.europa.eu/LexUriServ/LexUriServ.do?uri=OJ:C:2008:091:0004:0009:EN:PDF (last accessed on 14 August 2015).

India's total services exports. According to an RBI estimate, during 2010–2011, India's total software services exports (computer services and ITeS/BPO services exports) was US$47.6 billion, of which computer services exports accounted for nearly 73.7 per cent (RBI, 2012). The UNCTAD estimate indicates that in 2012, computer and information exports (including software and hardware) amounted to US$47.8 billion.[20]

On average, large Indian companies such as TCS Limited and Infosys BPO Limited have been exporting computer software services to over 145 countries every year. Table 6.1 shows the exports of some Indian companies and foreign wholly-owned subsidiaries.

India's export market is more robust than the domestic market for the IT/ITeS sector (Figure 6.1).

Between 2005 and 2007, although the European and the US IT/ITeS markets grew at the same rate, the share of the US in India's total trade remained higher than that of the EU. In 2008 and especially in 2009,

Table 6.1
Company-wise Exports of Computer Software Services in 2009–2010

Company Name	Total Exports (US$ million)
Tata Consultancy Services Ltd.	5119.94
Infosys BPO Ltd.	4456.37
Wipro Ltd.	3516.23
Cognizant Technology Solutions India Pvt. Ltd.	3284.36
HCL technologies	2129.85
IBM India Pvt. Ltd.	1357.93
Accenture Services Pvt. Ltd.	940.98
Tech Mahindra Ltd.	905.78
Mphasis Ltd.	816.61
Patni Computer Systems Ltd.	624.61

Source: Electronics and Computer Software Export Promotion Council (2010).

[20] Calculated using data obtained from UNCTAD Database on 'International Trade - Services', available at http://unctadstat.unctad.org/TableViewer/tableView.aspx (accessed on 2 March 2012).

Figure 6.1
Performance of India's IT/ITeS Sector

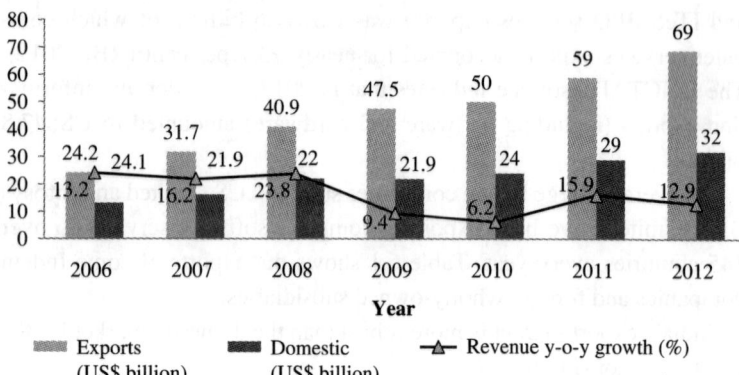

Exports (US$ billion)　Domestic (US$ billion)　Revenue y-o-y growth (%)

Source: Compiled from NASSCOM (different years).

trade with the EU declined (shown in Table 6.2) because of the decline in purchases by European businesses and governments. The EU recession has been relatively harsher than the US recession because of a greater shift towards small-scale outsourcing projects and lower price points in the European IT outsourcing market.

In 2010, the EU, followed by India, ranked first among WTO member countries as an exporter of information and communications services. In 2009, the EU accounted for 58.5 per cent of the world's total exports and India accounted for 19 per cent.[21] Globally, India and EU's trade in the IT/ITeS sector (or as defined by the UNCTAD database, trade in computer and information services) has been growing consistently.

As shown in Table 6.2, a comparison between the global trade figures of India and the EU indicates that both economies are net exporters of computer and information services. The sector has consistently recorded a positive trade balance. Except for the year 2009, which reflects the impact of the global slowdown on trade, the two economies have recorded a consistent rise on both measures of trade in computer and information services.

[21] http://www.wto.org/english/res_e/statis_e/its2011_e/its2011_e.pdf (accessed on 1 June 2015).

Table 6.2
Trade in Computer and Information Services by India and the EU with the Rest of the World for Select Years (in US$ billion)

Computer and Information	India 2000	EU 2000	India 2006	EU 2006	India 2007	EU 2007	India 2008	EU 2008	India 2009	EU 2009	India 2010	EU 2010	India 2011	EU 2011	India 2012	EU 2012
Exports	4.73	24.72	29.09	73.40	37.49	91.03	49.11	112.1	46.66	106.64	56.7	113.3	43.6	128.6	47.8	134.9
Imports	0.58	14.91	1.96	37.18	3.58	45.63	3.79	55.09	2.27	52.60	2.53	54.51	1.46	59.07	2.15	64.6
Trade Balance	4.15	9.81	27.13	36.22	33.91	45.40	45.32	56.96	44.39	54.05	54.1	58.80	41.75	69.58	45.65	70.3

Source: Calculated using data obtained from UNCTAD Database on International Trade—Services, http://unctadstat.unctad.org/ TableViewer/tableView.aspx (accessed on 7 June 2013).

Table 6.3
Trade in Computer and Information Services: EU 27 with India (in US$ billion)

	2003	2004	2005	2006	2007	2008	2009	2010
Total trade with India	(0.17)	(0.26)	(0.44)	(0.45)	(0.71)	0.34	0.62	0.37
Total exports to India	0.09	0.20	0.23	0.46	0.76	2.00	2.41	2.40
Total imports from India	0.27	0.46	0.07	0.12	0.14	1.66	1.80	2.03
India's share in Total trade (%)	(1.69)	(2.52)	(4.14)	(3.01)	(3.59)	1.31	2.37	1.23

Source: Compiled and calculated from the European Commission (2009, 2012c).

Bilateral trade between India and the EU has been fluctuating. As shown in Table 6.3, India had a negative trade balance with the EU in 2010.

Although the trade balance has shown a fluctuating trend, exports by India and the EU to each other's territory have been increasing. Figure 6.2 shows that after 2006, the EU's exports to India rose sharply, whereas India's exports to the EU flattened. In 2009–2010, the EU was India's second largest export market (after the US), accounting for 26.5 per cent of the total trade; of this, the UK alone accounted for 12.4 per cent. Within the EU, the UK has been the most important destination for India's exports followed by other EU Member States such as the Netherlands (7.96 per cent), Hungary (2.80 per cent), France (1.27 per cent) and Finland (0.99 per cent).[22]

The latest data on India's position in the EU's trade in computer and information services is not available, but the US remains the largest trading partner of the EU. India is an important trading partner, but its share is only about 1 per cent.

Although bilateral movement of persons is a key component of trade in IT/ITeS services, the EC, its Member States and India do not have accurate data on the movement of IT professionals between the two

---

[22] Electronics and Computer Software Export Promotion Council (2010).

Figure 6.2
Bilateral Trade between India and the EU in Computer and Information Services

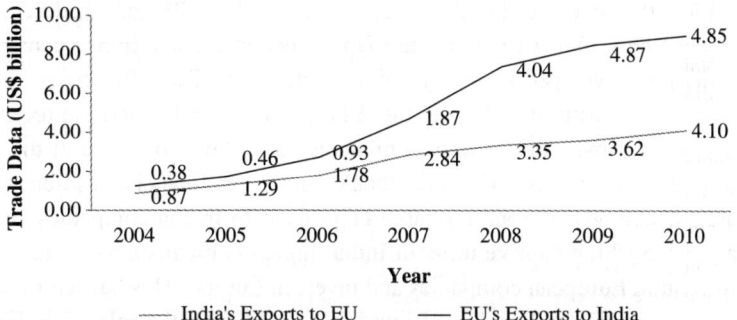

Source: Eurostat, available at http://ec.europa.eu/eurostat/data/database (accessed on 14 August 2015).

regions. Individual companies record the number of people that they send abroad for different types of services such as getting business, attending meetings and project delivery. Most research studies on India–EU trade in IT/ITeS services are, therefore, based on primary surveys (for example, Chanda, 2009) that help capture different modes of trade, barriers and policy requirements.

Key Findings of the Survey

A pan-India survey of 30 Indian and EU companies along with Indian policy-makers, representatives from EU embassies and consulates (such as the British High Commission and the European Commission) and industry chambers (such as FICCI and NASSCOM) was conducted between July 2012 and September 2012. In addition, a stakeholders' consultation was organised jointly with FICCI in New Delhi on how companies visualise the impact of the BTIA and how they make their trade and investment decisions beyond the BTIA. The survey was conducted using open-ended questionnaires through in-depth and one-on-one interviews. Questions were asked about the factors determining growth of trade in IT/ITeS services; perceptions about the markets, government policies and schemes; future market demand; barriers to trade and investments; expectations of the BTIA; and policy recommendations.

Overall, the survey confirmed that India–EU trade in IT/ITeS sector is more than two decades old. It began in the early 1980s and accelerated in the 1990s after the Indian and EU markets liberalised. In due course, India has developed as a major outsourcing hub. The Y2K crisis, the economic downturn following the 9/11 attack in the US and the recent economic downturn did impact bilateral trade flows, but overall there has been an increase. European banks and other financial institutions are increasingly outsourcing large IT projects to Indian companies and are establishing captive units in India. Indian companies have started to acquire European companies and invest in Europe. This has led to an increase in bilateral trade and investment. Although the role of global companies is immense, India's advantage in terms of its abundant pool of labour, huge population of software engineers, education institutions and government support has contributed greatly in shaping this industry.

This can be illustrated using the *Porter Diamond Framework* by Michael E. Porter,[23] as shown in Figure 6.3. The model explains how some nations and industries within nations become competitive on a global scale. The competitive advantage of nations is the outcome of five interlinked factors—factor endowments, demand conditions, related and supporting industries, chances and government support. Using this model, Kapur and Ramamurthi (2001) explained India's success in the IT sector and why clusters emerged in India in tradable services such as software. Here, we use it to explain the evolution of the Indian IT/ITeS industry and the role of EU companies in this evolution. It also helps identify complementarities and areas for future cooperation between India and the EU.

Factor Conditions

Factor conditions or the natural endowments of a nation play a role in developing its competitive advantage. In terms of factor endowments, India is a source of abundant labour. A huge population base of 1.21 billion, as recorded in the Census 2011, provides India with a competitive edge over

---

[23] The model was introduced in his book 'The Competitive Advantage of Nations' based on intensive research of the patterns of competitive success in ten leading trading nations over a period of four years. For details see Porter (1990).

Figure 6.3
Porter Diamond Model

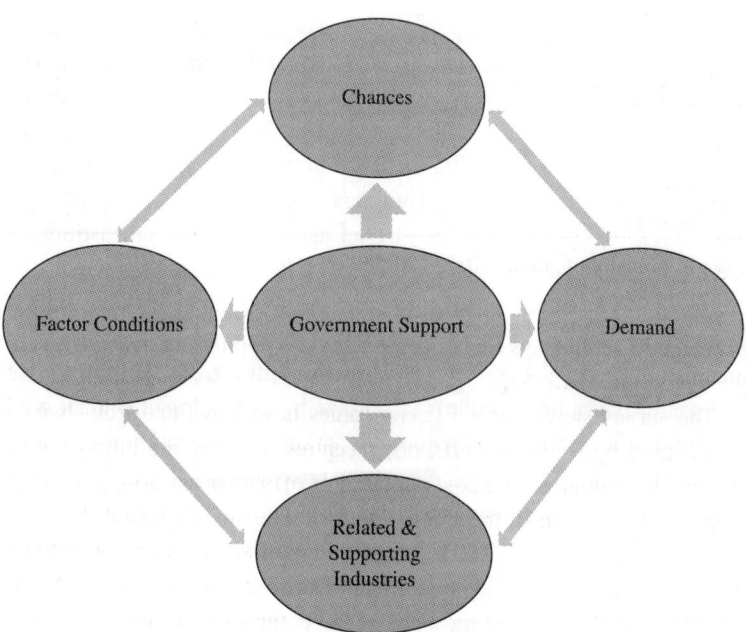

Source: Author's representation from Porter (1990).

countries such as the EU. India's population recorded a decadal growth of 17.64 per cent between the period 2001 and 2011, growing at the rate of 1.64 per cent annually. India's population accounts for 17.5 per cent of the world's population, which is expected to increase to 17.9 per cent by 2030. A large percentage of India's population is literate. In 2011, India's literacy rate was at 74.04 per cent, up from 64 per cent in 2001. Indian states have also shown an improvement in their respective literacy rates. This is especially true of the Indian states that form the IT conglomerate in India (Table 6.4).

India has a large pool of skilled IT personnel. According to NASSCOM, the number of IT graduates and postgraduates increased from 0.48 million in 2008 to 0.71 million in 2011. This makes it relatively easy for companies of all sizes to recruit workers and build development teams in response to client demands. The supply of skilled labour in India is not

Table 6.4
Population and Literacy Profile of Select States (in %)

State	Population Growth Rate	Share in India's Total Population	Literacy Rate
Andhra Pradesh	11.1	7	67.66
Delhi	21.0	1	86.34
Karnataka	15.7	5	75.60
Maharashtra	16.0	9	82.91

Source: Ministry of Home Affairs (2011).

expected to saturate, as 65 per cent of India's population in 2011 was in the age group of 15–64.

The survey showed that EU companies have benefitted from India's labour pool by setting up offshoring centres in India and hiring young Indian IT graduates. The cost per head of offshoring is 30–35 per cent lower in India than in the US or the EU. The survey found that Cap Gemini S.A., which has had a presence in the Indian market for nearly a decade, expanded its employment team from 200 employees in 2001 to 40,000 in 2012. Thus, the presence of EU companies in India has generated substantial employment in India's IT/ITeS sector. It has also led to the movement of high-skilled personnel from EU Member States to India, mostly in managerial and technical positions. They offer a wide range of services including training and dissemination of technical know-how.

The EU faces a labour shortage that has contributed to increased movement of people from India to the EU. Indians go to the EU in multiple capacities—for business, as independent professionals, as intra-corporate transferees or as contractual service suppliers.[24] The survey found that there have been some changes in labour movement; unlike the earlier practice of body shopping, Indian companies now send intra-corporate

[24] Business Visitor (BV) person who visit another country specifically for (a) business negotiations and/or (b) for preparatory work for a short duration to establish a presence; independent professional (IP) is a self-employed person who enters another country to perform a service on contract basis; intra-corporate transferee (ICT) is an employee of a company who transferred from originating country's office to an office of the same company in another country and contractual service supplier (CSS) is an employee of a foreign company who enters another country temporarily in order to perform a service pursuant to a contract.

transferees and contractual service suppliers (who go to work on specific projects) to the EU. The presence and establishment of Indian companies in the EU have further increased the movement of people.

When asked about recent labour movement regulations in the EU and the measures taken by the EU to harmonise the labour market for foreign nationals, survey participants pointed out that although the Blue Card Directive and the Single Permit Directive are a step in the right direction, the gains are greater for individuals than for companies. Also, these Directives look at migration rather than short-term movement. The Directive on conditions of entry and residence for third-country nationals in the framework of an intra-corporate transfer[25] proposed by the EC in 2010 is more beneficial for Indian companies. It will help Indian and EU companies in several ways. Indian companies will have a common set of rules and requirements, and EU companies will have better and faster access to global talent to meet their staffing needs for managers, specialists and graduate trainees, which will help it secure a knowledge-based and innovative economy that attracts investment, thereby creating jobs. In addition to fast tracking the entry procedure and the single application for a combined work and residence permit, the Directive proposes to include more attractive residence conditions for families of professionals and enhance mobility within the EU. Intra-corporate transferees will also benefit from the same working conditions offered to posted workers whose employer is established within EU territory.

Demand Conditions

Strong and high-quality domestic demand can improve the competitiveness of local export companies. The survey found that the structure of India's domestic IT/ITeS industry is pyramidal with very few large enterprises at the top and a huge pool of SMEs at the bottom of the pyramid. The SMEs engage with domestic companies to provide IT services and also work with the few large firms as subcontractors. This laid the foundation for domestic demand. With the entry of MNCs into India, several of these SMEs either directly engaged with them or became subcontractors to the large enterprises working with the MNCs. As a result, exports of IT/ITeS services increased. According to the survey, although

[25] http://eur-lex.europa.eu/LexUriServ/LexUriServ.do?uri=COM:2010:0378:FIN:EN:PDF

at present the exports of the IT/ITeS sector are greater than domestic demand, domestic demand is rising at a rapid pace and the share of domestic revenue in total revenue is rising.

In recent years, there has been an increase in the use of IT services across all sectors in India. Increase in domestic demand has helped Indian companies grow despite the global slowdown. It has also helped them consolidate. Indian companies that earlier provided only outsourcing services such as voice-based services and data processing are consolidating their offerings to provide a broader range of services. This saves clients from approaching different service providers for different services. The survey found that several IT graduates have begun their own start-ups. The total number of start-ups in India is now around 10,000, with 5,000 start-ups in Bangalore, followed by Mumbai, Delhi and Chennai. Several Indian start-ups are now moving up the value chain and providing more integrated and sophisticated services to their clients. To provide more sophisticated services to clients worldwide, Indian entrepreneurs innovated various online database application platforms that facilitate the design, delivery and use of data applications such as Software-as-a-Service (SaaS) and Platform-as-a-Service (PaaS) using only a web browser.

At the same time, with the EU's expansion, the nature of demand from European companies has been evolving, especially from countries in Eastern Europe. As a result, Indian IT/ITeS firms has evolved from the stage when EU companies established captive units in India to the emergence of Indian companies acting as venture funded third-party IT/ITeS firms, and Indian companies have expanded their reach in continental Europe with the help of acquisitions or by hiring local residents in senior roles.

Related and Supportive Industries

India's education sector has contributed greatly to India's development as a global outsourcing hub. There are 3,393 engineering colleges in India including 16 globally acclaimed Indian Institutes of Technology (IITs),[26] which have helped create a large number of skilled IT professionals and meet the growing needs of this sector. According to a report by the All

---

[26] As of August 2015. For details see http://mhrd.gov.in/iits (accessed on 14 August 2015).

India Council for Technical Education (AICTE), India produced 4.6 lakh engineers in 2004–2005, of which 31 per cent were computer engineers and in 2005–2006, 5.2 lakh engineers graduated. Among engineering colleges, 65 per cent are in the south of India (close to IT hubs like Bangalore) and 35 per cent in the north. Engineering colleges in India have a capacity of 14.85 lakh seats. The survey found that campus placements and collaboration between universities and companies have given a major boost to the employment rate of this sector.

Newer centres of engineering excellence in cities such as Indore, Jodhpur, Jaipur and Bhopal are emerging, with the government adding new IITs and National Institutes of Technology (NIT) to the existing list in Tier II cities and with the emergence of private institutes. As a result, hiring from Tier II and III cities is increasing. Even industry associations have engaged in various initiatives for skill creation. For instance, NASSCOM has developed the NASSCOM Assessment of Competence (NAC) to assess and certify IT professionals. There is strong interaction between industries, industry associations and education institutes in developing skills for the IT/ITeS sector. On-the-job training offered by both Indian and European companies has enhanced skill levels in India. Some Indian IT training institutes such as NIIT have globalised and have offices in EU Member States such as the UK, Belgium, the Netherlands, Germany and Spain.

The Indian government is encouraging foreign investment in the education sector and to this effect several bills including the Foreign Educational Institutions Bill, 2010 are being mulled over. Once the Bill is passed, the sector will benefit greatly, since it will encourage EU–India collaboration with universities that can enhance skill levels in both economies. In fact, a few Indian students pointed out that they have greatly benefitted from the UK–India Education and Research Initiative (UKIERI), which exposes them to global best standards and greater employment opportunities.

Survey participants said that the rapid growth of the telecommunications sector in terms of the use of technologies such as broadband, video conferencing, instant messaging and Internet telephony has supported the growth of the IT/ITeS sector in India.

The survey also highlighted the growing role of EU–India collaborative research programmes initiated under the Euro–India Research

Centre (EIRC) in the growth of the IT/ITeS sector. The EIRC helps Indian organisations access and benefit from EU funding in R&D. It provides a permanent platform for cooperation between India and the EU that promotes cooperation in research. In India, the National Contact Point (NCP) is the entity that supports scientific and business communities in accessing European funds for R&D.

In addition, over 140 Indian research organisations have been selected to fund around 90 EU projects under the Seventh Framework Programme (FP7). The EU has now launched Horizon 2020, a seven year research and innovation programme (2014-2020) for funding research projects across the world.

Chances

The reforms since the 1990s in sectors such as telecommunications facilitated growth in the sector. India is an active proponent of services liberalisation, especially liberalisation of IT/ITeS services in the WTO and has signed several bilateral agreements to encourage foreign investments in the services sector. India is willing to bind the liberal autonomous regime in IT/ITeS in its trade agreements that give operational certainty to foreign companies. India has autonomously liberalised several services sectors for foreign investments and the reform process is ongoing. More recently, India has partially liberalised sectors such as multi-brand retail, and there are opportunities for IT/ITeS companies to provide back-end services to foreign retailers.

The survey found that economic and policy reforms in infrastructure are likely, and IT services are expected to act as the strategic lever to bring efficiencies in these sectors. For instance, in the retail sector, there is tremendous scope for IT diffusion through back-end infrastructure upgrades, the revamp of supply chains and augmentation of front-end customer experiences. Even in the aviation sector, a surge of investments in the BPO-based customer service operations for airlines is expected. Hence, there is immense scope for EU companies to benefit from such policy changes.

Another factor that has supported India's image as a global outsourcing hub is India's resilience during both the global slowdown and the Eurozone crisis. Indian companies highlighted that the crisis led to the depreciation of the rupee, which benefitted the IT services sector. The EU companies highlighted that although there is a downturn in investments due to the slowdown, in the IT/ITeS sector, companies have or are planning to set up more captive units in India. The survey found that between 2008 and 2010, 37 new captive units were set up in India, of which 23 were set up in 2010. At present, there are over 750 MNC captive units in India.

The majority of the EU companies highlighted that the Indian public procurement market is untapped; it offers attractive investment opportunities and they are seeking greater market access in terms of access to the state-level procurement market and raising the threshold limit for contracts. The Indian companies were asked if they would be willing to invest in the government procurement market of EU Member States. They pointed out that the public procurement markets are different in the two economies. Some of the responses highlighting the differences across the Indian, UK and Western European government procurement markets are shown in Table 6.5.

While the UK is a fairly accessible market, Western European countries are relatively untapped and difficult to access. Indian companies have the opportunity to enjoy an early mover advantage and access the public procurement market in Western Europe, if it opens up after the BTIA is signed between the two economies. Since it is difficult to break into this market, they will have to develop a robust market entry strategy.

Role of the Government

Support from the Indian government for both domestic and foreign players in the IT/ITeS sector has acted as a major catalyst to its growth. Major fiscal incentives provided by the government in this sector have been for EOUs, STPs and SEZs. The government earmarked IT investment regions for special benefits and rebates and various start-ups are being supported through subsidies on capital expenditure.

Several companies highlighted that government support in the form of a 10-year tax holiday to IT firms setting up ventures in notified IT parks and SEZs and exemption from the Industrial Disputes Act, 1947 have also contributed to this growth. As a result, EU companies have enjoyed the benefits of low-operation costs, higher profit margins and a hassle-free labour market. Both the Indian and EU companies pointed out that their scale of investments has increased and they have started investing in developing innovation centres and R&D facilities. They

Table 6.5

Public Procurement Market in India, the UK and Western Europe

Parameters	India	UK	Western Europe
Onshore delivery	No preference. Depends on connections.	Majority (but less than 100%)—emphasis on offshoring	Onshore delivery conditions apply
Lobbying	Important. Some contracts are through lobbying, even with tendering process		
Emphasis on brand awareness and localisation	Brand awareness is low, but there is a push towards localisation of jobs and contracts	Very important	Important
Local job creation	Coming up as an important condition with the government emphasis on NREGA and other schemes.	Very important	Important
Transparent procedures—Open bidding, competition	Not very transparent; open bidding held but corruption continues to plague process	Transparent and ensures open competition	
Maintenance of open books—disclosing margins, listing subcontractors, onsite components of project, etc.	Present, but only in name. Several details are often not kept in hard copy	Yes	

Central government level-Delays in decision-making and gestation period	Takes a long time. Most delays last for years.	Decision-making takes long	Long gestation period
Scrutiny at state level	Lax scrutiny	Low scrutiny	
Cap on outsourced public sector contracts	No cap	£100 million cap on outsourced public sector contracts to avoid overdependence on a single service provider and encourage SMEs through subcontracting	
Language barriers	Not a barrier	Not a barrier	High—Delays caused in fulfilling RFP procedures
Labour laws	Obscure, with different states having different labour laws in various forms.		Stricter than the UK; not many contracts are awarded on the condition that government employees will be used instead of winner's own employees

Source: Compiled from NASSCOM (2011).

pointed out that these benefits have strengthened the ancillary industries and even the supporting education sector.

The EU Member States also offer various incentives to investments in the sector. The survey found that in order to increase R&D activities in the information and communications technology industry, the German government has taken the initiative to invest and spend around 3 per cent of the national GDP on R&D. The French government has also extended fiscal incentives such as complete abolition of local business tax from 1 January 2010 for productive investment. The French government has an attractive tax policy for investors. It has completely abolished taxes such as annual fixed tax and stock exchange tax for investors. Various Indian companies reported that they have benefitted from these and other incentives.

The survey found that, on the one hand, Indian companies face problems because the EU Data Protection Directive is very restrictive; on the other hand, EU companies complain that they feel data sharing is not secure in India. To overcome this, the Indian government further amended the existing Information Technology (Amendment) Act, 2008 in the year 2011. Indian companies expect that after this amendment, India will be accorded Safe Harbor Nation status by the EU and it will become easier to do business. The EU companies expressed interest in open access to the Indian public procurement market.

Barriers

Both Indian companies in the EU and EU companies in India face barriers, but the barriers are market-specific rather than company-specific. For instance, both Indian and EU companies refer to certain common barriers in each other's market; addressing these barriers will not only enhance trade but will also enable the domestic sector to grow. Some of the issues are related to the bilateral negotiations. There is limited data and secondary information on trade. Since neither India nor the EU systematically collects data on the bilateral movement of IT professionals, it is difficult to estimate the volume of temporary movements of service providers. This data is crucial for the ongoing negotiations since India and the EU are negotiating the number of service providers that can be given liberal entry to the EU market; without data, the basis for ascertaining the number of professionals permitted to enter the EU is contentious.

Another issue in the context of the ongoing India–EU bilateral negotiations is the difficulty of ensuring comprehensive coverage of the sector. The nature of IT services is complex since these services are cross-sectoral and have been evolving. Despite several modifications to the UNCPC, some BPO services, such as payroll, customer care service and web-enabled technical support services for electronic equipment, do not have a corresponding entry in the W/120. In addition, services like advertising, placement and supply of personnel and translation and interpretation are related to BPO services. These are classified under CPC 87 of the UNCPC. However, broadly CPC 84 of the UNCPC corresponds to IT/BPO services. Hence, in order to make commitments in BPO services, India and the EU need to make commitments in both CPC 84 and 87 at the two-digit level. Unless there is comprehensive sector coverage, certain sectors may not be liberalised under the bilateral agreement.

In addition to these common barriers, there are country-specific barriers that are discussed below.

Barriers in India

With the growing importance of the Indian IT/ITeS sector in the global market, the demand for IT products and services is rising at a considerable rate. While the demand seems robust, it is important that the supply-side constraints are dealt with. The main concerns are summarised below.

Underdeveloped Infrastructure

Survey participants said that inadequate infrastructure facilities such as the availability of uninterrupted power supply, lack of well-constructed roads, airports and mass transportation connectivity and traffic congestion, among others, are escalating the operational costs of IT/ITeS companies in India. Companies have to invest in upgrading infrastructure facilities such as setting up in-house electricity generation units. In fact, arbitrary government policies such as the closure of Bangalore airport in early 2012 for maintenance also raised operating costs and caused delays. The concentration of the IT sector in a few states has led to overcrowding and saturation of infrastructure facilities. Rising real estate costs is another cause for concern. Due to the poor supporting infrastructure, the rate of IT adoption is low in rural areas and in sectors like agriculture. Lack of adequate infrastructure facilities has generated regional heterogeneities in terms of the IT industry spread, which tend to locate in large metro cities. Since most of the prospective states, in terms of investment and presence of IT firms, are near saturation, foreign players are expanding their operations across India's competitors such as Vietnam and the Philippines. In fact, within the EU, Member States such as Romania, where Indian companies are trying to relocate, will offer competition to India in future.

Inadequate Supply of Skilled Workforce

Although India has a large workforce, there is a shortage of qualified and trained manpower, high attrition rates and rising salaries. Approximately 5,000 people are needed every year to meet the demand generated in the IT/ITeS sector, but the total production from educational and training institutes is only a third of this figure.[27] The skill levels and employability of the existing pool is diminishing (CRISIL, 2010). According to the survey, this has been the trend over the past four to five years. The time taken to train students from acclaimed institutes such as the Indian Institute of Technology (IIT) is the same as that required to train non-IIT graduates. The number of regional engineering colleges/private colleges (approximately 300) in India is insufficient and the level of skills that they impart is below the required global standards.[28] This is leading to a supply-side crunch and companies are offering high salaries to retain the existing personnel and attract new ones. Job hopping due to attractive salaries is increasing the costs of frequently hiring and training employees. According to a Hewitt report,[29] the IT/ITeS sector projects an average salary increase of 10.1 per cent for 2013. While urban human capital resources are becoming saturated, human capital in the rural areas is not appropriately skilled and has limited access to education and training institutes. The rise in labour costs and shortage of adequate skills will

[27] Statistical Year Book, 2009–2010, Electronics and Computer Software Export Promotion Council.

[28] http://articles.economictimes.indiatimes.com/2011-10-05/news/30246922_1_iit-students-indian-institutes-coaching-classes

[29] Aon Hewitt 17th Annual Salary Increase Survey 2013, available at http://www.aon.com/india/attachments/Aon_Hewitt_SIS_2013_Feb_20_2013_release.pdf (accessed on 1 June 2015).

reduce India's competitiveness in the global market and drive companies to other investment destinations.

Regulatory Bottlenecks

The IT/ITeS sector is affected by different government regulations at the central, state and local levels. Regulatory uncertainties in allied sectors particularly those related to spectrum allocation such as second generation (2G) and third generation (3G) licensing in telecommunications have created operational uncertainties. Several Indian and EU companies pointed out that uncertainty related to government incentives such as the discontinuation of the exemption granted to the IT/ITeS sector from adhering to the Industrial Employment (Standing Orders) Act, 1946 will adversely affect the sector. Companies will be required to comply with social security schemes and minimum wage requirements. While this will protect the labour pool in this sector, it will increase the operating costs of companies.

Information security is also a major problem. The existing acts—Information Technology (Amendment) Act, 2008 and the Copyright Act, 1957—are weak. The amendment to the Copyright Act is overdue and the enforcement mechanism needs to be strengthened. Several respondents pointed to delays in litigation and lack of provisions for piracy cases as key issues. Survey participants said that the General Financial Rules, 2005, that govern public procurement in India are weak. These rules do not create any rights in favour of the public or potential suppliers. Nor do they provide a fair and effective mechanism for dispute resolution, thus virtually denying any recourse against unfair and arbitrary decisions of the procuring entities. A robust Public Procurement Act is required if the government plans to allow EU companies access to the Indian procurement market.

During the survey, various IT/ITeS companies located in SEZs pointed out that their tax liability and, thus, costs have increased with the introduction of the Minimum Alteration Tax of 18.5 per cent with effect from April 2012. The industry views this as a move to discourage investments in SEZs that are attractive because of the tax exemption.

Lack of R&D Initiatives

The main growth in the IT/ITeS sector is in software and BPO services, and India mainly exports low-technology products. This is because

India lacks adequate R&D facilities and initiatives. India's total R&D investment is only 0.8 per cent of GDP, which is very low compared to countries like China (1.6 per cent) and Japan (3.5 per cent) (Battelle, 2012). Even though India is emerging as a hub for outsourcing and IT software services, investments in R&D, particularly by the private sector, still remain low and are largely directed at the outsourcing market. The sector is heavily dependent on foreign technology due to limited domestic innovation; this increases operation costs. New inventions are making global markets highly competitive. For instance, software robots and humanoids invented at the UK-based Blue Prism Ltd. automate and deliver IT projects at a cost that is less than one-fourth the billing rates of engineers from TCS and Infosys.[30] This is likely to displace jobs for Indian IT professionals. To combat this, R&D facilities in India need a paradigm shift from tinkering with low-level procedures to using research in artificial intelligence, robotics and speech recognition, among others.

Weak Hardware vis-à-vis Software Sector

In India, both in terms of exports and the domestic market, software ousts the hardware sector. Although increased government initiatives have driven up FDI inflows and domestic demand in the hardware sector, India has a comparative advantage only in consumer electronics; for other segments, India is dependent on imports. In the IT/ITeS sector, for both finished and intermediate components, Indian manufacturers rely on foreign partners such as Unisys Corporation and Hewlett-Packard Company. Since the hardware and software industries are complementary, it is important to develop the Indian hardware industry in order to reduce dependence on external sources and develop India as a complete hub for IT software and hardware services and products. This will attract higher investments that are at present routed to countries such as Taiwan, Philippines, China and Thailand.

Other

Other barriers, such as trade union demonstrations and labour unrest/strikes, exchange rate fluctuations, changes in the domestic tax regime including retrospective taxes and uncertainties over the direct tax code

---

[30] http://epaper.livemint.com/epaper/viewer.aspx

and the single goods and services tax (GST), adversely affect the operations of foreign players.

Barriers in the EU

At present, both India and the EU have strong trade ties in the IT/ITeS sector and continue to have an interest in each other's economy. However, the EU's trade policies are somewhat restrictive and certain broad issues hinder free trade in services between India and the EU. The EU lacks a single market for trade in services and this is the foundation for most of the barriers discussed below.

Barriers to Labour Mobility

1. *Work Permits and Visas*

   In the EU, visa and work permit regulations are not harmonised and vary across Member States. The survey participants pointed out that even for temporary stay and business visits, separate visas are required for states outside the Schengen region. Also, with a Schengen visa, service providers have to first enter the country that issues the visa and the visa is for a short period. Countries have different immigration and entry rules and regulations that constrain movement across Member States for professionals from Indian companies that have multiple offices in the EU. Employees of Indian origin posted in the EU offices find it difficult to visit plants and factories spread across different Member States due to the state-specific visa requirements. From the perspective of service providers, the movement of people is based on requirements. For instance, at the beginning of a project, Indian professionals need business visas for short visits to understand the project, but to implement and monitor the project, longer stays are needed. However, the visa and work permit regimes of different Member States do not take into account the requirements of the IT/ITeS sector. State-specific regulations and delays in issuing visas make the process time-consuming and cumbersome and cause operational difficulties for both Indian companies and their clients. Some survey participants pointed out that it is more difficult to obtain visas, work permits and resident permits for some EU countries than for the US. This finding is in line with other survey-based studies (Upadhya, 2006).

In an attempt to harmonise the EU labour market, the Blue Card Directive was introduced in 2009. However, this Directive has limitations, since each Member State will maintain the right to determine the number of immigrant workers that can be admitted into the domestic labour market through the Blue Card. In addition, while a few Member States such as Austria, Cyprus and Greece have not yet transposed the provisions of the EU Blue Card into their respective national legislations, others such as the UK and the Netherlands are not in favour of the policy. As a result, Indian companies that have to move their employees across EU Member States still have to meet cumbersome legislative requirements. Across Member States, visa processing can vary from one week to six months. There is no provision for long-term multiple-entry business visas, and there are restrictive conditions on the entry of dependents and visa extensions and renewals.

The EU *Single Permit Directive* (2011/98/EU*)* also has limitations. It does not cover long-term residents, seasonal workers or intra-corporate transferees and posted workers. If the intra-corporate transferee Directive is not implemented soon, Indian IT professionals will continue to face problems during entry and movement across EU Member States.

2. *Economic Needs Tests and Other Labour Market Regulations*
   In the EU's Revised Offer, the services market has been liberalised, but there are still certain restrictions that inhibit the movement of professionals between India and the EU. The economic needs test (ENT) or labour market test[31] are mandatory for non-EU nationals applying for jobs in the EU. There are rigid labour market restrictions in Member States like Germany on hiring and firing workers, working hours and unemployment compensations. In some Member States, there are minimum wage requirements.

3. *Changes in Immigration Policies*
   Of late, especially after the economic slowdown, there have been sudden and sporadic changes in immigration policy without

---

[31] ENT requirement is that a firm employing a foreign worker has to prove that a local employee is not available for that specific job.

prior notice. For instance, in April 2012, the UK government discontinued the Tier I Post-Study Work Visa for Indian students; there is a cap on the number of Tier II visas issued to Indian nationals and an increase in the base salary of professionals eligible to get a visa for five years.

4. *Restrictive Mode 4 Commitments in Trade Agreements*
In the WTO Revised Offers and in their respective bilateral trade agreements, India's Mode 4 offers and commitments seems to be more liberal for each category of service providers than those of the EU. For instance, in the EU's Revised Offer in the Doha Round, a Business Visitor (BV)[32] is only permitted to stay for 90 days, while Contractual Service Suppliers (CSS)[33] and Independent Professionals (IP)[34] can stay for six months in a year. On the other hand, in its Revised Offer, India has offered to allow business visitors to stay for 180 days in a maximum period of five years and this has also been scheduled in India's commitments to Republic of Korea. India also allows CSSs and IPs for one year. In addition, there are slight differences in the definition of two of the four broad categories under the horizontal commitments. The EU, unlike India, does not cover Executives[35] under ICTs in its horizontal commitments; instead it covers Graduate Trainees,[36] whose stay is restricted to one year.

---

[32] A person who visits another country specifically for business negotiations and/or for preparatory work for establishing a presence for a short duration.

[33] Employee of a company who is transferred from an office in the country of origin to an office of the same company in another country.

[34] A person of a country who enters another country to perform a service on contract basis is called a self-employed person.

[35] In India's Revised Offer, TN/S/O/IND/Rev.1, 24 August 2005, Executives are defined as persons who are in senior positions within a juridical person, including a branch, who primarily direct the management, have wide decision-making powers and are either members of the board of directors or receive directions from the board or the general body of shareholders (WTO 2005c).

[36] In the EU's Revised Offer, TN/S/O/EEC/Rev.1, 29 June 2005, Graduate Trainees are defined as persons with a university degree who are transferring for career development purposes or to obtain training in business techniques and methods. The recipient country in the EU may be required to submit a training programme covering the duration of the stay for prior approval, demonstrating that the purpose of the stay is training (WTO 2005b).

5. *Other Barriers to Labour Movement*
    Labour movement is adversely affected by economic slowdowns, unemployment in the domestic market and anti-outsourcing sentiments. Non-familiarity with the European culture and language also impacts labour mobility.

Barriers to Investment

In the EU, a company is treated differently based on its mode of operation. A foreign company is treated as an EU company only if it is a wholly owned subsidiary; and setting up a wholly owned subsidiary involves high costs. This restricts companies that operate on a project-by-project basis. This limitation is highlighted in the EU's Revised Offer to the WTO. Other restrictions in the EU's Revised Offer and the survey are given in Box 6.1. The survey participants pointed out that investment requirements vary across the Member States and it takes two to six months to establish an office. They also highlighted the high incidence of corporate tax and stringent accounting and auditing requirements that add to the cost

---

Box 6.1: Barriers to Investment

Restrictions across all EU Member States
- Subsidiaries of companies from third countries do not enjoy national treatment unless an *effective and continuous link* with the economy of a Member State can be established.
- Branches, representative offices and agencies of companies from third countries do not enjoy national treatment.

Restrictions by Individual Member States
- Hungary, Poland and Sweden impose legal entity-related restrictions.
- Initial entry as a branch is restricted in Hungary.
- Poland restricts the establishment of a branch.
- Finland has specified market access limitations for all sectors (except telecommunications) on citizenship and residency requirements for Board of Directors.
- Restrictions on purchase and rentals of real estate in Poland, Hungary, Ireland, the Czech Republic and Finland.
- Residency and legal entity requirements in Sweden.

Source: Compiled from the EC's Revised Offer, TN/S/O/EEC/Rev.1, 29 June 2005 WTO (2005b) and the survey.

---

of operations. India has signed social security agreements with Member States including Germany, France, Belgium, the Netherlands, the Czech Republic, Denmark, Hungary, Luxembourg and Norway.[37] In the case of other Member States, especially the UK, which has the maximum number of Indian IT/ITeS professionals, non-EU nationals have to make social security contributions, even if they do not avail of its benefits.

Barriers to Data Protection

Data Protection Directive 95/46/EC restricts the transfer of personal data to locations outside the EU unless the importing country ensures adequate data protection under domestic regulations or international commitments. Regulations for data protection in the EU are cumbersome since they require the creation of government data protection agencies, registration of databases with those agencies and, in some cases, prior approval before personal data processing can be done. The EC, which is empowered to identify whether a third country ensures an adequate level of data protection, has identified a limited number of countries, but India is not among them. As a result, Indian companies and even subcontracting parties have to meet the lengthy requirements laid down under the EU Directive on data protection. These laws are not simple and impose various legal barriers on Indian companies. For instance, Indian companies engaged in cloud computing can transfer data within the EU or to locations outside the EU only after ensuring that such transfers are covered by legally binding agreements such as binding corporate rules (BCRs). Adhering to them is complicated and expensive since drafting the codes while transfers are being made requires approval from the national and other multiple authorities of each Member State. The survey found that Indian call centre companies that work with live customer data and jobs that involve outsourcing live and confidential data on European citizens to India are the most affected due to the data protection regulations.

The Indian government amended the Information Technology Act, 2000 in 2011 and the new rules are in line with the safe harbour principles adopted by the US (see Table 6A.1 in Appendix). The EU has accorded the US the status of a Safe Harbor Nation, but India has not received similar status from the EU.

---

[37] Deloitte (2011).

Barriers to Public Procurement

Survey participants pointed out that the Indian government is mulling over the Public Procurement Bill. The Indian government plans to open the public procurement market to European companies on the condition that Indian companies can also bid for European government contracts. The provisions are yet to be finalised, but there are some concerns for Indian companies. First, the EU is a member of the WTO's Government Procurement Agreement (GPA) and has also entered into public procurement agreements with countries such as Chile, Mexico and the Caribbean Forum (CARIFORUM, which is a subgroup of the African, Caribbean and Pacific Group of States). In contrast, India has not entered into any bilateral agreements and is not a member of the GPA. Hence, Indian companies that bid for European government contracts will be governed under each Member State's legislation, since there is no uniform mandate for EU Member States. Second, Indian companies might have to face severe competition from other foreign companies that are more aware of the market and the procedures for bidding. Several foreign companies have subsidiaries in the EU that raise bids on behalf of the parent company under indirect cross-border procurement because the chances of winning are higher than in direct cross-border procurement,[38] as subsidiary companies have access to local expertise and inputs and the transaction costs are lower. Indian companies that do not have subsidiaries in the Member State where the bid is opened might be at a disadvantage. Third, the EU government has reserved 25 per cent of the contracts for domestic SMEs. This condition discriminates against Indian companies.

Apart from these EC-wide restrictions, there are restrictions specific to a Member State. The survey found that the UK government imposes a limit on the value of outsourced public sector contracts. A US$163 million (£100 million) cap is imposed on outsourced contracts to avoid overdependence on a single service provider and to encourage SMEs through subcontracting.

According to the USTR (2012), the lack of transparency in awarding contracts is common across Member States such as Bulgaria, Germany,

---

[38] Under direct cross-border procurement, the parent company residing outside the native country bids for a contract raised by the native country government.

Greece, Hungary and Ireland. The governments of these and other Member States such as Portugal and Austria tend to favour EU firms. Foreign companies are more successful when they bid as part of a consortium or joint venture with EU firms. Other problems include long and cumbersome procedures and legal formalities, budgetary decision delays, lack of clarity in tendering documentation and opacity in bid evaluation.

Other

High barriers to entry in Western Europe such as onsite delivery conditions, strict labour laws, such as compulsory hiring of EU nationals irrespective of the skill disparity, and multilingual requirements make the market restrictive for Indian companies.

The BTIA and Beyond: Need for Reforms

The preceding discussion confirms the existence of trade and investment complementarities between India and the EU. These complementarities can be enhanced by removing barriers to trade and investment under the BTIA. However, both economies should also initiate some domestic policy reforms that will not only support their commitments under the BTIA, but will also enable the sector to grow irrespective of the trade agreement.

To ensure uniform development of the IT/ITeS sector and to create employment opportunities, the Indian government needs to formulate policies that focus on infrastructure and skill development across all states so that foreign players can set up operations across the country. To avoid overcrowding in a few cities and saturation of the infrastructure, the focus should be on developing Tier II and III cities. By establishing IT parks in these cities, the government can reduce inter-state migration and increase employment opportunities in Tier II and III cities. This needs to be complemented with higher investments in infrastructure in terms of better road connectivity, power supply, optical fibre infrastructure, and so on.

The Indian government also needs to invest in enhancing education standards and skill levels to overcome the problem of declining skill levels among IT graduates. The focus should be on strengthening education standards at primary and secondary school level along with collaboration between Indian and foreign universities to create a pool of skilled IT professionals. The government should encourage collaboration between the government/universities and foreign universities, especially from the EU. This will expose Indian students to global standards and increase their employability. The government should also set employment standards in collaboration with IT companies. The IT companies can outline the skills required in the IT/ITeS sector, which should be adopted in the curriculum of education institutes. A greater focus on developing and promoting R&D facilities in educational institutes such as the Indian Institute of Technology (IIT) and in IT companies will automatically increase the skill levels of students and professionals.

Skill development can be complemented with greater innovation in this sector. The Indian government needs to support investments in developing R&D facilities in India. It could initiate programmes similar to FP7. Greater collaboration with attractive benefits can be offered to international institutes to encourage innovation. R&D facilities should focus on inventing hardware technology to support India's hardware industry. This will foster domestic demand and supply.

To keep track of the movement of IT professionals between India and the EU, a robust data collection mechanism is imperative. This is especially important when the two countries are negotiating on the number of Indian professionals who would be allowed to enter the EU. The Indian government needs to identify a department that should maintain such data so that India can strengthen its negotiating position in the bilateral negotiations. Category-wise data should be collected on the number of Indian professionals entering the EU each year and vice versa.

To facilitate greater bilateral trade in the IT/ITeS services sector, the EU needs to relax restrictions on visas issued to Indian IT professionals. The one-year limit on a student visa can be removed and they should be allowed to work in the EU for at least one year after completing their education. The employer can then assess whether or not the students should be granted a work permit for an extended stay. This will provide EU Member States access to high-skilled IT professionals.

At present, one of the pressing issues restricting labour movement in the EU is lack of harmonisation across Member States. To overcome this, the EU needs to harmonise labour market policies across all Member States in order to ease the movement of Indian IT professionals across Member States. This should be allowed at least for ICT and business visitors, since they need to make temporary visits to different Member States.

Further, indirect barriers such as those related to data protection and public procurement can be overcome if the EU accords India the status of a Safe Harbor Nation. At the same time, while Indian authorities need to be more vigilant in the implementation of data security regulations, Indian companies need to take steps to ensure data privacy.

Also, the EU can adopt a liberal policy towards India when it opens the EU public procurement market to Indian companies. As discussed in the previous section, Indian companies may be at a disadvantage compared to EU companies and other companies from GPA members; they can be initially offered a five-year exemption from the US\$162 million cap on outsourced contracts and SME reservation.

To overcome regulatory bottlenecks, the Indian government needs to expedite the implementation of the Public Procurement Bill and Foreign Educational Institutions Bill, 2010. The units in SEZs should be given incentives such as exemption from the minimum alternate tax, which has been withdrawn. Additional benefits should be given to SEZ units that have high employment and low attrition rates to compensate for the rise in operation costs resulting from these regulatory changes. Since there are no disciplines on subsidies in services and most developing countries continue to subsidise IT/ITeS sector, India should also continue to subsidise the sector. This can retain investments and attract new investors to this sector. The government also needs to modify the Information Technology Rules, 2011 to include an enforcement clause that ensures accountability. An independent authority should be identified that clearly defines the procedures and penalties in the case of failure to comply. This is important to make the Data Protection clause meet international standards.

The EU also needs to take steps to streamline the regulatory mechanism. It is essential that all Member States, especially the UK, transpose their labour market provisions to the Blue Card Directive. The EU needs to expedite the implementation of the ICT Directive in order to harmonise and facilitate the movement of ICTs across Member States. For greater transparency, Indian companies can register with the EC and their employees can be granted visas based on prior company certification and authentication. This will reduce time and effort in issuing repeat visas and hasten the movement of professionals, especially in the case of temporary and frequent visits. In addition, the EU can revise its WTO Revised Offer to include Executives under the ICT category of its horizontal commitments. The ENT requirement should also be phased out. There is a need to harmonise the EU market to introduce single window clearance to fast track both the movement of natural persons (Mode 4) and investment approvals for establishing commercial presence (Mode 3) in EU Member States. Visa issuance guidelines and timelines and investment procedures and timelines should be harmonised across Member States.

Some measures can also be taken at the company level to facilitate trade and investment. As shown in Figure 6.4, the strategy of Indian companies to enter the EU market should involve building strong relationships in the EU market. The Indian IT/ITeS companies largely operate on an outsourcing model and have failed to develop strong onsite delivery models. For greater resilience, the industry should focus on moving up the value chain, expanding their global presence and strengthening onsite delivery models. For this, they need to build resources internally

Figure 6.4
Steps to be Taken by Indian Companies to Access the European Market

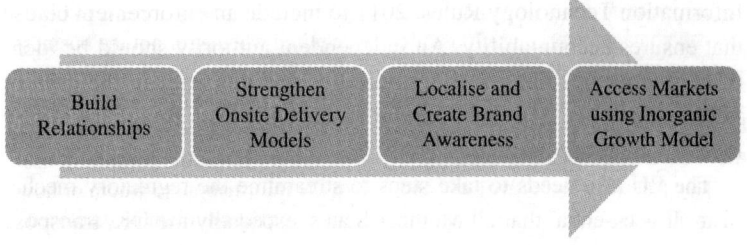

Source: Author's compilation.

by training local talent and customising and creating brand awareness. Using this strategy, Indian companies should target unexplored Western EU Member States. To overcome multilingual barriers, local hiring and training should be the key. Companies can adopt the inorganic growth strategy that involves acquiring domestic companies in the Western EU region so that it is easy to access the market.

EU companies, especially SMEs, that dominate the sector and have been the worst hit by the financial crisis, need to strengthen their position. They can bid for public procurement projects and also enter into partnership with Indian SMEs. They can conduct R&D and share technical know-how with Indian SMEs and access third-country clients jointly. This will strengthen their position and increase market access. Both economies have a lot to offer to each other, but in order to facilitate that they have to negotiate for greater market access and the removal of restrictions on Mode 4 commitments.

Appendix

Table 6A.1
Comparative Analysis of the US–EU Safe Harbor Framework and Information Technology Rules, 2011

S. No.	The US–EU Safe Harbor Framework's Requirements	India's Offering—Information Technology Rules, 2011
1.	Notice Organisations must notify individuals about the purposes for which they collect and use information about them. They must provide information about how individuals can contact the organisation with any inquiries or complaints, the types of third parties to which it discloses the information and the choices and means the organisation offers for limiting its use and disclosure.	Privacy policy Every business is required to have a privacy policy to be published on its website. The business has to also appoint a Grievance Officer. The privacy policy appears to be required whether or not the business deals with sensitive personal data or information (SPD). The privacy policy must describe what information is collected, the purpose of use of the information, to whom or how the information might be disclosed

(Table 6A.1 Continued)

(Table 6A.1 Continued)

S. No.	The US–EU Safe Harbor Framework's Requirements	India's Offering—Information Technology Rules, 2011
		and reasonable security practices followed to safeguard the information.
		Notification The business should ensure that the provider of the information is aware that the information is being collected, the purpose of use of the information, the recipients of the information and the name and address of the agency collecting the information. Prior consent is required for disclosure of the infor-mation to any party other than the government.
2.	**Choice** Organisations must give indi-viduals the opportunity to choose (opt out) whether their personal information will be disclosed to a third party or used for a purpose incompatible with the purpose for which it was originally collected or subsequently authorised by the individual. For sensitive informa-tion, affirmative or explicit (opt in) choice must be given if the infor-mation is to be disclosed to a third party or used for a purpose other than its original purpose or the purpose authorised subsequently by the individual.	**Consent for collection** A business cannot collect SPD unless it obtains the prior consent of the provider of the information. The consent has to be provided by letter, fax or email. The business must also, prior to collecting the informa-tion, give the option to the provider of the information to not provide such information. In such a case, the business can cease providing goods and services for which the informa-tion is sought.
3.	**Onward transfer (transfers to third parties)** To disclose information to a third party, organisations must apply	**Transnational transfer** A business can only transfer the SPD or information to a party over-seas if the overseas party ensures the

(Table 6A.1 Continued)

(Table 6A.1 Continued)

S. No.	The US–EU Safe Harbor Framework's Requirements	India's Offering—Information Technology Rules, 2011
	the notice and choice principles. Where an organisation wishes to transfer information to a third party that is acting as an agent, it may do so if it makes sure that the third party subscribes to the Safe Harbor Privacy Principles or is subject to the Directive or another adequacy finding. As an alternative, the organisation can enter into a written agreement with such third party requiring that the third party provides at least the same level of privacy protection as is required by the relevant principles.	same level of protection provided for under Indian rules. Further, the information can be transferred only if it is necessary for the performance of a lawful contract between the body corporate and the information provider or where the information provider has provided his/her consent to such transfer.
4.	Access Individuals must have access to personal information about them that an organisation holds and be able to correct, amend or delete that information where it is inaccurate, except where the burden or expense of providing access would be disproportionate to the risks to the individual's privacy in the case in question, or where the rights of persons other than the individual would be violated.	Right of access, correction and withdrawal The business should permit the provider of the information the right to review that information and should ensure that any information found to be inaccurate or deficient be corrected. The provider of the information also has the right to withdraw its consent to the collection and use of the information.
5.	Security Organisations must take reasonable precautions to protect personal information from loss, misuse and unauthorised access, disclosure, alteration and destruction.	Security procedures The IT Act requires reasonable security procedures to be maintained in order to escape liability (see above). The rules appear to state that reasonable security procedures would be either (a) the IS/ISO/IEC 27001 on *Information Technology—Security*

(Table 6A.1 Continued)

(Table 6A.1 Continued)

S. No.	The US–EU Safe Harbor Framework's Requirements	India's Offering—Information Technology Rules, 2011
		Techniques—Information Security Management System—Requirements; or (b) a code developed by an industry association and approved and notified by the government. The security procedure has to be audited on a regular basis by an independent auditor, who has been approved by the Government of India. Such audit should be carried out at least once a year or as and when the body corporate has undertaken a significant upgrading of its computer resources.
6.	Data integrity Personal information must be relevant for the purposes for which it is to be used. An organisation should take reasonable steps to ensure that data is reliable for its intended use, accurate, complete and current.	Use and retention The business can use personal information only for the purpose for which it was collected. Also, the business cannot retain the SPD for longer than is required for the purposes for which the information may lawfully be used or is otherwise required under any other law.
7.	Enforcement In order to ensure compliance with the safe harbour principles, there must be (a) readily available and affordable independent recourse mechanisms so that each individual's complaints and disputes can be investigated and resolved and damages awarded where the applicable law or private sector initiatives so provide; (b) procedures for verifying that the commitments companies make to adhere to the safe harbour principles have been implemented; and (c) obligations	No particular rule has been designed concomitant with this principle.

(Table 6A.1 Continued)

(Table 6A.1 Continued)

S. No.	The US–EU Safe Harbor Framework's Requirements	India's Offering—Information Technology Rules, 2011
	to remedy problems arising out of a failure to comply with the principles. Sanctions must be sufficiently rigorous to ensure compliance by the organisation. Organisations that fail to provide annual self-certification letters will no longer appear in the list of participants and safe harbour benefits will no longer be assured.	

Source: Compiled by the author from the regulations, survey of policy-makers, legal experts and NASSCOM.

7

Accountancy Sector: High Potential beyond Higher Barriers

Parthapratim Pal

Introduction

Accounting services is among the fastest growing professional services in the world. The importance of this sector stems from the fact that accountancy is an essential service for any firm involved in the production of goods or services. Accountancy services help firms in the collection, retention and dissemination of financial information. They also help companies by providing advice and assistance on taxation matters, financial reporting and commercial strategy. Accountancy can also be viewed as a strategic tool to attain good corporate governance. Statutory audit, which is an important component of accountancy services, is a crucial element for the proper functioning of any market-based economy. In a stock market-based financial system, external auditors play the important role of independently certifying the performance of a firm and its management to its shareholders. Credibility and fairness of audit and accountancy firms is the cornerstone of a market economy. Consequently, there are strong positive social externalities associated with a well-functioning accounting sector. Moreover, a well-functioning accounting and auditing sector allows the implementation and enforcement of prudential requirements and other financial regulatory measures. It also safeguards reliable financial information, which reduces the possibilities of financial fraud. The existence of an independent, reliable and accountable control and reporting system is, therefore, crucial in the smooth functioning of capital markets and the financial system as a whole (Rubalcaba, 2007).

Due to the critical role of the accountancy sector in an economy, strong regulatory requirements are often imposed on this sector. This is particularly true for the largest subsector of accountancy services, which is auditing. Due to the special nature of auditing services, it is treated as an accredited profession, similar to medicine and law. For accredited professions, the right to practice is generally restricted and the profession is subject to various accreditation requirements and procedures, including licensing or authorisation. In such services, 'the professional is expected to maintain high professional conduct and standards and to uphold the welfare of clients and society over and above pursuing pure profit maximisation' (UNCTAD, 2004:7,8). As a result, most countries impose domestic regulations including local qualification and licensing requirements for this sector. Though the extent of restrictions is somewhat less for other subsectors of accountancy services, the overall regulatory restrictions faced by this sector are quite high.

High levels of domestic regulations have traditionally restricted international trade in this sector. An analysis of barriers to trade in accountancy services reveals that trade is severely restricted by local qualification and licensing requirements for individual practitioners as well as conditions on the ownership and management of firms. In other words, for most countries around the world, accounting firms are required to be locally owned and independent.[1] This becomes evident from the Services Trade Restrictiveness Index (STRI)[2] developed by the World Bank (see Figure 7.1). The STRI shows that in most regions of the world, professional services, which is composed of legal and accountancy services, is the most restricted services sector.

---

[1] Unlike most other professional services, which are practised at an individual level, accountancy services in most countries are conducted through partnerships and firms.

[2] World Bank Services Trade Restrictions Database, available at: http://iresearch.worldbank.org/servicetrade/home.htm (accessed on 10 August 2013).

Figure 7.1
Services Trade Restrictiveness Index (STRI) by Sector and Region

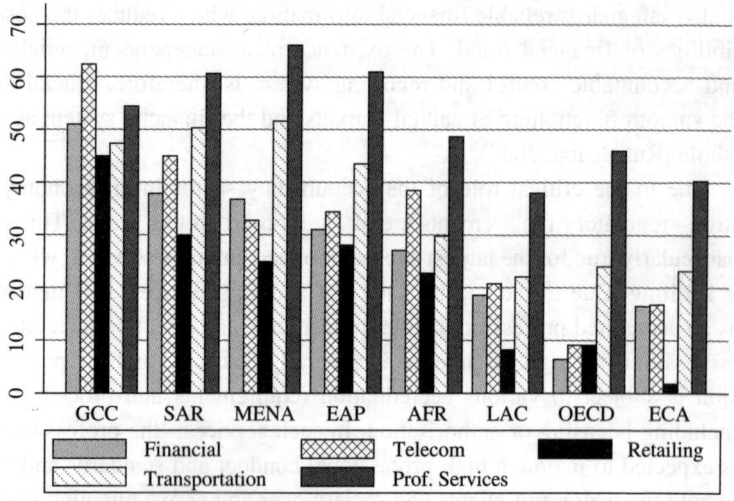

Source: Extracted from Borchert, Gootiiz and Mattoo (2012), Figure 3, Page 23.
Notes: The services trade restrictions index (STRI) at the regional level is
           calculated as a simple average of individual country's STRIs. The
           STRI in the cross-border air passenger transportation subsector comes
           from the QUASAR database of WTO (2007). Regional abbreviations:
           HNO – High income non-OECD, SAR – South Asia, EAP – East Asia
           and Pacific, MENA – Middle East and North Africa, AFR – Sub-Saharan
           Africa, LAC – Latin America and Caribbean, ECA – Europe and Central
           Asia, OECD – High income OECD.

With the rapid spread of globalisation, the inward-looking structure of this sector is gradually changing. The Big Four firms, namely
Deloitte, Ernst and Young (E&Y), KPMG and PricewaterhouseCoopers
(PwC), which dominate the global accounting market have a presence
in more than 140 countries. With the increasing relocation of the global
production process and cross-listing of firms in international capital
markets, it has now become extremely important to internationalise
and standardise the accounting process. Also, with the increased integration of global capital markets and a heightened focus on corporate
transparency, the demand for international accounting standards is on
the rise. Increased globalisation and this new wave of standardisation

of accounting practices are gradually liberating the accountancy sector from the clutches of domestic regulations and are opening up huge possibilities for international trade in accountancy and audit services. Some recent events and trends have helped the growth of this sector. The global financial crisis of 2007–2009 prompted several countries to introduce stricter prudential norms and regulatory mechanisms that require a higher level of compliance. Also, several companies are implementing better corporate social responsibility (CSR) practices. These new developments have created new markets for accounting professionals.

India has a strong export interest in this sector since it produces a large number of trained accountants who are conversant with English and are considered to be highly proficient and globally competitive. This gives India a major advantage in Mode 4 (movement of natural persons) of services exports in this sector. Also, with rapid improvements in telecommunication technology, cross-border trade in this sector is increasing. This has resulted in a significant increase in the financial and accounting outsourcing (FAO) business. Several BPO and KPO firms based in India have made significant progress in this area. Consequently, India has developed an aggressive export interest in Mode 1 in this sector.

Europe is a large potential market for Indian accountancy professionals because countries such as the UK and Ireland have accounting norms similar to India and have a long tradition of association with the Institute of Chartered Accountants of India (ICAI). At the same time, EU countries such as Germany, France, the Netherlands, Sweden and Denmark are the headquarters of large multinational companies and, therefore, are also large potential markets for Indian accountancy professionals. This chapter studies the trade potential between India and EU in the accountancy sector. This analysis is important because India and the EU are negotiating a bilateral free trade and investment agreement, and improved market access for professional services such as accountancy is an important issue in the negotiation. Given India's export interest in this sector, it may have strong implications for India's services exports.

This chapter is based on a field study and secondary data. For this study, we conducted in-depth interviews with several professional accountants, ICAI members and experts in various accounting firms. We interviewed professional accountants practising in India and in some EU countries. Some top executives of Big Four companies in India were also interviewed.

Global Overview of the Accountancy Sector

As per the WTO Services Sectoral Classification List (MTN. GNS/W/120), the accountancy sector is composed of the following subsectors:

Accounting, auditing and bookkeeping services (CPC 862)

- CPC 8621 Accounting and auditing services
  - CPC 86211 Financial auditing services
  - CPC 86212 Accounting review services
  - CPC 86213 Compilation of financial services
  - CPC 86219 Other accounting services
- CPC 8622 Bookkeeping services, except tax returns

The global accountancy sector has a market turnover estimated to be around US$400 billion. According to the Datamonitor report (2012), in 2011 the total revenue of the global accountancy market was around US$394.2 billion, which is expected to reach around US$500 billion by the end of 2016. The audit segment was the dominant subsector with total revenues of US$189.6 billion that accounted for 48.1 per cent of the sector's overall revenue.

One of the most important features of the accountancy sector is that internationally this sector is characterised by unusually high market concentration. In accountancy, four large firms (called the Big Four) dominate the market. These four firms, namely Deloitte, E&Y, KPMG and PwC, are structured as a network of separate and independent firms, each of which works under the same brand name and network agreement, but they are legally separate entities. To work under the same brand name, these member firms have to follow a common set of principles and policies. In return, they have access to common resources and expertise. Thus, each of the Big Four accounting firms can be described as a network of independent member firms bound together by a contractual relationship across countries. These firms provide a wide variety of accountancy services, and they are also major players in the advisory and consulting business. Among their various business activities, audit has always been the largest grossing service, accounting for about 45 per cent of total revenue. However, in recent years, advisory and consulting services have emerged as the fastest growing segments for the Big Four.

The market power of the Big Four firms can be judged from their spread across the world and the volume of their business. According to the annual reports of these companies, in 2012, each of these four companies had a presence in more than 140 countries around the world and together they employed more than 690,000 people. Their combined revenue in 2012 was more than US$110 billion (Table 7.1). Estimates suggest that the Big Four audit more than 78 per cent of all US public companies, representing 99 per cent of public company sales (Bloom and Schrim, 2005). In the UK, the Big Four firms audited all of the FTSE 100 companies and 343 of the FTSE 350 companies in 2004 (Cousins, Mitchell and Sikka, 2004).

Table 7.1
Basic Statistics on the Big Four Firms of Accounting for the Year 2012

	Presence in Countries	Employment	Revenue of all Member Firms (US$ billion)	Rate of Growth of Revenue (%)
Deloitte	More than 150	193,359	31.3	8.7
E&Y	More than 140	167,225	24.4	6.7
KPMG	156	152,390	23.0	4.4
PwC	158	180,529	31.5	7.8

Source: Collated from company reports—PwC Global Annual Review, 2012, E&Y Integrated Annual Review, 2011/12, Deloitte 2012 Global Report and KPMG International Annual Review, 2012.[3]

---

[3] These company reports can be accessed at PwC Global Annual Review 2012; http://www.pwc.com/gx/en/annual-review/2012/assets/pwc-global-annual-review-2012.pdf; E&Y Integrated Annual Review 2011/12; http://www.ey.com/Publication/vwLUAssets/Jaarverslag_-_2011-2012/$FILE/Annual%20Review%20-%202011-2012.pdf; Deloitte 2012 Global Report; http://public.deloitte.com/media/0564/pdfs/DTTL_2012GlobalReport.pdf; KPMG International Annual Review 2012; http://www.kpmg.com/TW/zh/Documents/2013reports/iar-2012.pdf (accessed on 3 July 2013).

Apart from the Big Four firms, there are medium-sized and small firms in this sector. In the middle, there are several companies that are smaller than the Big Four but still have a formidable presence in the sector; examples of such firms are Grant Thornton, BDO and McGladrey LLP.[4] Some of them provide services to larger clients including some Fortune 1000 companies. At the bottom end of the sector, there are small proprietorship or partnership firms that cater to small and medium businesses and local clients. Sometimes, the smaller firms become associates of the Big Four and work as their domestic partners. For example, KPMG had more than 8,000 such partners in 2012.

The second feature of this sector is that along with accountancy and audit services, most large firms often provide a bouquet of services that include advisory, management and consultancy activities. It is argued that audit services are not very profit-making and large accountancy firms often use auditing as a *loss leader* to market more profitable non-audit services such as management and consultancy. Along with these services, these big firms specialise in insolvency services, tax advice, investment services and management consulting. The global spread and outreach of these firms also allows them to provide investment banking and risk advisory services to new entrants, particularly in developing country markets. Because of the large basket of services provided by the Big Four firms, they have become the world's largest suppliers of consultancy and advisory services.

The tight oligopolistic market structure of the global accountancy sector and the increased presence of these firms in advisory and consultancy services have raised concerns among regulators. In the US, the EU and the EU Member States such as the UK, regulators have expressed concerns that due to this high market concentration, companies do not have much choice when selecting auditors for their firms. This may lead to a situation where a long-term understanding develops between the management and the auditors, which may prevent auditors from carrying out their role with objectivity. Then, regulators are worried that if audit

---

[4] These firms are not small firms by any means, although they are smaller than the 'Big Four'. For example, McGladrey has 700 offices in 86 countries. BDO has 1,118 offices in 135 countries with more than 48,000 partners and professional staff. Grant Thornton employs more than 35,000 people in more than 100 countries across the world. Source: Websites of these firms.

firms and their audit clients enter into business relationships, such as strategic alliances, co-marketing arrangements and other forms of advisory and consultancy services, it may lead to a serious conflict of interest between auditors and their clients. These concerns have intensified after the financial crisis when the top audit firms were heavily criticised for not adequately informing shareholders about the financial exposures and extent of leverage of various banks. The financial crisis highlighted the extent of systemic risk embedded in the financial sector and the importance of the role that auditors play in such a system. Therefore, the regulators feel that it is imperative to adopt measures that will restore trust in the capital markets, improve audit quality and restore confidence in the role of the auditor.

To attain these goals, over the years regulators have introduced stricter discipline. In the US, after the Enron crisis, the Sarbanes–Oxley Act or the Public Company Accounting Reform and Investor Protection Act was introduced in 2002 to impose restrictions on auditing firms. More recently, the Dodd–Frank Wall Street Reform and Consumer Protection Act (2010) made several significant changes to financial regulation in the US. Similarly, the European Commission has proposed a set of stringent new regulations since 2010. These include mandatory rotation of auditors by companies after a stipulated number of years, the possibility of employing two auditors for important companies and, most importantly, forbidding audit firms from offering any other services to check the problem of conflict of interest.[5] These proposals have not yet been implemented, but the Competition Commission of Britain has recently made it compulsory for British companies to put their auditing contract out to fresh tender every five years. There are provisions in this law that stipulate that companies will not be allowed to restrict their choice to the Big Four firms. The Netherlands has also introduced mandatory audit rotation for Dutch public interest entities. It is not clear whether other proposals made by the European Commission will be accepted, but if some of those proposals are implemented, the business methods of this sector will have to change quite significantly.

[5] A copy of these proposals can be found at: http://ec.europa.eu/internal_market/auditing/reform/index_en.htm (accessed on 1 June 2015).

Accountancy Sector in Europe

In Europe, the accounting services sector is categorised under the broad group of Legal and accounting services (Division 69 under NACE Revision 2). According to Eurostat, in the EU-27 under this broad group, there are over one million enterprises that employ more than 3.3 million people. This broad sector employs about 29.8 per cent of the total workforce engaged in professional, scientific and technical activities. The value-add generated by the EU-27's legal and accounting services was €169.4 billion ($224.75 billion)[6] in 2010, which is approximately 30.2 per cent of total professional, scientific and technical activities. Based on employment measures, this sector is the largest among the seven NACE divisions within professional, scientific and technical activities.

The accounting services sector is composed of accounting, bookkeeping and auditing activities and tax consultancy (Group 69.2). In the broad grouping of legal and accounting services, the subsector of accounting, bookkeeping and auditing activities and tax consultancy has an employment share of 56.7 per cent in the EU-27, implying employment generation of about 1.9 million in this sector.[7]

According to Datamonitor (2012), the European accountancy market had total revenues of US$132.6 billion in 2011. Audit is the largest segment within this subsector with revenue of US$57.3 billion, which is 43.2 per cent of the overall turnover of the subsector. The growth rate of this subsector has been low since 2008 due to the slowing growth rate of the EU. However, it is projected that the sector may grow at a CAGR of 3.9 per cent for the five-year period 2011–2016, which may allow the turnover of the sector to reach US$160 billion by 2016.

Like the global market, the European accountancy market is dominated by the Big Four firms. From the annual reports of the Big Four firms, it is notable that the EMEA region (the Big Four firms typically combine Europe with Middle Eastern and African nations for a giant Europe, Middle East and Africa region) accounts for about 44 per cent

---

[6] Converted using www.oanda.com using the average exchange rate for the year 2010 of 1 Euro = 1.3267 dollars.

[7] These figures are from Eurostat where the year for which latest data are available for this sector is 2010. At that time EU had 27 members.

of global revenues of these firms. While the Eastern European countries showed spectacular growth as there is increased demand for sophisticated audit, tax and transaction services, economic stagnation in Western Europe led to overall slow growth of revenue from the EMEA region.

For the accountancy sector as a whole, Eurostat data show that among the 27 countries of the EU, the two largest markets in 2010 were the UK and Germany. This is not surprising since London has been a global financial hub for several years and Germany is home to a large number of multinational companies. Germany is also one of the largest exporters of goods and services in the world. Eurostat data show that for the subsector of accounting, bookkeeping and auditing activities and tax consultancy, these two countries account for more than 49 per cent of the total turnover of the EU-27. The Netherlands, Spain and Italy are other important players in this area. Table 7.2 shows the share of major EU countries in different service categories of this subsector.

As far as international trade is concerned, in most EU countries accounting and particularly auditing are protected sectors. A look at the regulations in this sector shows that in EU countries, accountants typically must satisfy education and practical experience requirements and a local residency requirement; in some countries, they must also pass a qualifying or licensing examination. The organisation structure of accounting firms is often limited to partnerships or sole proprietorships; corporate forms are often prohibited; and ownership of accounting firms is often limited to accounting professionals. Also, accounting standards and auditing procedures are usually regulated. In several countries, restrictions or bans are placed on advertising or on other forms of promotion and price competition.

In the accountancy sector, a country-wise look at the barriers to the accounting and auditing subsectors reveals that auditing is almost always more restricted than accounting. The accountancy sector is fairly open in a few EU countries, such as Greece and the Netherlands; for example, Greece has no restrictions on Mode 1 and Mode 3 in accounting, although there are some restrictions in Mode 4. The Netherlands has a similar barrier, where there are only some restrictions in Mode 4 while other modes are open. The two large markets in the accountancy sector, viz. the UK and Germany, have kept Mode 1 open but have restrictions on Modes 3 and 4. A closer look at the restrictions imposed by

Table 7.2
Share of Major EU Countries in Total Turnover of Service Categories in 'Accounting, Bookkeeping and Auditing Activities and Tax Consultancy' (2010)

	Financial Auditing Services	*Accounting Services*	*Accounting Review Services; Compilation Services of Financial Statements; Bookkeeping Services*	*Payroll Services*	*Other Accounting Services*	*Tax Consultancy Services*	*Insolvency and Receivership Services*	*Total Sector (Accounting, Bookkeeping and Auditing Activities and Tax Consultancy)*
United Kingdom	24.71	22.21	13.58	36.91	32.79	28.59	88.49	25.88
Germany	24.96	22.63	27.86	20.82	8.12	27.98	2.83	23.27
Netherlands	13.62	13.05	18.34	5.77	4.33	14.85	0.30	13.02
Spain	7.72	12.07	7.54	9.34	28.66	4.64	4.25	9.74
Italy	0.00	11.41	8.87	18.63	11.37	3.75	0.17	7.46
Sweden	7.33	1.94	2.77	0.78	0.63	1.63	0.06	2.96
Denmark	4.54	1.94	3.24	0.41	1.17	1.89	0.47	2.52
Austria	2.07	2.57	3.25	2.08	0.95	3.33	0.03	2.50

Norway	4.70	2.04	3.20	0.54	0.00	0.65	0.38	2.32
Belgium	2.03	2.42	3.67	0.28	0.80	2.69	0.00	2.30
Poland	1.64	2.41	2.67	0.84	3.24	1.20	0.00	1.98
Ireland	3.29	1.06	0.80	0.23	2.75	2.83	2.81	1.86
Finland	1.38	1.68	1.44	2.18	1.86	0.66	0.21	1.41
Others	2.01	2.57	2.77	1.20	3.34	5.31	0.01	2.79
Total	100	100	100	100	100	100	100	100

Source: Eurostat, extracted on 28 July 2013. http://ec.europa.eu/eurostat/help/new-eurostat-website (last accessed on 7 August 2015).

these countries reveals that in Mode 3, there are several restrictions on ownership by non-locally licensed professionals. In Germany, foreign firms/accountants are not allowed to have more than 49 per cent ownership or control of an accountancy firm, provided that their qualifications are substantially similar to German requirements. In the UK also, there are limits on ownership or control by non-locally-licensed professionals; 75 per cent of the votes must be held by qualified persons. Also, any single shareholding of more than 5 per cent must be approved by a special monitoring body within the profession. In Mode 4, the restrictions are more stringent. In most of these countries, there are local education requirements and there is no automatic recognition of foreign licences. Foreign-licensed professionals are eligible to practise only subject to conditions of a certain number of years of work experience. A common feature among the countries of the EU is that they recognise only professional licensing from other countries within the bloc. Also, there are mandatory residency requirements in some countries in order to be licensed to practise and even to be admitted to the professional accountancy associations. However, in accountancy, entry is allowed through intra-corporate transferee or service-supplying employee (SSE) routes. In some countries, there is a numerical ceiling on the SSE route. A summary of restrictions for Mode 4 in the accountancy subsector is shown in Table 7.3.

For auditing, Mode 1 is completely restricted in most EU countries except Austria and Sweden. In most cases, Mode 1 is also tied to commercial presence in the country (Mode 3). In most EU countries, Mode 3 is restricted in auditing since there are numerous requirements for ownership or control by non-locally-licensed professionals. In some cases (like Italy), access through Mode 3 is restricted to natural persons. In Mode 4 for the auditing subsector, there are again barriers related to lack of recognition of foreign degrees. There are also requirements related to nationality, residency, local education and local experience. In most of these cases, professionals from the European Economic Area (EEA)[8] receive more favourable treatment than other foreign nationals. A list of barriers for Modes 1, 3 and 4 for the auditing sector for select EU countries is given in Table 7A.1 in the Appendix.

[8] EEA or the European Economic Area comprises the Member States of the European Union (EU), except Croatia, plus Iceland, Liechtenstein and Norway.

Table 7.3
Restrictions on Mode 4 in Accountancy in Select EU Countries

	Automatic Recognition of Foreign Licence Granted	Foreign-licensed Professionals Eligible to Practise Subject to Conditions	Type of Entry Available	Quota for Foreigners	Labour Market Test Required	Economic Needs Test Require
Austria	No	Only for EEA	ICT, SSE, IPE, IPC	No	No	No
Belgium	No	Only for EEA	ICT, SSE, IPE, IPC	Quota for SSE	Yes	No
Denmark	No	Yes	ICT, SSE	Quota for SSE	No	No
Finland	No; yes for EEA	No	ICT, SSE, IPE, IPC	No	Yes	Yes
France	No	No	ICT, SSE	No	No	No
Germany	No	Only for EEA	ICT, SSE	Quota for SSE		Yes
Greece	No	Only for EEA	ICT, SSE	No	No	No
Ireland	No	Yes, based on MRA	ICT, SSE	Yes	No	No
Italy	No	Only for EEA	ICT, SSE, IPE, IPC	No	No	No
Netherlands	Yes	No	ICT	No	No	No
Spain	No	Only for EEA	ICT	No	No	No
Sweden	No	Only for EEA	ICT, SSE	No	No	No
UK	No	No	ICT, SSE	No	Yes	No

Source: World Bank Services Trade Restrictions Database, available at: http://iresearch.worldbank.org/servicetrade/home.htm (accessed on 10 August 2013).

Notes: ICT = Intra-Corporate Transferee, SSE = Service-Supplying Employee, IPE = Independent Professional as Employee of a local firm, IPC = Independent Professional as Contractual Service Provider. MRA = Mutual Recognition Agreement.

Overall, it is evident that the market for the accountancy and auditing sector in EU is large and growing. As the EU is slowly coming out of a major slowdown, this sector is expected to grow faster. However, this market is restricted and there are major entry barriers for non-EU countries. The rules and regulations across EU countries are not harmonised and there are significant policy differences across countries. Moreover, there are likely to be major changes in the EU's approach towards these sectors since the European Commission has suggested a substantial overhaul in policies.

From India's point of view, it is of concern that Mode 4 is heavily restricted both for accounting and auditing services. While Mode 1 is relatively open for accounting, it is completely closed for the auditing segment. Mode 3 is restricted in both cases and countries outside the EEA face strong disadvantages vis-à-vis countries within the region (see Table 7.4).

Accountancy Sector in India

Unlike the global accounting scenario where a few firms dominate the industry, the Indian accounting sector is characterised by small- and medium-sized firms. Small firms typically have 2–3 Chartered Accountants with a few Article Clerks, while medium-sized firms employ around 5–6 Chartered Accountants. According to the ICAI website, there are around 50,000 such audit firms in India and some of them are associates of the global large players. Table 7.5 shows the distribution of audit firms in India. Compared to the global accountancy sector, the market concentration in India is much lower.

The different structure of the Indian accountancy sector is an outcome of the Chartered Accountants Act, 1949, and regulations imposed by the ICAI. According to the Chartered Accountants Act, an accountant is prohibited from soliciting customers and paying commission, brokerage or share of profits to anybody other than another accountant; there are also restrictions on publishing advertisements about their products and services. Due to these restrictions, in India, there is a dearth of large accountancy firms. Most of the bigger Indian firms are

Table 7.4
Services Trade Restrictiveness Indicators (STRI) for Select EU Countries

Country	Accounting				Auditing			
	Overall	Mode 1	Mode 3	Mode 4	Overall	Mode 1	Mode 3	Mode 4
Austria	50	0	50	75	55	25	50	75
Belgium	50	0	50	75	60	100	25	75
Denmark	40	0	25	75	60	100	25	75
Finland	30	0	25	50	60	100	25	75
France	50	100	50	25	50	100	50	25
Germany	40	0	50	50	60	100	50	50
Greece	10	0	0	25	40	100	0	50
Ireland	20	0	0	50	60	100	50	50
Italy	70	100	50	75	70	100	50	75
Netherlands	10	0	0	25	60	100	50	50
Spain	30	0	0	75	50	100	0	75
Sweden	20	0	0	50	55	75	50	50
UK	40	0	50	50	60	100	50	50
EU-20	45	25	50	50	55	75	50	50

Source: World Bank Services Trade Restrictions Database, available at: http://iresearch.worldbank.org/servicetrade/home.htm (last accessed on 10 August 2013). STRI scores imply the following levels of trade restrictions: Completely open (0); Virtually open but with minor restrictions (25); Major restrictions (50); Virtually closed with limited opportunities to enter and operate (75); Completely closed (100).

Table 7.5
Structure of the Accountancy Sector in India

Profile	No. of Firms	% of Total No. of Firms
Proprietary Firms	34,996	70.66
Firms with 2 to 5 members	13,145	26.54
Firms with 6 to 10 members	1,188	2.40
Firms with more than 10 members	199	0.40
Total	49,528	100.00

Source: Provided by Patel (2012).

associates of the global large players. These regulations have also not allowed accountancy firms to increase their spread. There are only a handful of accountancy firms that operate on an all-India basis. The fragmented nature of accountancy in India has generated a significant number of jobs for local accountants. But during the interviews done for this study, most Chartered Accountants (CAs) were of the opinion that the lack of large players in India's accountancy sector is restricting the country's ability to take full advantage of the potential offered by the global market in accountancy services. It is also notable that in India the large global firms are not allowed to undertake audit work in their own name. KPMG, Deloitte and E&Y have local associates that undertake audit work in India, while the global partner provides management consulting, taxation, company law and various other services. However, an ICAI panel recommended in 2011 that multinational accounting firms, including the Big Four, should be prohibited from offering management consultancy services under their current names. After the audit fraud in Satyam Computer Services in 2011, ICAI has alleged that several multinational accounting firms are flouting its rule through their proxy operations and has asked the government and the central bank to act against these companies (ICAI, 2011). However, it seems that even the surrogate presence of the Big Four is leading to changes in the structure of the domestic accountancy sector. The increased preference shown by Indian corporates and public sector firms towards the Big Four firms for their audit work has forced smaller CA firms down the value chain. It is also forcing some Indian chartered accountants to do low-value-added work for foreign firms in India.

Like the rest of the world, regulations for the accountancy and auditing sector are changing in India. On 8 August 2013, India passed the Companies Bill, 2012, which includes several new regulations for companies in their accounting and auditing practices and a clause to introduce mandatory rotation of auditors in India. This new regulation also prohibits auditors from rendering specified non-audit services to their client company or its subsidiaries. Existing companies will get a transition period of one year to comply with this new rule. There are differences of opinion about whether these new rules will benefit the Indian accountancy sector, but from media reports, there seems to be consensus that this new Bill will address the broader objective of improving corporate governance and transparency in the system. These new rules will also make Indian regulations more uniform with global best practices.

As far as international trade openness is concerned, the Indian accountancy sector is almost closed. The STRIs for accounting and auditing in Modes 1 and 3 are 100, implying that these are completely blocked. Overall, both the subsectors, viz. accounting and auditing, have an STRI of 90, which is among the highest in the world. India's strong protectionist position is said to have been adopted on the grounds of reciprocity. Since most developed countries do not accept Indian professional degrees, ICAI also does not recognise any foreign qualifications. The STR database points out that to be eligible to provide services requiring certification or authentication of financial data in India, applicants must be members of the ICAI, must have a qualifying degree from a recognised university in India and must pass an examination. However, the sector is more open in Mode 4 since India allows the entry of foreign accountants as ICTs or SSEs. Although the accountancy sector in India appears to be completely closed in Mode 1 and no FDI in this sector is allowed, all the Big Four firms are present in India, but as management and consultancy service providers. Globally, the Big Four firms are audit and accounting firms that provide other advisory services; however, it is the reverse in India where these firms are legally management and consultancy firms that render services that come under the domain of accountancy and auditing services (ICAI, 2011).

Opportunities for the Indian Accountancy Sector in the EU

India produces a large number of English-speaking accountants who are one of the most price-competitive in the world. Our interviews and survey showed that as international trade in the sector is being liberalised, Indian accountants are becoming more aware of the huge potential of the international market. India's advantage in this sector comes from different factors. India's main advantage in this sector is the huge number of trained accountants it produces every year. According to the ICAI website, there are more than 192,000 professional chartered accountants in India. Then, Indian accountants are price-competitive. Greene (2006) estimates that while the wage rate for an accountant is US$23.35 per hour in the US, it is around US$6–10 in India. While this may have changed in 2013, it would not be unfair to assume that the exchange rate adjusted hourly wage in India is significantly lower than for accountants in developed countries. Along with lower wages, familiarity with international accounting standards and expertise in English also provide Indian accountants with an edge. From the demand side, several factors have led to higher international trade in accountancy services; these factors include the growing presence of foreign firms in developing countries, a steep rise in global FDI flows including a boom in mergers and acquisitions, the development and spread of electronic commerce and requirements to follow a common, accepted set of accounting principles. As several of these services are increasingly being served through Mode 1, India's dominant position in the BPO and KPO industry makes it a potential large player in the accountancy market. Moreover, as the EU is going through a demographic transition, a shortage of professional service providers is expected in the near future. India, with its vast number of professionally trained accountants, is likely to be in a position to take advantage of this opportunity. These factors, taken together, are likely to open up significant market access for India in Modes 1 and 4 in the EU market. However, India has a disadvantage in Mode 3. Domestic regulations in the accountancy sector have resulted in an industry structure that is dominated by small- and medium-sized firms; this is in contrast to the international accountancy sector where a few very large firms dominate. This means that while India has strengths in Modes 1 and 4, in Mode 3

Indian firms are likely to find it difficult to compete with international large players.

If one juxtaposes India's strengths in the accountancy and auditing sector with the services trade restriction indicators shown in Table 7.3, a few things become clear. First, Mode 1 for accounting services in EU is relatively open. Apart from France and Italy, other countries do not seem to have major market access barriers. Therefore, there is a fairly large market in the EU that Indian accountants can explore. Accounting services that can be traded through Mode 1 includes work related to (a) statutory books and records, (b) management books and records, (c) IT implementation, (d) preparation and compilation of accounting documents (financial statements/annual reports), (e) preparation of periodic financial statements and (f) organisation of accounting systems and related internal control. So far, in the accountancy sector, Indian BPOs and KPOs have mainly dealt with the US market, and business with the European market is only gradually increasing. But Indian firms are extremely keen on the European market as well for their business expansion.

There are a few concerns about the laws of different EU countries regarding Mode 1 service provision. In most EU countries, commercial presence is required to provide services in this sector. For example, the STRI database mentions that among EU countries, there is a commercial presence requirement for Mode 1 service provision in Belgium, Denmark, Finland, Germany, Greece, Ireland, Italy, the Netherlands, Portugal, Spain and the UK. Removal of this requirement is one of India's requests in the multilateral forum. Issues regarding data protection and privacy have not yet created much problem for service providers in this sector, but these are potential problem areas that should be taken care of.

The largest potential market India has in the EU in the accounting sector is in Mode 4. Tables 7.3 and 7.4 show that Mode 4 is highly restricted in most EU countries, the exceptions being France, Greece and the Netherlands. Most EU countries also do not recognise a foreign licence to practice accountancy in their respective countries (Table 7.4). But among the countries listed in Table 7.4, seven countries allow foreign-licensed professionals from within the EU to practise (subject to certain conditions). Also, there are requirements of residency and local experience (See Appendix Table 7A.2 for details). All these requirements make it difficult for Indian professionals and accountants to take advantage of the EU market.

As far as audit services is concerned, Table 7.3 shows that it is virtually closed in the EU and there is very limited opportunity to enter and operate in these markets. This is not surprising because globally audit is the most protected segment of accountancy services. It must be highlighted here that the licence to provide statutory audit is an additional certification for professional accountants. For example, even if a professional is a certified chartered accountant, s/he still needs to get a *practicing certificate* by meeting further requirements, such as purchasing adequate insurance and undergoing regular inspections. This registration of statutory auditors is organised in different ways across EU Member States. In a few EU countries (e.g. the Netherlands and France), individuals who are not members of a professional accounting body are permitted to carry out statutory audit, usually in the case of small companies or not-for-profit organisations. Additionally, public registration with the local authorities is mandatory.

One way to improve market access for Indian accountants in the EU's accounting and audit market is to sign Mutual Recognition Agreements (MRAs) with EU countries. An MRA between two countries allows professionals from one country to practise in the other country without having to completely re-credential themselves. While negotiating an MRA with another country, the ICAI generally follows the approach of recognising each other's qualifications and, if necessary, supplementing it with a bridging mechanism (such as a requirement to qualify in an additional paper) to ensure knowledge of local systems. There is a strong belief that MRAs with several European countries are feasible because of the standardisation of accounting practices both within the EU and in India. In particular, there is similarity between the accounting system, tax laws and company laws of India and the UK/Ireland. Also, given that the UK is one of the largest markets for the accounting sector in the EU, it is not surprising that the ICAI has prioritised it for MRA negotiations.

The ICAI has initiated negotiations to sign MRAs with some professional accounting associations in the UK and Ireland and has signed a Memorandum of Understanding (MOUs) with them. The ICAI has signed an MRA with the CPA (Certified Public Accountants) Ireland. It has started the process of entering into an MRA with the Institute of

Chartered Accountants in England and Wales (ICAEW), but no MRA has been signed so far. Several legal barriers regarding professional qualifications can be overcome if MRAs can be signed with important EU countries. It may also open up the market for statutory audit for Indian accountants. It is worth reiterating that in this sector, it will be extremely important for the ICAI and the respective professional associations in the EU countries to make tangible progress through MRAs. In the trade negotiations between the EU and India, the role of the government and the negotiators can be to act as facilitators or a catalyst for such dialogues.

Although the signing of MRAs will be useful for Indian accountants, it must be highlighted that there could be other regulations that prevent Indian accountants from accessing the EU market. For example, obtaining visa and work permits could be one of the major problems in doing business with EU countries; this was confirmed by almost all the accountants and business managers interviewed during this study. According to them, streamlining the visa procedure should be an important target for Indian negotiators. This issue is not specific to this sector but is a horizontal issue that the negotiators should try to address. Another barrier that acts as a quantitative restriction for the services market is the Economic Needs Test (ENT) that is required in certain EU countries. The ENT should be abolished as it goes against the basic premise of trade and competitiveness. In the Revised Offer of 2005,[9] the EU has suggested removing the ENT for several sectors, including professional services. Also, India has asked for the removal of the ENT in the GATS negotiations and this stance should be maintained.

Another crucial factor for market access both through Modes 1 and 4 is that in accountancy sector, countries often make service delivery through these two modes conditional on commercial presence. Internationally, Mode 3 or commercial presence is the dominant mode of delivery for accountancy services, mainly because domestic regulations in most countries require that accounting firms are locally owned and independent. Accountancy firms also prefer a local presence since it allows them to serve their clients better by using knowledge of the local market and domestic laws. Local presence also helps these firms expand

---

[9] WTO document number TN/S/O/EEC/Rev.1 dated 29 June 2005.

their business by diversifying into related consultancy services for local firms and foreign firms operating in the local market. For long-term market access in this sector, this mode offers the maximum potential for a country such as India that has a proven comparative advantage in audit and accountancy services. Moreover, this mode has strong and positive inter-sectoral linkages. Mode 3 facilitates the movement of labour (Mode 4) in the form of intra-corporate transfers. It also leads to increased cross-border supply (Mode 1) in the form of delivery of offshore services through voice, satellite or electronic means. As India has strong comparative and cost advantages in both Modes 1 and 4, increased commercial presence should help India increase business through these modes.

Unlike Modes 1 and 4, India's position in Mode 3 is somewhat weak. The regulations of the Indian accountancy sector have created a market structure that is fragmented and dominated by several small and medium firms. Most of these firms lack the economies of scale or the resources to have a commercial presence in a foreign market. The larger Indian firms, on the other hand, are already associates of the Big Four in the Indian market and they may not want to compete with other associates of the Big Four in a foreign market. For medium-sized Indian firms, it is possible to have a Mode 3 presence in Europe, but there are some other impediments that restrict their access to EU countries. One major impediment is the lack of brand equity of Indian firms. Since auditing is a sensitive sector, reputation and brand name play a larger role in this sector than the cost of the services provided. As most Indian firms have not yet developed a global brand name, they tend to lose out in these services. However, this is true only of audit services; for non-audit services this problem is less important. Also, Indian firms appear to be less comfortable having a Mode 3 presence in non-English-speaking countries. Finally, there are some horizontal issues that restrict firms from accessing the EU market through Mode 3. For example, several firms find it difficult to open an office in France for a short to medium timeframe because it is extremely difficult to hire local staff on a short-term basis.

Overall, it can be said that in the accountancy sector, Mode 3 presence is important because it not only allows firms to better serve their clients by customising their service according to local laws and norms, but also in several cases Mode 3 presence is a prerequisite for providing services through Modes 1 and 4; for example, Austria has this requirement in the EU Revised Offer. Given India's commercial interest in these two modes, it is advisable that Indian firms and the ICAI take steps to remove the barriers that constrain the abilities of Indian firms to have offices abroad.

Possible Negotiating Issues and Conclusion

It is evident from the earlier discussion that India possesses strong export interest in Mode 1 and Mode 4 of accountancy and audit services. India is less competitive in Mode 3, but it will be important to develop a commercial presence in Europe, because in accountancy and auditing, access through Mode 1 and Mode 4 are often linked with commercial presence. The role of the government and the ICAI in promoting exports in these three modes will be an important strategy.

Then, in most European countries, it is difficult to get the licence to carry out statutory audits, and there are several restrictions on auditors. Given these difficulties, it is not clear whether there is much market access potential in this subsector in the short run. As the new EU proposals on audit services intend to impose even stricter rules, it is unlikely that this sector will open up in the near future. But there will be some business generation for Indian accountants. The new EU rule will impose restrictions only on the auditor who signs the audit report, but it does not preclude the use of non-EU accountants for the preparation of audit reports. A possible downside is that without the ability to sign audit reports, the market value of these accountants will be less than it would have been otherwise. Moreover, there will be significant business opportunities for accounting professionals and Indian firms beyond the few audit services that are heavily regulated. There are non-statutory audit services that are less regulated and there are tax, accounting and consultancy services. In fact, these services account for more than 60 per cent of the revenues of large accounting firms in Europe. Modes 1, 3 and 4 are the possible modes for delivering these services. Indian accountancy service providers are more likely to gain market access in these services. For increased export opportunity for the accountancy sector, it is imperative that India strongly seeks better market access in the EU in these modes.

On the flipside, there is likely to be a strong quid pro quo in the negotiations on the accountancy sector. The EU is home to some of the largest accountancy firms in the world, and they are very keen to access the Indian market. In particular, firms in the UK have an aggressive export interest in the Indian market due to their familiarity with the accounting system and language in India. But India in its Revised Offer to the WTO has kept Mode 3 unbound both under market access and national treatment for accounting and bookkeeping services. Audit services have been excluded from the scope of offers. Interpretation of the Indian FDI rules also suggests that FDI in audit and accountancy is prohibited under Indian law (ICAI, 2011). The STRI suggests that although FDI is not allowed, a liaison office can be established with an Indian firm. Given India's highly defensive position in Mode 3, it will be difficult to negotiate for improved market access in the EU unless India is ready to relax some of its barriers in Mode 3.

In the negotiations between India and the EU on the accountancy sector, there seems to be a lack of convergence between their views. According to information, negotiators from the EU are demanding Mode 3 access from India that is similar to that granted by Republic of Korea in the EU–Korea Free Trade Agreement of 2011. Republic of Korea has allowed phased entry of EU firms in the legal and accountancy sector of Republic of Korea and stipulated that in five years Republic of Korea will allow joint ventures between EU and South Korean firms in these two sectors with the restriction that the South Korean partner will have at least 50 per cent stake in the company. However, India has not agreed to allow the EU similar access. India's offer to the EU is very similar to what India allowed Republic of Korea in Comprehensive Economic Partnership Agreement (CEPA) signed in 2005, in which India has not opened up Modes 3 and 4 for Republic of Korea, but it has imposed no restrictions on Modes 1 and 2. There is reasonable understanding that India will not go beyond this level of liberalisation vis-à-vis the EU unless there is some major market opening from the EU.

Since opening up Mode 3 is crucial for negotiations in the accountancy sector, it is important to analyse the dynamics of commercial presence in this sector. All the Big Four firms of global accounting are present in India;

they are not allowed to do audit works, but they have tied up with Indian partners who provide audit jobs to the companies. So, despite Mode 3 restrictions and domestic regulations that prohibit these firms from practising in India, the large accountancy firms are already present in the Indian market through their (surrogate) partners. These Big Four firms mainly provide consultancy services to Indian companies. However, apart from these four firms, not many other large global accountancy firms are present in the Indian market, perhaps because their consultancy services business is not as large as that of the Big Four companies.

In spite of prohibiting global accounting firms from auditing in India, increasing numbers of corporate firms are procuring services from the Big Four. This trend has been largely market-driven because as Indian companies go for American Depository Receipts/Global Depository Receipts (ADRs/GDRs), seek foreign listings or plan to have acquisitions abroad, they have to appoint internationally renowned firms to do their auditing work since Indian auditors are not recognised in several developed countries. Therefore, if foreign accounting firms are legally prohibited in India, Indian MNCs will have to approach foreign subsidiaries of these global accounting firms. Market forces may lead to a situation where despite restrictions on Mode 3, most Indian corporate firms move to global accounting firms for auditing. ICAI (2011) has expressed some apprehensions on this possibility.

Against this backdrop, Indian negotiators may consider opening up Mode 3 for the accountancy sector. If Mode 3 is opened up, the threat will not come from the Big Four because they are already present in India, but it may come from the large accountancy firms of Europe that are on the next rung. This may not affect India adversely because it is unlikely that foreign accountants will come to India to compete with Indian accountants at Indian wage rates. Even if some foreign accounting firms come to India, they will have to hire Indian professionals, which will help Indian accountants.

Given such a scenario, market access in Mode 3 of the accounting sector can be used as a bargaining chip to gain reciprocal treatment in the EU market. Indian negotiators must emphasise that reciprocity is important for granting any market access to EU firms in this mode. The Indian accountancy sector should be ready to face the challenge from foreign firms in its domestic market, provided EU countries simultaneously open up Mode 1 and Mode 4 access to India. But there may be two caveats here. First, in the accountancy sector sometimes Mode 1 and Mode 4 are tied to commercial presence. It needs to be ensured that this requirement does not hamper India's market access in these two key modes. Also, it is important to ensure that this trade-off is implemented without any hidden barriers from the other side. The history of trade negotiations with developed countries has shown several instances where developed countries have managed to insert clauses or rules that allow them to circumvent some of their commitments. Indian negotiators must remain cautious about this possibility. This is especially true for the accountancy sector where there are myriad domestic regulations in the EU countries. Finally, it is important to understand that there are several horizontal issues that prevent full Mode 4 access to the EU's accountancy market. In countries like Germany, France, Italy, Belgium and the Scandinavian countries, the labour unions tend to be extremely strong and protectionist. There is no reason to believe that professional associations for the accountancy sector will be much different, and it is unlikely that these bodies will allow Mode 4 access without resistance. Indian negotiators and accountancy professionals should take note of this issue while negotiating reciprocity in this sector.

Overall, the EU offers a large market for Indian accountants, but there are significant barriers that make it difficult to access this market. The analysis in this chapter suggests that as a strategy, Indian negotiators may negotiate for better market access and use Mode 3 access to India as a bargaining chip. The majority of Indian accountants interviewed during this study suggested that such negotiating trade-offs must take care of reciprocity, and the concessions to each other must be granted on a simultaneous basis. Given the changing nature of the global economy and the rise of protectionist trends across the world, it is better to avoid sequential moves unless it allows India a first-mover advantage. In the context of the overall negotiation, it is important for India to gain advantages in professional services because it is widely recognised that if India signs the India–EU bilateral trade and investment agreement, it is likely to have a disadvantage in the manufacturing sector and in certain services sectors such as financial services and insurance services. However, some of these disadvantages may be offset if India gets better market access for its professionals in various business services, including the audit and accounting sector.

Appendix

Table 7A.1
Restrictions in Different Modes for the Audit Sector in Select EU Countries

Country	Mode 1	Mode 3	Mode 4
Austria	Allowed, but statutory audits are reserved for locally licensed professionals.	Foreign auditors are not permitted to form a partnership with local firms. There are limits on ownership or control by foreign nationals: only foreign accountants from GATS member countries may hold up to 25%. At least 51% must be held by locally qualified and resident professionals. Managing directors must be resident in Austria. There are restrictions on the use of a foreign firm name.	A nationality requirement applies, except for nationals of EEA countries. For these, the conditions for practising in Austria are: (a) A residency requirement. (b) An education requirement; foreign degrees from EEA countries may be recognised. (c) Five years' training; foreign training from EEA countries may be recognised. (d) Passing a local examination.
Belgium	Not allowed. Commercial presence is required.	There are limits on ownership or control by non-locally-licensed professionals: 100% must be held by registered professionals, 50% of which must be resident in Belgium. There are restrictions on the name: a foreign name can be used only if it is that of a partner (natural or legal person) in the firm.	There is a nationality requirement, but exceptions may be made for nationals of EU Member Countries. For these, the conditions for practising in Belgium are: (a) A residency requirement; maintenance of local presence is required for regular practice. (b) An education requirement. (c) Three years' work experience. Entry as an SSE is not allowed. The other two types (ICT, IP) are available. Foreign-licensed professionals are subject to LMT. The employer must apply for a work permit. For a non-EU national

(Table 7A.1 Continued)

(Table 7A.1 Continued)

Country	Mode 1	Mode 3	Mode 4
			to work as a self-employed person, he or she must apply for a Professional Card; the application process can take up to a year. Professional cards are limited to a precise field of practice.
Denmark	Not allowed. Commercial presence is required.	Allowed, except permission required to establish partnership with Danish authorised auditors.	Nationality is normally required, but there are certain exceptions. In these cases, the requirements for foreign-licensed lawyers are: (a) Residency, although only for non-EEA nationals. (b) Education; foreign degrees are generally not recognised, but professional qualifications acquired in other Nordic countries are recognised. Additional courses in tax and commerce law in Denmark are usually required. (c) Local training in Denmark may be required. (d) Passing a local examination is necessary. Entry only as ICT is permitted. LMT applies, but not for transfers within international networks. There is a minimum wage/wage parity requirement.
Finland	Not allowed. Commercial presence is required.	There are limits on ownership or control by non-locally-licensed professionals. At least two-third of partners or board members must be, or at least two-third of all shares and voting rights must be held by, auditors authorised by the Central Chamber of Commerce. The chairman and vice-chairman or the managing director and deputy managing director, if any, must	Foreign-licensed professionals are eligible to practise, subject to certain conditions. (a) There is an education requirement; foreign degrees may be recognised only if from EEA countries. (b) Three years of training are required; foreign experience may be recognised only if from EEA countries. (c) Passing a local examination is necessary. While Finnish nationality is not required to practise as an auditor, in a statutory audit of a Finnish limited liability company at least one of the auditors must have Finnish nationality. Entry is allowed as an ICT only. LMT is for specialists only. Foreign-licensed professionals are subject to ENT.

		be authorised auditors. In a statutory audit of a Finnish limited liability company, at least one of the auditors must have Finnish nationality.	
France	Not allowed.	Ownership or control by non-locally-licensed professionals is limited to 25%. Restrictions on clientele: state-owned enterprises are audited by an auditor appointed jointly by the Ministry of Finance and the relevant sector ministry. Independently, the Court of Auditors examines the accounts and management of state-owned enterprises.	Non-EC professionals may be permitted to provide services by a decision of the Minister of Economics, Finance and Industry, in agreement with the Minister of Foreign Affairs. The requirement of residence cannot exceed five years. There is an education requirement; foreign degrees may be recognised if considered equivalent to those required in France to practice as *commissaire aux comptes* or *expert-comptable*. For non-EU nationals, there is training/work experience requirement; foreign experience is recognised. Passing a professional examination is necessary, but there is the possibility of a reduced examination.
Germany	Approval is necessary; prerequisites include professional and educational standards and a commercial presence.	A branch is not allowed. Provision of services through legal forms such as *GmbH and CoKG* and *EWIV* is not allowed. Majority ownership must be with locally qualified and resident professionals. Foreign firms/auditors may hold up to 49% of ownership or control, provided that their qualifications are substantially similar to German requirements.	Foreign-licensed professionals are eligible to practise subject to certain conditions if they are nationals of EEA countries. (a) There is a residency requirement. (b) Education: this may be taken into account for admission as an accountant (*Wirtschaftsprüfer*). This requirement may be waived for EEA nationals after an aptitude test. (c) Four years of work experience in Germany are necessary, but this may be waived for EEA nationals after an aptitude test. (d) Passing a local examination is necessary. Entry as ICT is permitted. Foreign-licensed professionals are subject to ENT. No permits for stay are granted to self-employed individuals from non-EU countries, but exceptions may be granted in the public interest.

(Table 7A.1 Continued)

(Table 7A.1 Continued)

Country	Mode 1	Mode 3	Mode 4
Greece	Not allowed. Commercial presence is required.	The majority of board of directors/ managers must be nationals or residents.	Automatic recognition of foreign licences granted if licensed to practise in other EU Member States. Otherwise, must have: (a) relevant higher education degree; (b) 7 years of work experience; and (c) passing an exam. Entry as ICT possible. No economic needs test for ICTs. SSE & IP—Unbound. The limit on stay is ICT up to three years; extensions are not allowed.
Ireland	Not allowed. Commercial presence is required.	Entry is allowed only through partnership. Ownership or control by non-locally-licensed professionals is limited to 49%.	There is an education and training requirement; foreign degree and training may be recognised if from an EU country. Passing a professional examination is required. EU countries set up a procedure for approval of statutory auditors from other EU countries, based on EU registration, equivalence of education, training, and examination; an aptitude test may be required. Entry is allowed only through ICT. Membership of professional association and residency requirements apply. The limit on duration of stay is three years; extensions are not allowed.
Italy	Not allowed. Commercial presence is required.	Access is restricted to natural persons. Professional association (not incorporation) among natural persons is permitted.	A nationality requirement normally applies, but there are certain exceptions. Statutory auditors from other EU countries may practise in Italy subject to certain requirements. (a) There is an education requirement; foreign education may be recognised. (b) Three years of training are required. (c) Passing a local examination is necessary.

Nether-lands	Not allowed. Commercial presence is required.	Allowed, except that ownership or control by non-locally-licensed professionals is limited to 49% if the firm is incorporated and carries out statutory audits.	Statutory auditors from other EU countries may practise in The Netherlands subject to some requirements. An aptitude test may be required. Statutory auditors from non-EU countries must meet the same requirements as Dutch applicants. (a) Education; foreign education may be recognised. (b) Three years of training in The Netherlands are required, but an exception may be made for EU-licensed auditors. (c) Passing a local examination is necessary. Entry is possible as an ICT only. Nationals of certain countries are exempt from the resident visa (EU, EEA, Switzerland, Japan, Australia, New Zealand, Canada and the US), but a VTV resident permit is needed if the stay is longer than six months. There is a minimum wage/wage parity requirement.
Spain	Not allowed. Commercial presence is required.	Allowed.	Applicants must be EU nationals. (a) There is an education requirement; foreign degrees may be recognised. (b) Three years of work experience are required; foreign experience may be recognised. (c) Passing a local examination is necessary. Entry is possible only as ICT.
Sweden	Statutory auditing services may only be provided by auditors approved in Sweden. A Swedish examination, work experience, and	A separate legal entity is not allowed. There are limits on ownership or control by non-locally-licensed professionals. In the case of a partnership, all partners must be locally licensed. In case of a limited company, the managing director and at least three-quarter of Board of Directors	Statutory auditors from other EU countries may practise in Sweden, subject to some conditions. Statutory auditors from non-EU countries must meet the same education and training requirements as Swedish applicants. Alternatively, one could become a *revisor* and perform non-statutory audits, public sector accounting and book-keeping with just three to four years of higher education. The requirements for practising as a statutory auditor are: (a) Residency; this is required for training; EEA

(Table 7A.1 Continued)

Country	Mode 1	Mode 3	Mode 4
	residency are required for approval.	members and their deputies must be locally licensed, and at least three-quarter of the shares and voting power must be held by locally licensed professionals. Exemptions may be possible to the extent that locally licensed auditors maintain the majority.	residence is accepted. (b) Education; foreign degrees may be recognised, if from EEA countries. (c) Three to five years of training—three years to become a *godkandarevisor* (*approved public accountant*) and five to become an *auktoriserad* (*authorised public accountant*). Foreign training may be recognised, if from EEA countries. (d) Passing a local examination. Entry is possible only as ICT.
United Kingdom	Not allowed. Commercial presence is required.	There are limits on ownership or control by non-locally-licensed professionals; 75% of the votes must be held by *qualified persons*. Also, any single shareholding of more than 5% must be approved by a special monitoring body within the profession.	Foreign-licensed professionals are eligible to practise, subject to certain conditions. (a) There is an education requirement; foreign education may be recognised. (b) Two years of work experience in the UK are required. (c) Passing a local examination is necessary. Entry is possible only as ICT. There is a point-based visa programme; points are awarded for education, prior earnings, age, UK experience and English language proficiency. Foreign-licensed professionals are subject to LMT.
Poland	Allowed	An audit firm organised as a limited partnership must be exclusively owned by auditors or audit firms licensed in an EU Member Country. Otherwise, an audit firm must be majority-owned and controlled by auditors or audit firms	Foreign-licensed professionals may become eligible to practice in Poland by meeting certain conditions based on the principle of reciprocity, unless already licensed in another EU Member State. The requirements are: (a) a university degree, which must be determined to be equivalent to a Polish degree (foreign degrees may be accepted); (b) 3 years of practical training or work

		licensed in an EU Member Country. The firm must become a member of the National Chamber of Statutory Auditors	experience (foreign experience may be accepted); and (c) passing an exam on Polish economic law. Education and work experience requirements may be waived if licensed in an EU Member State. Entry as an ICT is possible. No economic needs test for ICTs. SSE and IP—Unbound.
Portugal	Not allowed. Commercial presence is required	Ownership or control held by non-locally-licensed professionals is limited to 25%. The firm must be organised as a professional association and registered with Ordem dos RevisoresOficiais de Contas.	Portuguese or EU nationality is normally required, but exemption is given to foreigners from countries providing reciprocity. Other conditions are: (a) a university degree (foreign degrees may be accepted); (b) 3 years of practical training or work experience (foreign experience may be accepted); and (c) passing an exam. Education and work experience requirements may be waived if licensed in an EU Member State. Entry as ICT or SSE is possible. No economic needs test for ICTs, but a numerical ceiling may apply to SSEs. IP—Unbound. There is a limit on stay: ICT is three years, extensions are not allowed.

Source: World Bank Services Trade Restrictions Database, available at: http://iresearch.worldbank.org/servicetrade/home.htm (last accessed on 10 August 2013).

Table 7A.2
Restrictions in Mode 4 for the Accountancy Sector in Select EU Countries

Country	Mode 4
Austria	A nationality requirement applies, except for nationals of EEA countries. For these, the conditions for practicing in Austria are: (a) A residency requirement. (b) An education requirement; foreign degrees from EEA countries may be recognised. (c) Five years' training; foreign training from EEA countries may be recognised. (d) Passing a local examination.
Belgium	There is a nationality requirement, but exceptions may be made for nationals of EU Member Countries. For these, the conditions for practising in Belgium are: (a) A residency requirement; maintenance of local presence is required for regular practice. (b) An education requirement. (c) Three years' work experience. There is a quota; SSEs are subject to a numerical ceiling. Foreign-licensed professionals are subject to LMT.
Denmark	Nationality is normally required, but there are certain exceptions. In these cases, the requirements for foreign-licensed lawyers are: (a) Residency, although only for non-EEA nationals. (b) Education; foreign degrees are generally not recognised, but professional qualifications acquired in other Nordic countries are recognised. Additional courses in tax and commerce law in Denmark are usually required. (c) Local training in Denmark may be required. (d) Passing a local examination is necessary. Entry as ICT or SSE is possible. There is a quota: SSEs are subject to a numerical ceiling. LMT applies, but not for transfers within international networks.
Finland	Automatic recognition of foreign licences is granted for EEA countries. LMT is for specialists only. ENT applies to all but ICT.
France	Entry allowed through ICT or SSE. Non-EC professionals may be permitted to provide services, by a decision of the Minister of Economics, Finance and Industry, in agreement with the Minister of Foreign Affairs. The requirement of residence cannot exceed 5 years. There is an education requirement; foreign degrees may be recognised if considered equivalent to those required in France to practice as *commissaire aux comptes* or *expert-comptable*. For non-EU nationals, there is training/work experience requirement; foreign experience is recognised. Passing a professional examination is necessary, but there is the possibility of a reduced examination.

(Table 7A.2 Continued)

(Table 7A.2 Continued)

Country	Mode 4
Germany	Foreign-licensed professionals are eligible to practise subject to certain conditions if they are nationals of EEA countries. (a) Education; this may be taken into account for admission as an accountant (*Wirtschaftsprufer*). This requirement may be waived for EEA nationals after an aptitude test. (b) Four years of work experience in Germany are necessary, but this may be waived for EEA nationals after an aptitude test. (c) Passing a local examination is necessary. Entry as ICT or SSE is permitted. There is a quota: SSEs are subject to a numerical ceiling. Foreign-licensed professionals are subject to ENT. No permits for stay are granted to self-employed individuals from non-EU countries, but exceptions may be granted in the public interest.
Greece	Automatic recognition of foreign licences granted if licensed to practice in other EU Member States. Otherwise, must have: (a) relevant higher education degree; (b) 7 years of work experience; and (c) passing an exam. Entry as ICT or SSE possible. No economic needs test for ICTs, but a numerical ceiling may apply to SSEs. IP—Unbound. The limit on stay as an ICT is up to three years, SSE for 6 months; extensions are not allowed.
Ireland	There is an education and training requirement; foreign degree and training may be recognised if from an EU country. Passing a professional examination is required. The Institute of Chartered Accountants has agreements with chartered accountant organisations in other countries, including England and Wales, Scotland, Australia, New Zealand, South Africa, Canada and Hong Kong, and with the US AICPA. Entry is allowed through ICT and SSE. SSEs come at the request of the consumer and are subject to a numerical ceiling: modalities of application and level are to be determined. The limits on duration of stay are as follows: ICT—up to three years, SSE—up to 12 months; extensions are not allowed.
Italy	Applicants must be EU nationals. Foreign professionals may practice under home country title if there is a reciprocity agreement. Otherwise, they must meet: (a) An education requirement; foreign education may be recognised. (b) Three years of training are required. (c) Passing a local examination is necessary.

(Table 7A.2 Continued)

(Table 7A.2 Continued)

Country	Mode 4
Netherlands	Automatic recognition of foreign licences is granted. Entry is allowed as an ICT or SSE. The candidate must be professional and qualified, and employed at least six months outside The Netherlands (if employed by a non-EU company). Nationals of certain countries are exempt from the resident visa (EU, EEA, Switzerland, Japan, Australia, New Zealand, Canada and the US), but a VTV resident permit is needed if the stay is longer than 6 months. There is a minimum wage/wage parity requirement.
Poland	Automatic recognition of foreign licences is granted. Entry as an ICT or SSE is possible. No economic needs test for ICTs, but a numerical ceiling may apply to SSEs. IP are unbound.
Portugal	Portuguese or EU nationality is normally required, but exemption is given to foreigners from countries providing reciprocity. Other conditions are: (a) residency; (b) a university degree (foreign degrees may be accepted); (c) some practical training or work experience (foreign experience may be accepted); and (d) passing an exam. Entry as ICT or SSE is possible. No economic needs test for ICTs, but a numerical ceiling may apply to SSEs. IP—Unbound. Limit on stay: ICT 3 years, SSE-6 months per year. No extension possible.
Spain	Applicants must be EU nationals. (a) There is an education requirement; foreign degrees may be recognised. (b) Three years of work experience are required; foreign experience may be recognised. (c) Passing a local examination is necessary. Entry is possible only as ICT.
Sweden	Statutory auditors from other EU countries may practise in Sweden, subject to some conditions. Statutory auditors from non-EU countries must meet the same education and training requirements as Swedish applicants. Alternatively, one could become a *revisor* and perform non-statutory audits, public sector accounting and bookkeeping with just three to four years of higher education. The requirements for practising as a statutory auditor are: (a) Residency; this is required for training; EEA residence is accepted. (b) Education; foreign degrees may be recognised, if from EEA countries. (c) Three to five years of training. Foreign training may be recognised, if from EEA countries. (d) Passing a local examination. Entry as ICT or SSE is possible.

(Table 7A.2 Continued)

(Table 7A.2 Continued)

Country	Mode 4
United Kingdom	Foreign-licensed professionals are eligible to practice, subject to certain conditions. (a) There is an education requirement; foreign education may be recognised. (b) Two years of work experience in the UK are required. (c) Passing a local examination is necessary. Entry as ICT or SSE is possible. There is also a point-based visa programme; points are awarded for education, prior earnings, age, UK experience and English language proficiency. Foreign-licensed professionals are subject to LMT. Note: apart from the reserved areas of company audit, insolvency work, and investment advice, the accountancy profession remains unregulated.

Source: World Bank Services Trade Restrictions Database, available at: http://iresearch.worldbank.org/servicetrade/home.htm (last accessed on 10 August 2013).

8

Strengthening India–EU Relations in Health Services: Opportunities and Challenges*

Rupa Chanda

Introduction

Healthcare is a key social sector in which governments must invest for inclusive long-term growth and the development of human capital. Across countries, governments play an important role in the provision of healthcare, though the mix between public and private spending varies depending on fiscal, regulatory, social and other considerations. Given the public good orientation of health services, there has always been a tension between opening up the sector and the possible equity-efficiency trade-offs that may arise if there is greater commercialisation of healthcare. And yet, given the emerging demographic, technological, fiscal and economic trends, it cannot be denied that there is growing scope for the globalisation of healthcare and for expanding developing–developed country relations in health services. It is in this context that

* The author is grateful to Sasidaran and Kirthiga Balasubramaniam for their research assistance and to the several industry stakeholders who shared their views and insights on the subject.

the possibilities for enhancing India–EU bilateral relations in health services assume importance.

The healthcare sector constitutes a significant and growing share of GDP in the EU with the government playing the dominant role through national health trusts and programmes. In India, the sector is growing rapidly and its share in GDP as well as employment is significant. However, the private sector accounts for around 70 per cent of healthcare delivery (IBEF, 2013). Although health services is not a high profile sector for the India–EU BTIA and lies outside the scope of the EU Services Directive, several factors make this sector conducive to expanding India–EU relations across a wide range of segments, activities and modes of delivery. This chapter examines these opportunities. It looks beyond the commercial aspects of this bilateral relationship and highlights the associated regulatory and other challenges. It further outlines the main issues that need to be discussed and the strategies that need to be pursued in the BTIA and beyond to deepen cooperation between India and the EU in the health services sector.

Sectoral Coverage of the Health Services Sector

Health services are covered in two separate sectors under GATS. These are the health-related and social services sector and professional services in the business services sector. The coverage of the health services sector (professional- and establishment-related and others) along with the associated Central Product Classification (CPC) and the activities covered under these subsectors are given in Table 8.1.

Overview of the Health Services Sector in the EU

Healthcare is considered a vital and strategic sector in EU countries. The health sector constitutes around 9 per cent of GDP in the EU and employs almost 10 per cent of the total workforce.[1] Health spending has

---

[1] See http://ec.europa.eu/enterprise/policies/innovation/policy/lead-market-initiative/ehealth/ (accessed June 2013).

Table 8.1
Health and Social Services in the GATS Scheduling Guidelines and CPC

Sectoral Classification List	Relevant CPC No.	Definition/Coverage in Provisional CPC
Business Services		
A. Professional Services		
[...]		
h. Medical and dental services	9312	Services chiefly aimed at preventing, diagnosing and treating illness through consultation by individual patients without institutional nursing...
i. Veterinary services	932	Veterinary services for pet animals and animals other than pets (hospital and non-hospital medical, surgical and dental services).
j. Services provided by midwives, nurses, physiotherapists and paramedical personnel	93191	Services such as supervision during pregnancy and childbirth... nursing (without admission) care, advice and prevention for patients at home.
k. Other[a]	n.a.	N.A.
Health-related and Social Services		
A. Hospital Services	9311	Services delivered under the direction of medical doctors chiefly to in-patients aimed at curing, reactivating and/or maintaining the health status...

B. Other Human Health Services	9319 (other than 93191)	Ambulance Services; Residential health facilities; Services other than hospital services; Other human health services n.e.c.[b]
C. Social Services	933	Social services with accommodation;[c] Social services without accommodation
D. Other	N.A.	N.A.

Source: WTO (1998a), Table A1, p. 22.

Notes: 1. N.A. refers to Not available.

2. The scope of this chapter is limited to the following subsectors.
- Medical and dental services (CPC 9312)
- Services provided by midwives, nurses (CPC 93191)
- Hospital services (CPC 9311)

[a]Relates to all professional services (including sub-sectors (a) to (g) some of which are not listed above).

[b]Services in the field of morphological or chemical pathology, bacteriology, virology and immunology, and services, such as blood collection services, not elsewhere classified.

[c]Welfare services delivered through residential institutions to old persons and the handicapped (CPC 93311) and children and other clients (93312); other social services with accommodation (93319).

[d]Child day-care services including day-care services for the handicapped (93321); guidance and counselling services n.e.c. related to children (93322); welfare services not delivered through residential institutions (93323); vocational rehabilitation services (excluding services where the education component is predominant) (93324); other social services without accommodation (CPC 93329).

risen faster than the GDP in the EU and is estimated to reach 16 per cent of GDP by 2020. One of the most important characteristics of the EU healthcare sector (goods and services) is the high levels of total and per capita expenditure. As shown in Table 8.2, per capita health expenditure is significant in all EU Member Countries, ranging between US$2,000 and US$5,000. The average healthcare expenditure per capita is around US$2,457.[2] The UK is a particularly important market within the EU from the Indian perspective, with total health expenditures amounting to 9.3 per cent of GDP in 2011, up from 7 per cent of GDP in 2000.[3]

Table 8.2
Health Expenditure in Select EU Member Countries (in million at constant 2005 US$)

Country	Total Expenditure		Expenditure Per Capita		Expenditure as Share of GDP (%)		Private Expenditure as Share of GDP (%)	
	2007	2011	2007	2011	2007	2011	2007	2011
Austria	33,647	36,582	4,053	4,344	10.3	10.6	2.5	2.6
Belgium	38,270	43,242	3,603	3,939	9.6	10.6	2.6	2.5
Denmark	26,739	28,474	4,897	5,113	10.0	11.2	1.6	1.7
Finland	18,388	19,696	3,477	3,655	8.0	8.9	2.1	2.2
France	249,682	262,480	3,915	4,027	11.1	11.6	2.4	2.7
Germany	310,264	337,095	3,772	4,122	10.5	11.1	2.5	2.7
Greece	24,490	18,942	2,188	1,675	9.8	9.0	3.9	2.9
Ireland	15,745	17,476	3,607	3,892	7.6	9.4	1.8	2.8
Italy	155,858	163,834	2,625	2,697	8.6	9.5	2.0	2.2
Netherlands	71,701	79,714	4,378	4,776	10.8	12.0	1.7	1.7
Spain	93,442	100,966	2,082	2,189	8.5	9.4	2.4	2.5
Sweden	36,935	40,355	4,037	4,274	8.9	9.4	1.7	1.8
United Kingdom	204,364	220,206	3,351	3,510	8.4	9.3	1.6	1.6

Source: WHO Global Health Expenditure Database, http://apps.who.int/nha/database/DataExplorer.aspx?ws=2&d=1 (accessed 20 June 2013).

[2] WHO Global Health Expenditure Database (accessed June 2013).
[3] WHO Global Health Expenditure Database (accessed June 2013).

Coverage of Healthcare

The public segment dominates the healthcare sector in the EU (although the private segment has been growing in recent years due to the gradual privatisation of health services in some EU countries). As seen in Table 8.3, public spending on healthcare constitutes around 70 to 80 per cent of this spending, with a share of around 8 to 11 per cent of GDP across member countries. The private sector's share in healthcare spending relative to GDP ranges between 1.6 per cent in the UK to 2.6 per cent in Germany and averaged around 2 per cent of GDP in most EU countries in 2011.[4]

The dominance of the public sector reflects the universal or near-universal public coverage for health in EU Member Countries as part of a wider system of social protection. Public coverage is extended to health services that are prescribed by health professionals or institutions that are registered with the health insurance system or which figure on the country's positive list of approved procedures or of drugs and medical devices. Private insurance accounts for less than 20 per cent of total healthcare financing, mostly complementing the coverage under statutory insurance and covers services such as dental or alternative treatment that may be partially covered by statutory user charges or excluded altogether or options elected by patients.[5] Statutory reimbursement of pharmaceuticals tends to be based on a positive list of drugs drawn up by National Medical Agencies in these countries. In recent years, the EU has moved from a heavily regulated insurance market with controls over prices and products towards a subsidiary principle of insurance where governments are free to decide on the appropriate form of regulation depending on the context. The aim has been to give patients wider choice of providers and faster access to services. Coverage of alternative treatments by the statutory healthcare system tends to be excluded. Treatments such as homeopathy and spa treatment are not covered by most statutory healthcare systems in EU countries.

Although health services are excluded from the scope of the EU Services Directive, there are several initiatives to promote cross-border cooperation among member countries in healthcare and to harmonise

---

[4] WHO Global Health Expenditure Database (accessed June 2013).
[5] WHO Global Health Expenditure Database (accessed June 2013).

Table 8.3

Public and Private Expenditures on Healthcare, 2011 (values in million at constant 2005 US$; share as % of total health expenditure)

Indicators	France Value	France Share	Germany Value	Germany Share	Sweden Value	Sweden Share	United Kingdom Value	United Kingdom Share
General government expenditure on health	201,428.6	76.7	255,701.0	75.9	32,661.0	80.9	182,108.3	82.7
Ministry of Health[a]								
Social security funds[a]	191,911.7	73.1	229,419.3	68.1			171,726.3	78.0
Private expenditure on health	61,051.5	23.3	81,394.2	24.1	7,693.5	19.1	38,097.6	17.3
Private insurance	36,457.7	13.9	32,483.2	9.6	104.3	0.3	7,153.5	3.2
Out-of-pocket expenditure	19,586.6	7.5	41,829.4	12.4	6,830.0	16.9	20,218.7	9.2
Non-profit institutions serving households (e.g. NGOs)	32.8	0.012	1,400.7	0.4	73.6	0.2	8,374.1	3.8

Source: WHO Global Health Expenditure Database, available at http://apps.who.int/nha/database/DataExplorer.aspx?ws=2&d=1 (accessed 20 June 2013).

Note: [a]Ministry of Health and Social Security Fund expenditures are part of general government expenditures. Cells are blank where such data is not separately provided under general government expenditures.

internal systems to the extent possible while also giving room to individual member governments to retain their national legislation and regulatory frameworks to address concerns of consumer safety, standards and accountability. Within the EU, Member States have the right to healthcare for emergency treatment in another member country or a EEA member country. EU nationals can also elect to get treated in another member country for pre-approved procedures or cases of undue delay if they carry a European Health Insurance Card (EHIC), also called the EU Medical Card (which has replaced the earlier E111 form). The EHIC lasts for 3–5 years and entitles the holders to receive free or reduced cost emergency healthcare when visiting EEA countries. It authorises reimbursement by the home country of the patient in such cases. There is also an initiative to standardise health cards across the member countries by providing an interoperable format that would help a patient prove entitlement to healthcare from different national health services or to medical insurance schemes in Member States (European Commission, 2003). Treatment is also possible in other countries under reciprocal agreements.

IT Integration[6]

An important aspect of the healthcare system in EU countries is the adoption of IT in healthcare delivery. The e-health industry in the EU was estimated at €20 billion ($27.84 billion) in 2011.[7] The main push for adoption of technology in healthcare delivery comes from ageing populations and rising operational costs coupled with the need to improve service access and quality. However, the approach to IT integration varies in the EU and the member countries are at different levels of adoption. Countries such as the UK, France, Germany, Netherlands and Sweden spend comparably more in absolute and per capita terms than others such as Spain, Italy and Poland. Some have launched e-health initiatives.

The objectives vary across member countries. While cost control and efficiency dominate Sweden's IT strategy, in Germany, the consolidation of records across different providers is seen as the main problem to be

---

[6] Eurohealth, 2002; European Commission, 2007a.

[7] Converted using www.oanda.com historical exchange rates for the year 2011; where 1€ = US$1,3924. http://ec.europa.eu/information_society/doc/factsheets/009-ehealth-en.pdf (last accessed 29 June 2013).

addressed through IT. Some countries such as Sweden have gone the farthest in the health informatics area by facilitating the use of IT in information provision and transaction support, including electronic prescriptions and tele-diagnostics. The German government has launched an IT strategy for various public services including health, which proposes a programme of coordinated IT investment to bring Germany to the level of its main competitors. This includes issuance of health insurance smartcards on an optional basis, issuance of 300,000 ID cards for health professionals, electronic trade in medicines and electronic prescription. Security and tele-medicine are other high-priority areas for local IT investment in Germany.

The most widely perceived opportunity is electronic patient records (EPR) and interoperability between the record-keeping systems of different doctors and hospitals to improve patient safety and cut costs. However, there are concerns about patient privacy and whether citizens can trust their government and its privacy laws. The UK is in favour of centralised control of patient records to safeguard privacy, whereas other governments such as Sweden, the Netherlands, Germany and France favour a more decentralised system. Overall, there remain challenges in the adoption of IT within the countries and the wider EU membership due to market fragmentation, lack of inter-operability across countries in the EU, lack of legal certainty, inadequate financial support and government procurement norms that limit intra-regional delivery.

Key Regulations

Healthcare is a highly regulated sector. The health services market is highly fragmented in the EU, with different countries having their own sets of regulations in addition to EU-wide guidelines. Two areas of regulation are relevant to a discussion of trade and investment in health services in the EU: (a) data protection, data privacy and information security, which is pertinent to e-health delivery and (b) accreditation, registration and standards, which is pertinent to the cross-border movement of health professionals and the prospects for medical tourism and tele-medicine (Busse, Wismar, and Berman, 2002; Busse et al., 2006; Commission of the European Communities, 2004, 2007a and 2007b;

EHPH, 2005, Eur-Lex, 1995, 2000, 2005, 2006, 2007; European Commission, 2001; European Commission, 2005b, 2006d).

1. *Data protection and privacy*

   The EU-wide Directive on Data Protection takes a regulatory and comprehensive approach to data privacy. These regulations establish strict guidelines for processing personal information and trans-border flows of personal data outside the EU so as to ensure personal privacy. The EU's data protection law is governed by three Directives, namely the General Directive, the Directive on Privacy and Electronic Communications, and the Directive on Data Retention. Each EU Member is required to enact national laws that give effect to these Directives. The primary principles on which the General Directive is based include: (a) legitimacy: personal data may only be processed for limited and legitimate purposes; (b) finality: personal data may be collected only for specified, legitimate purposes and may not be further processed for any other purpose; (c) transparency: data subjects must receive information about the processing of their personal data; (d) proportionality: personal data must be relevant and not excessive relative to the purpose for which they are collected and processed; (e) confidentiality and security: technical and organisational measures must be in place to ensure the confidentiality and security of personal data; and (f) control: data protection authorities must enforce data protection laws.

   Thus, the Directive requires all personal information to be processed fairly and lawfully, such as requiring that the person whose personal information is being collected and used be informed about the proposed uses, or that the use of personal information is limited to the purpose first identified and to other compatible uses. The EU Directive imposes certain institutional requirements on member countries and companies. It requires companies processing the data to appoint a data controller who must register with government authorities. The data controller must notify the government authorities before processing any data. This notification includes informing the individual of the purpose of the processing, providing a description of the data subject and of the recipients to whom the data might be disclosed, proposed transfers to third countries and a description to ensure that basic security requirements have been met. Technical and organisational measures are also required to protect the data against destruction, loss, change or unauthorised disclosure or access. Users of e-health applications are required to ensure that they respect the fundamental rights of the individuals concerned and also comply with the legal obligations for the protection of personal data of patients. Certain data may be deemed sensitive and is not permitted for processing. The Directive also requires the establishment of an independent public authority to oversee data processing activities.

With respect to data transfers to countries outside the EU, the Directive requires Member States to enact laws that prohibit such transfers if the third country is deemed unable to ensure adequate privacy protection. The Data Protection Commissions and Member States are required to inform each other in such cases. This approach is different from that of the US, which uses a sectoral approach to data privacy that relies on a mix of legislation, regulation and self-regulation. Some countries have entered into 'safe harbor agreement' with the EU, which ensure that EU organisations know that the companies from countries that are engaged in data processing work provide adequate privacy protection as required by the EU Directive.

The EU's Privacy Rule establishes regulations for the use and disclosure of Protected Health Information (PHI), which refers to any information about health status, provision of healthcare, or payment for healthcare that can be linked to an individual. This is interpreted rather broadly and includes any part of a patient's medical record or payment history. Covered entities must disclose the PHI to the individual within 30 days upon request. They also must disclose the PHI when required to do so by law, such as reporting suspected child abuse to state child welfare agencies.

The Security Rule complements the Privacy Rule. While the Privacy Rule pertains to all Protected Heath Information (PHI) including paper and electronic, the Security Rule deals specifically with Electronic Protected Health Information (EPHI). It lays out three types of security safeguards required for compliance: administrative, physical and technical. For each of these types, the Rule identifies various security standards, and for each standard, it names both required and addressable implementation specifications.

2. *Registration, accreditation and standards*[8]

There are numerous regulations concerning standards and eligibility requirements for healthcare providers (persons and establishments) in the EU. These regulations concern who can provide services, what conditions he/she must fulfil, how the operations must be conducted, their liabilities and various accountability issues. There are, for instance, registration requirements with the concerned regulatory bodies, language certification requirements, insurance coverage requirements and compliance requirements with EU-wide as well as national-level legislation in areas like tele-medicine, clinical trials and research activities. There are also requirements in some areas to adhere to established EU or international standards.

Health professionals are regulated at the level of Member States and, to some extent, at the EU level to ensure that only properly qualified professionals provide health services. EU legislation has established different systems of recognition of professional qualifications that would enable the migration of high-quality professionals within the region. There are two different regimes for recognition of qualifications:

- The sectoral system, based on common minimum training standards defined in the relevant sectoral Directives. The minimum common criteria lead to the automatic recognition of the diploma, without any need for ad hoc evaluations of diplomas that meet the minimum requirements.
- The general system, which may require a case-by-case evaluation of the diploma by national authorities with the option to impose compensation measures. Ad hoc evaluation is a key obligation to allow recognition in Member States other than the one in which the diploma was awarded.

---

[8] The discussion is based on the following sources: Eur-Lex (2005 and 2007), Gerlinger and Schmucker (2007), Polak (2007).

Dentists, medical doctors, midwives, nurses, pharmacists and veterinarians are covered by the sectoral system; all other health professionals are covered by the general system. These recognition requirements include competence assessment, certification requirements, specification of minimum training and other conditions for the medical profession.

Challenges Facing the EU Healthcare Sector

The healthcare systems in EU Member Countries face numerous challenges. These include issues such as ageing populations and pressures on healthcare spending, the demography of the medical profession and limited human resources in healthcare, the need to modernise and redesign national health services, the need for improved management of the healthcare system, cost and sustainability of public health expenditures, the role of the private sector, long waiting times and the need to give patients greater choice.

Problems of access to public healthcare providers are evident from the long waiting times that characterise many of the national health services. A 2012 Euro Health Consumer Index finds that waiting times for elective surgeries are significant in almost all EU Member Countries, with 50 per cent or more of patients having to wait over three months to obtain treatment. Waiting times for diagnostics such as CT scans and outpatient consultations may also range between 1 and 12 weeks (Bjornberg, 2012). An earlier report found that in the UK 22 per cent of patients waited more than 13 weeks for their first outpatient appointment and 27 per cent of patients waited six months or more for an in-patient admission. Patients waited for the first appointment with a general physician, for the initial consultation with a specialist, for diagnosis and for treatment. Patients needing heart bypasses had to wait over a year for treatment, one in four cardiac patients died while waiting and one in five lung cancer patients waited so long that they become untreatable. Those with painful skin conditions, children needing speech therapy or elderly patients needing hip replacements had to wait several years for the treatment (European Observatory on Health Systems, 2002). In part, these waiting times reflect the shortage of healthcare personnel in EU countries. For example, the UK's National Health Service (NHS) has faced severe shortages of capacity, with fewer doctors per head than several other EU countries.

It has had to import nurses and doctors from the rest of the world. Some EU countries have initiated programmes to expand their health workforce along with targets for service improvements.

Although some EU governments have introduced national legislation that provides waiting time guarantees for critical illnesses and general waiting time guarantees to improve access to healthcare and there are initiatives to facilitate intra-EU patient mobility and e-health, the problem persists and has grown after the financial crisis. Long waiting times have resulted in increased pressure from patients in several EU countries to access services across borders, and sickness funds in some EU countries have contracted hospitals across borders to alleviate this pressure. In addition, there is a demand for unauthorised and non-contracted care in other EU countries.

In light of such emerging challenges, some EU Member Countries have initiated reforms by undertaking quality assurance programmes, providing guarantees of reduced local waiting times, restructuring healthcare delivery, adopting IT strategies and developing health plans for citizens.[9] Regional agreements and collaboration are also being used to address supply-side constraints. In turn, such challenges and the associated initiatives suggest opportunities for healthcare providers in non-EU countries like India to alleviate the cost and accessibility pressures in EU countries through cross-border delivery of healthcare services (telemedicine, movement of professionals, back-office support functions, and so on).

Overview of the Health Services Sector in India

The Indian healthcare delivery market was estimated at US$72 billion in 2011 (IBEF, 2011) and employed around four million people,[10] making it one of the largest service sectors in the economy today. Total national

---

[9] In the UK, the gross cost of the NHS in per capita terms has risen from £1,287 in 2003/04 to £1,979 in 2010/2011. http://www.nhsconfed.org/priorities/political-engagement/Pages/NHS-statistics.aspx (accessed 17 June 2013).

[10] http://www.cii.in/Sectors.aspx?enc=prvePUj2bdMtgTmvPwvisYH+5EnGjyGXO9h LECvTuNu2yMtqEr4D408mSsgiIyM/ (accessed 3 July 2013).

healthcare spending constituted 5 per cent of GDP in 2011.[11] Health-care expenditures recorded a CAGR of 12.1 per cent for the 2008–2011 period. Per capita health expenditure increased at a CAGR of 10.3 per cent in the 2008–2011 period amounted to US$57.9 billion in 2011 and was projected to reach US$88.7 billion in 2015 (IBEF, 2013). The sector is expected touch US$280 billion by 2020 or over 8 per cent of GDP.[12] This growth and potential is due to the growing demand for specialised and quality healthcare services in the Indian market, which is driven by rising incomes, a growing propensity to spend on healthcare, a shift to lifestyle-related diseases and ageing among other factors.

Structure of the Sector

India's healthcare sector comprises several segments that include medical care providers (physicians and nurses), medical care establishments (hospitals, clinics and nursing homes), diagnostic service centres and pathology laboratories, medical equipment and device manufacturers, contract research organisations that conduct clinical trials and research, pharmaceutical manufacturers, tele-medicine providers, health insurance providers and health services outsourcing providers. Estimates are available for some of these segments. Of the total healthcare revenue, hospitals account for 71 per cent, pharmaceuticals for 13 per cent, medical equipment and supplies for 9 per cent, medical insurance for 4 per cent and diagnostics for 3 per cent (IBEF, 2013).

The largest segment, which is the hospital services market, is expected to be worth US$81.2 billion in 2015[13] with the bulk of the contribution coming from the private sector. The medical tourism market was valued at US$1.9 billion in 2011, with around 100,000 foreign patients coming each year, mostly from Africa, the Commonwealth of Independent States (CIS) Member countries, the Gulf and the SAARC region for organ transplants and orthopaedic, cardiac and oncology treatments. The segment

---

[11] http://www.cii.in/Sectors.aspx?enc=prvePUj2bdMtgTmvPwvisYH+5EnGjyGXO9h LECvTuNu2yMtqEr4D408mSsgiIyM/ (accessed 3 July 2013).

[12] http://www.oifc.in/Resources/Spotlight/Spotlight-Healthcare-Sector-in-India (accessed 3 July 2013).

[13] http://www.oifc.in/Resources/Spotlight/Spotlight-Healthcare-Sector-in-India (accessed 3 July 2013).

is expected to expand at a CAGR of 27 per cent over the next few years. Another rapidly growing segment is the healthcare information technology market. The electronic medical record services segment is seen as having high growth potential, with an estimated CAGR of 13.5 per cent between 2009 and 2016. Large investments were undertaken by Indian healthcare providers on IT integration at an estimated spend of US$1.05 billion in 2013.[14] Contract research has also grown rapidly, as foreign players have entered the clinical trials segment to reduce their costs. In 2010, over 1,00,000 clinical trials were carried out covering some 12 million patients. There is outsourcing of pathology and laboratory tests by foreign hospital chains due to the lower costs in India. The domestic pathology industry is estimated at US$500 million and has been growing at an estimated CAGR of 20 per cent in recent years. The domestic diagnostics market is worth over US$1 billion and is growing at 15–20 per cent per year. There are some 40,000 laboratories in the country, including pathology laboratory chains and hospital-run diagnostic centres. The healthcare sector is also attracting capital from investors and the emergence of de-centralised healthcare delivery models is making the sector attractive to private equity and venture capital investors. In 2012, the industry absorbed US$1.2 billion across 48 deals.[15] The healthcare business outsourcing market has been expanding rapidly, providing employment to around 200,000 people. Other growth segments include the health imaging market and the hi-tech medical devices market; the latter has grown at around 12–15 per cent per year and is among the top 20 markets in the world. It was worth an estimated US$2.6 billion in 2011 (KPMG, 2012). The medical equipment and diagnostics industry is expected to see a surge in investment. The potential in the health insurance market is also huge given the less than 10 per cent health insurance penetration at present.[16]

---

[14] http://www.oifc.in/Sectors/Healthcare/Healthcare-in-India (accessed 3 July 2013).

[15] http://www.oifc.in/Resources/Spotlight/Spotlight-Healthcare-Sector-in-India (accessed 3 July 2013).

[16] http://www.cii.in/Sectors.aspx?enc=prvePUj2bdMtgTmvPwvisYH+5EnGjyGXO9h LECvTuNu2yMtqEr4D408mSsgiIyM/http://www.cii.in/Sectors.aspx?enc=prvePUj2bdM tgTmvPwvisYH+5EnGjyGXO9hLECvTuNu2yMtqEr4D408mSsgiIyM/ (accessed 3 July 2013).

A key feature of India's healthcare system is the significant and growing role of the private sector in healthcare delivery and total healthcare expenditures. Public health expenditure accounts for less than 1 per cent of GDP compared to 3 per cent of GDP for developing countries and 5 per cent for high-income countries. The private healthcare sector in India accounts for around 70 per cent of total healthcare expenditure in the country and is one of the largest in the world. An estimated 65 per cent of primary care centres and more than 40 per cent of hospitals, 75 per cent of dispensaries and 80 per cent of all qualified doctors are in the private sector. An estimated 95 per cent of new hospital beds in recent years has come up in the private sector (IBEF, 2013). The growing spending power of the middle class has been driving growth opportunities for corporate healthcare providers. Earlier studies by the Central Bureau of Health Intelligence show that the majority of Indians trust private healthcare, despite a higher average cost of US$4.3 compared to US$2.7 in government-owned healthcare agencies (IBEF, 2011). Only 23.5 per cent of urban residents and 30.6 per cent of rural residents chose government facilities, reflecting the widespread lack of confidence in the public healthcare system. The private sector's role is expected to grow, providing over 80 per cent of the sector's future investment requirements, including the development of the hospital industry. However, according to an earlier Technopak report (2007), private healthcare delivery in India remains highly fragmented with over 90 per cent of private healthcare being serviced by the unorganised sector. Some 2 to 3 per cent of hospitals are 200+ beds, some 6–7 per cent consists of 100–200 beds, and the bulk or 80 per cent of private sector hospitals have fewer than 30 beds (Technopak, 2007). Firm-level data indicates a total of 133 companies engaged in health services in the Indian market (SACEPS, 2011).

In future, government spending on healthcare infrastructure is projected to rise because the government has decided to increase health expenditure to 2.5 per cent of GDP by the end of the 12th Five-Year Plan (2012–2017) from its existing level of around 1.5 per cent. The government also plans to increase insurance penetration from the current average of 15 per cent to 50 per cent by 2020, so as to increase the affordability of healthcare.[17]

---

[17] See http://www.oifc.in/Sectors/Healthcare/Healthcare-in-India, May 2013 and http://www.cii.in/Sectors.aspx?enc=prvePUj2bdMtgTmvPwvisYH+5EnGjyGXO9hLECvTuNu2yMtqEr4D408mSsgiIyM/ (accessed 3 July 2013).